Improving Disability Laws under Nigeria's Fourth Republic

Improving Disability Laws under Nigeria's Fourth Republic

Ten Measured Steps into the Future

Philip C. Aka and Joseph Abiodun Balogun

LEXINGTON BOOKS
Lanham • Boulder • New York • London

Published by Lexington Books
An imprint of The Rowman & Littlefield Publishing Group, Inc.
4501 Forbes Boulevard, Suite 200, Lanham, Maryland 20706
www.rowman.com

86-90 Paul Street, London EC2A 4NE

British Library Cataloguing in Publication Information Available

Library of Congress Cataloging-in-Publication Data

Names: Aka, Philip Chukwuma, author. | Balogun, Joseph A., 1955- author.
Title: Improving disability laws under Nigeria's Fourth Republic : ten measured steps into the future / Philip C. Aka and Joseph A. Balogun.
Description: Lanham : Lexington Books, 2022. | Includes bibliographical references and index.
Identifiers: LCCN 2022026104 (print) | LCCN 2022026105 (ebook) | ISBN 9781666914177 (cloth) | ISBN 9781666914184 (ebook)
Subjects: LCSH: People with disabilities--Civil rights--Nigeria. | People with disabilities--Legal status, laws, etc.--Nigeria.
Classification: LCC HV1559.N6 A335 2022 (print) | LCC HV1559.N6 (ebook) | DDC 362.404809669--dc23/eng/20220602
LC record available at https://lccn.loc.gov/2022026104
LC ebook record available at https://lccn.loc.gov/2022026105

For our families. To the estimated 25–30 million persons living with disabilities in Nigeria

Contents

Preface

In January 2018, Nigerian lawmakers passed into law the Discrimination Against Persons with Disabilities (Prohibition) Act (DPDP or Nigerian Disabilities Act) of 2018. The passage occurred over seven years after Nigeria's ratification of the Convention on the Rights of Persons with Disabilities (CRPD), along with its acceptance of the individual-complaint and inquiry procedures under the multilateral treaty's Optional Protocol, both in September 2010. The auspicious turn of events affords an opportune moment for a midrange examination of the Nigerian national government's implementation of its international obligations related to the welfare of persons living with disabilities (PLWDs) in the country.

PLWDs are individuals imbued with inalienable human rights whose talents and potentials Nigeria's governments should harness in their perennial pursuit of economic development. However, under Nigeria's Fourth Republic since 1999, implementation of laws relating to PLWDs has been lethargic at best. Taking these propositions as starting point, this book explores measures for improving the capacity of the Nigerian national government to implement international agreements on disability Nigeria is a state party to, especially the CRPD and its Optional Protocol.

This book is divided into four chapters, plus an introduction and conclusion. The Introduction is an entrance into the book, encompassing several threshold issues converged around the purpose of the study, including a primer on Nigeria, definition of key terms, argument of the book and animating themes, recent developments that inspired and lent impetus to the research, and the location of the book within four sub-approaches to disability studies.

Chapter 1 traces the history of disability in Nigeria, using the past to understand the present and to gauge the future. The sketch is organized around three interrelated features enshrined equally in three eras. The features are: sources of disabilities and prevalence, representative laws and policies, and societal attitudes toward disabilities and individuals living with these conditions. The three eras are: the precolonial, colonial, and postcolonial periods, with the last broken into the timeframes before and after 1999. A constant that runs through the three eras is an invariably negative attitude toward PLWDs.

Chapter 2 unpacks the global and regional disability regimes pertaining to Nigeria. Proper understanding of the responses of the Nigerian government toward matters relating to the welfare of disabled persons or lack thereof must be predicated on an outline of the specific laws involved. Thus, the task of Chapter 2 is to pinpoint those international measures and the domestic laws meant to facilitate their implementation as Nigerian domestic law.

Chapter 3 examines the record of the Nigerian national government since 1999 under the Fourth Republic. To provide heuristic benchmarks for realistic assessment of the labor of the government, the chapter analyzes in some detail the Nigerian Disabilities Act of 2018, a signature legislative achievement of the Fourth Republic pertaining to disabilities, followed by a list of ten sectors of inaccessibility that impede the lives and prospects of persons living with disabilities in Nigeria. The chapter also includes a statement on the negative impact of sustained military rule in the country, spanning three decades until 1999, on disability rights.

Chapter 4 outlines workable measures for enhancing the capability of the Nigerian government under the Fourth Republic to implement disability laws. While Chapter 3 chronicles, arguably negatively, the failures of the national government relating to the welfare of PLWDs, this chapter looks, arguably positively, on what can be done to remediate or minimize the effect of those failures on the lives of PLWDs. Its highlights consist of proposals, packaged in a set of ten measures, for advancing disability laws in Nigeria under the Fourth Republic, underlain by the "auxiliary precautions" of improved civilian rule as predicate.

The book's Conclusion ties together the achievements of the book, with a look into the future, anchored on two recommendations: more robust provisions for disability rights in the Nigerian constitution, and the need for Nigeria to ratify the Protocol of the African Charter on Human and Peoples' Rights on the Rights of Persons with Disabilities in Africa. No different from their fellow citizens, PLWDs are *also* Nigerians, to whom the national government owes an obligation, freely and voluntarily assumed, of freedom from discrimination based on disabilities.

This book departs from similar or comparable works because of its increased emphasis on the human rights of PLWDs, and their untapped potentials to contribute to socioeconomic development that a progressive government must work hard to harness. Its key highlights and achievements include the set of ten sectors of inaccessibility that impedes the lives of PLWDs in Nigeria that it composes, and the set of ten targeted measures, underlain by the predicate of improved civilian rule, that it proposes, for improving disability laws in Nigeria under the Fourth Republic. Since the

1990s, Nigeria and many other African countries embarked upon a journey to more democratic and participatory governing processes, that will remain incomplete unless the governments of these countries change their policies toward PLWDs, in conformity with their obligations in international law. Nigerian constitutionalism imposes on the government definite duties toward the citizenry, that the national government has not successfully extended to its disabled communities. Concededly, a number of important works have been published recently in the field of disability studies. However, until this book, none of these studies dealt with Nigeria, particularly Nigeria under the Fourth Republic since 1999.

Every book is a work of collaboration and tribute to the solidarity of numerous parties whose antecedent energies made the work possible. This book is no different. Among the parties who deserve acknowledgment in this preface are the authors of the numerous sources in the references whose ideas we drew upon to support our argument in this work. We thank them immensely. We equally extend our appreciation to the anonymous reviewer whose expansive and engaging evaluation of our manuscript, within the best traditions of the peer-review process, immensely improved the quality of this book. Last but not least, we are indebted to Sydney Wedbush, Associate Acquisitions Editor for African and Africana Studies and Geography at Lexington Books, for her interest in this project and for meticulously shepherding it from start to completion. Sydney, you are such a pro and a joy to work with! Consistent with canons of academic practice, we alone take the blame for any errors of analysis and interpretation in this work. We gratefully acknowledge the permission of the United Nations Publications Board to reproduce the map of Nigeria on page xiii.

Table of Nigerian National and International Laws

African Charter on the Rights and Welfare of the Child. OAU Doc. CAB/LEG/24.9/49, 1999.

Child's Rights Act, Act No. 26 (2003). Reprinted in refworld.org/pdfid/5568201f.4.pdf

Constitution of the Federal Republic of Nigeria, 1999. Reprinted in Constitute Project. https://www.constituteproject.org/constitution/Nigeria_1999.pdf.

Convention on the Rights of Persons with Disabilities. UN General Assembly Resolution No. A/RES/61/106, Annex I. December 13, 2006. https://www.refworld.org/docid/4680cd212.html.

Discrimination against Persons with Disabilities (Prohibition) Act of 2018. Reprinted in *Nigeria Health Watch.* https://nigeriahealthwatch.com/wp-content/uploads/bsk-pdf-manager/2019/02/1244-Discrimination-Against-Persons-with-Disabilities-Prohibition-ACT-2018.pdf.

International Covenant on Economic, Social, and Cultural Rights. U.N. General Assembly Resolution No. 2200A (XXI) (December 19, 1966), 993 U.N.T.S. 3 (1976).

International Covenant on Civil and Political Rights. U.N. General Assembly Resolution 2200A (XXI) (December 16, 1966). 999 U.N.T.S. 171 (1976).

National Health Act, 2014. Federal Republic of Nigeria Official Gazette No. 101(145). October 27, 2014. https://nigeriahealthwatch.com/wp-content/uploads/bsk-pdf-manager/2018/07/01_-Official-Gazette-of-the-National-Health-Act-FGN.pdf.

Nigeria Independence Act, 1960. 1960 Ch. 55 8 & 9 Eliz. July 29, 1960. https://www.legislation.gov.uk/ukpga/1960/55/pdfs/ukpga_19600055_en.pdf.

Nigeria Republic Act, 1963. 1963 Ch. 57. December 18,1963. https://www.legislation.gov.uk/ukpga/1963/57/enacted.

Nigeria Social Insurance Trust Fund Decree 1993 (No. 73 of 1993). 1993. August 23. Published in Federal Republic of Nigeria Official Gazette, 80(24), A811-A27 (September 1, 1993). *Reprinted* in Laws Africa: Legislation Commons. https://commons.laws.africa/akn/ng/act/1993/73/eng@2002-12-31.pdf

Optional Protocol to the Convention on the Rights of Persons with Disabilities. UN General Assembly Resolution No. A/RES/61/106. Annex II. December 13, 2006. https://www.refworld.org/docid/4680d0982.html

Universal Declaration of Human Rights. U.N. General Assembly Resolution No. 217A. December 10, 1948.

Map 0.1 Map of Nigeria. Source: Map No. 4228, Rev. 1 (August 2014), set forth above, is gratefully reproduced with permission from the United Nations Publications Board.

List of Tables

Abbreviations

ACHPR	African Charter on Human and Peoples' Rights
ACRWC	African Charter on the Rights and Welfare of the Child
African Commission	African Commission on Human and Peoples' Rights
ADA	Americans with Disabilities Act
AIDI	African Infrastructure Development Index
AI	Amnesty International
ASCEND	Association for the Comprehensive Empowerment of Nigerians with Disabilities
AU	African Union, successor of the Organization of African Unity (OAU)
BRISIN	Basic Registry and Information System in Nigeria
CEDAW	Convention on the Elimination of All Forms of Discrimination against Women
COVID-19	The novel coronavirus, a respiratory disease that can result in serious illness or death. The disease is caused by a new strain of coronavirus not previously identified in humans that spreads easily from person to person. The World Health Organization declared it as a pandemic
CAT	Convention Against Torture and other Cruel, Inhuman or Degrading Treatment or Punishment
CCD	Center for Citizens with Disabilities
CRC	Convention on the Rights of the Child
CRMW	International Convention on the Protection of the Rights of All Migrant Workers and Members of Their Families
CRPD	Convention on the Rights of Persons with Disabilities
DTF	Disability Trust Fund
DRDP	Declaration on the Rights of Disabled Persons

DPDPA	Discrimination Against Persons with Disabilities (Prohibition) Act
DWAN	Deaf Women Association of Nigeria
DWYPD	Department of Women, Youth, and Persons with Disabilities (a South African government agency)
HIV/AIDS	HIV stands for Human Immunodeficiency Virus, the virus responsible for HIV infections. AIDS stands for Acquired Immuno-Deficiency Syndrome, the most advanced stage of HIV infection. The nature of the connection between HIV and AIDS is that HIV attacks and destroys the infection-fighting CD4 cells (CD4 T lymphocyte) of the immune system, an occurrence that makes it difficult for the body to fight off infections and certain cancers. Without treatment, HIV gradually destroys the immune system, causing HIV infection to advance to AIDS.
ICCPR	International Covenant on Civil and Political Rights
ICERD	International Convention on the Elimination of All Forms of Racial Discrimination
ICESCR	International Covenant on Economic, Social, and Cultural Rights
ICF	International Classification of Functioning, Disability, and Health
ICT	Information and Communications Technology
ICPPED	International Convention for the Protection of All Persons from Enforced Disappearance
IDPs	Internally-Displaced Persons
IDP Camp	Internally-Displaced Persons Camp
ILM	Independent Living Movement
ILO	International Labor Organization
JONAPWD	Joint National Association of Persons with Disabilities
MDGs	UN Millennium Development Goals. The program was replaced after 2015 by the Sustainable Development Goals (SDGs)
MS	Multiple sclerosis
MWASD	Ministry of Women Affairs and Social Development
NBS	National Bureau of Statistics
NCPD	National Center for Persons with Disabilities
NCPD	National Commission for Persons with Disabilities
NDHS	Nigeria Demographic and Health Survey
NEPAD	New Partnership for Africa's Development
NGOs	Non-governmental organizations

NIIMP	National Integrated Infrastructure Master Plan
NNAD	Nigeria National Association of the Deaf
NHRC	National Human Rights Commission
OAU	Organization of African Unity, predecessor of the African Union (AU)
OPCRPD	Optional Protocol to the Convention on the Rights of Persons with Disabilities
PACRD	Protocol of the African Charter on Human and Peoples' Rights on the Rights of Persons with Disabilities in Africa
PLWDs	Persons Living with Disabilities
PPPMI	Principles for the Protection of Persons with Mental Illness and the Improvement of Mental Health Care
R & D	Research and Development
Standard Rules	Standard Rules on the Equalization of Opportunities for Persons with Disabilities
TDR	Technological and digital resources
UDHR	Universal Declaration of Human Rights.
UK	[The] United Kingdom [of Great Britain and Northern Ireland]
UN	[The] United Nations
UNDP	United Nations Development Program
UNESCO	United Nations Educational, Scientific, and Cultural Organization
WCAG	Web Content Accessibility Guidelines
WHO	World Health Organization
WPA	World Program of Action Concerning Disabled Persons

Introduction

In January 2018, Nigerian lawmakers passed into law the Discrimination Against Persons with Disabilities (Prohibition) Act (DPDP or Nigerian Disabilities Act) of 2018.[1] The passage occurred over seven years after Nigeria's ratification of the Convention on the Rights of Persons with Disabilities (CRPD),[2] and its acceptance of the individual-complaint and inquiry procedures under the multilateral treaty's Optional Protocol, both of which took place in September 2010.[3] The cascade of auspicious events affords an opportune moment for a midrange examination of the Nigerian national government's implementation of its international obligations related to the welfare of persons living with disabilities (PLWDs)[4] in the country. This chapter is an entrance into the book and an embodiment of its purpose of study in seven integrated parts: primer on Nigeria, the geopolitical anchor and locus of the work; definition of key terms in the study; statement related to the changing nature of disability in modern times; argument of the book and animating themes; recent developments that inspired and lent impetus to the research; location of the book within four sub-approaches to disability studies; and a statement regarding the book's organization.

PRIMER ON NIGERIA

Nigeria is a key country in West Africa, a zone of immense geopolitical importance in Africa.[5] Nigeria has a population of over 208 million people in 2020.[6] It is bordered to the north by the French-speaking Niger Republic,[7] to the northeast by Chad, to the east by Cameroon, and to the west by Benin Republic.[8] Nigeria's southern coast rests on the Gulf of Guinea in the Atlantic Ocean.[9] Nigeria is a wholesale creature of British colonial overlords who, in 1914, merged two previously separate "protectorates," Northern and Southern, along with the colony of Lagos, to form the country.[10] These three entities encompass numerous ethnic groups that, before 1914, had no history of living together.[11] For good or bad, ethnicity plays a major role in Nigerian society and politics.[12] Altogether, there are over 250 ethnic groups in Nigeria.[13] Table I.1 provides a breakdown of the major ethnic groups of Nigeria as of 2018.

Table I.1. Major ethnic groups of Nigeria

Item No.	*Name of group*	*Share of the population as of 2018 (percentage)*
1.	Hausa	30
2.	Yoruba	15.5
3.	Igbo	15.2
4.	Fulani	6
5.	Tiv	2.4
6.	Kanuri/Beriberi	2.4
7.	Ibibio	1.8
8.	Ijaw/Izon	1.8
9.	Rest	24.7

Source: Author created with data from *Country Background Note: Nigeria* (London: Home Office, updated December 5, 2019), https://assets.publishing.service.gov.uk/government/uploads/system/uploads/attachment_data/file/856368/Nigeria_-_Background_-_CPIN_-_v2.0__January_2020__gov.uk.pdf (quoting CIA *World Factbook* data on Nigeria).

The first four groups, three when Hausa-Fulani are combined into one, make up nearly two-thirds of the country.[14] Nigeria's heterogeneity creates a complexity for governance; the three major ethnic groups—the Hausa-Fulani dominant in the North, the Igbo in the East, and the Yoruba in the West, unceasingly "vie with each other for political predominance and economic favor."[15]

Pre-1914, the areas that became Nigeria were known as the Slave Coast, in notorious testament to the commerce in humans that went on there before the abolition of the slave trade in 1807.[16] Nigeria won political independence from the United Kingdom (UK) in October 1960 after 46 years of colonial rule, counting from 1914.[17] It became a republic in 1963, in an act that eliminated residues of British control emblematized by the station in the new country of a governor-general who functioned as representative of the British Crown.[18] Nigeria is a federation of thirty-six states, a Federal Capital Territory based in Abuja, and 774 local governments.[19]

A slight reshaping of Nigeria's borders took place soon after independence when, in a referendum in spring 1961, Northern Cameroons voted to join Nigeria, while Southern Cameroons voted to join French-speaking Cameroon.[20] Before the referendum, these two Cameroons were UN Trust Territories that the UK administered as part of its Nigerian colony.[21] More recently, in 2002, the International Court of Justice heard a land and maritime dispute between Nigeria and Cameroon wherein it awarded ownership of the Bakassi Peninsula to Cameroon but a stretch of land in the area around Lake Chad to Nigeria.[22]

Without minimizing events pertaining to the welfare of disabled persons at the sub-national levels, for practical reasons, top of which is limited access to data, the focus of this book is on the national government. This is consistent with provisions in multilateral treaties, including those dealing with disabilities, which make the national government proxy for the whole country, in a federal system,[23] of which, as indicated in the preceding paragraphs, Nigeria ranks as one. Even so, sharp distinctions between national and sub-national levels can be unrealistic, since, as we will see later in this book, putatively national policies are sometimes shaped by events at the complementary sub-national level, consistent with the doctrine of "laboratories of democracy" that hallmarks a federal system.[24] Similarly, because of the more ample room it affords for critical analysis vis-à-vis previous eras, the focus in this book is on the Fourth Republic, the current installment of and experiment in civilian rule in the country since 1999.[25]

Two spells of prolonged military dictatorship spanning nearly three decades from 1966 until 1979 and 1983 to 1999 preceded the Fourth Republic.[26] The First Republic or era of civilian rule took place from October 1960 until January 1966 when the experiment was aborted by a military coup.[27] The Second Republic took place from 1979 until 1983 when it was terminated again by military rule, this time led by General Muhammadu Buhari,[28] president since 2015. A projected Third Republic became stillborn when elections designed to usher in that instalment of civilian rule was aborted by the military government under General Ibrahim Babangida in 1993.[29]

The preceding narrative is designed to introduce the Nigerian society and political system to an uninitiated reader while refreshing the memory of the reader already familiar with these basic facts. With the other threshold materials covered in this chapter, this narrative provides a canvas for what is to come, including the nature and origins of the rights of PLWDs, the nature and origins of the Nigerian national government's obligations related to these rights, the basis for assessing the government's performance with respect to these rights as inadequate, and the viable way forward.

DEFINITION OF KEY TERMS IN THIS BOOK

The beginning of academic wisdom, as the Chinese philosopher, Confucius (551–479 B.C.), famously advised, is to call things by their proper names by unambiguously defining them.[30] Because concepts are "abstract mental images" that, by their nature, are "fuzzy and imprecise,"[31] definition of key terms is critical in a study like this. Key terms of this book that, in this section need to be called by their proper names through unambiguous definition, are *regime*, *stigma*, *disability*, and *persons living with disability*. As the ensuing description makes clear, the last two terms are interlinked.

Regime

A *regime* is a term of art, with roots in international relations theory, that denotes a set of formal institutions, such as rules, norms, procedures, informal understandings, and expectations governing behavior in a certain issue-area.[32] Two complementary regimes implicated in this book are the global regime under the United Nations (UN), and the regional regime under the African Union, successor of the Organization of African Unity. Chapter 2 of this book elaborates the disability instruments associated with these two regimes.

Stigma

Stigma refers to the "attitudes and beliefs that lead people to reject, avoid, or fear those they perceive as being different."[33] It is a mark of disgrace associated with a particular entity, here PLWDs, that results in lowered status for the group in question.[34] The etymology of the term is Greek and refers to a mark or tattoo cut or burned into the skin of a victim, whether demonized as criminal, slave, or traitor, to mark out that victim as a member of a class, something of an albatross, to be avoided.[35] The trouble with stigma is the polar stereotypes that it can feed into, all of which are "self-fulfilling prophesies" that do not accurately portray the world of PLWDs.[36] On the one hand, it sees these individuals "as passive, weak, helpless, unable to make decisions or take responsibility for themselves, overly sensitive," or the like.[37] On the other hand, PLWDs who break out of the box, "are then seen as brave, amazing, having superhuman qualities" or the like.[38]

Stigma elicits varied negative responses toward PLWDs, such as anxiety, avoidance, disgust, hatred, hostility, and pity.[39] Similarly, stigma of PLWDs vary, based on factors, such as the severity of impairment, gender, socioeconomic status, and location or place of residence.[40] For example, PLWDs "with intellectual disabilities, severe mental health conditions, albinism, and sensory disabilities are often more stigmatized than people with physical disabilities[,]" and PLWDs "who can participate in their communities experience less stigma than those with more severe disabilities."[41] With respect to gender, "[f]emales who are disabled are doubly disadvantaged, due to the stigma associated with gender as well as disability."[42] This is matched against the reality, however, that, in some African societies, men living with disabilities "face high rates of dependency and divorce," and endure the taunts of portrayal as "liabilities to society due to depression caused by the notion that they cannot contribute to their community as" real men.[43]

Next to socioeconomic status, more likely than not, PLWDs born to poor families experience more discrimination than their counterparts from more well-off families.[44] Finally on place of residence, PLWDs resident in rural areas, where incidentally majority of the populace in developing countries live, are more likely to experience discrimination anchored on harmful practices than their counterparts in urban centers.[45] In rural communities, stereotypes against PLWDs are more searing because "[t]he lifestyle in these [communities] require physical strength to grow enough food and to support a family[,]" meaning that persons living with deafness or mental impairment "can lead a better life than the physically and visually disabled" if they are good manual workers.[46] In contrast, "[l]iving in urban areas depends more on being brainy than brawny[,]" and, therefore, "the ideal place for physically disabled persons because their survival depends on intelligence, creativity and ability to organize people."[47]

In addition to treatment from the rest of society, stigma may affect the way PLWDs perceive themselves. This happens when, for example, PLWDs act in ways that conform to the expectation of their tormentors.[48] That is also the case when stigma deprives disabled persons, such as those afflicted with mental impairment, the opportunity they need to seek treatment and gain recovery.[49]

Disability

A disability is any impairment, physical or mental, that makes it more difficult for a person living with that condition to engage in certain activities (activity limitation) and interact with the world around him or her (participation restrictions).[50] As we show shortly, disability is a composite term for "a great number of different functional limitations" within the population of a particular country.[51] This is a phenomenon that international treaties dealing with disabilities refer to as the "diversity of persons [living] with disabilities."[52]

The field of disability studies identifies four categories of impairment or a combination of the four: physical, intellectual or cognitive, sensory, and medical disability or mental illness.[53] *Physical* disabilities are deformities like multiple sclerosis, cerebral palsy, spina bifida, brain or spinal cord injury, epilepsy, and muscular dystrophy, that temporarily or permanently affect a person's physical capacity and mobility.[54] *Intellectual* or cognitive disabilities are developmental delays in communicating, learning, and retaining information, exemplified by deformities like Down's syndrome, Fragile X syndrome, and Prader-Willis syndrome.[55] *Sensory* disabilities are deformities like autism, blindness, and hearing loss, that affect the sufferer's sense of sight, hearing, smell, touch, taste, spatial awareness, or a combination of these senses.[56] *Medical disabilities* or *mental illnesses* are deformities like bipolarity, depression, schizophrenia, and eating disorders, that affect a person's thinking, emotional state, and behaviors.[57]

The CRPD,[58] a preeminent global disability instrument, elaborated in Chapter 2, and referred to repeatedly in this book, does not per se define *disability*. This is because the multilateral treaty regards *disability* as an "evolving concept" and a condition that "results from the interaction between persons with impairments and attitudinal and environmental barriers that hinders their full and effective participation in society on an equal basis with others."[59] This means that disability is not fixed but instead is a condition that can change from society to society, depending on the prevailing environment. However, the same instrument includes "[d]iscrimination on the basis of disability" on its list of defined terms.[60]

Disability is a human right issue;[61] discriminating against PLWDs, defined below, is "a violation of the inherent dignity and worth of the human person."[62] It is likewise an economic development issue.[63] This wisdom informs the assessment of the UN General Assembly to the effect that equalizing opportunities for persons with disabilities marks a major contribution to the global "effort to mobilize human resources,"[64] while simultaneously minimizing social factors like "ignorance, neglect, [and] superstition," that have served to isolate PLWDs and delay their development.[65] In Nigeria, the most prevalent forms of disability are physical and mobility, visual, hearing, mental (intellectual), and communication, impairments.[66]

Governments can empower PLWDs by "remov[ing] the barriers which prevent them [from] participating in their communities[,] getting a quality education, finding decent work, and having their voices heard."[67] One conceivable way of removing these barriers is by creating a more level-playing field that promotes human rights and socioeconomic development through reform of existing policies and laws, addressing barriers to financing and affordability, addressing barriers to service delivery, and addressing human resource barriers, as they work to fill gaps in data and research bearing on disability in their own societies.[68] As part of that level-playing field, governments may pay special attention to groups, some of whom historically have been victims of discrimination, like "women, children, the elderly, the poor, migrant workers, persons with dual or multiple disabilities, indigenous people and ethnic minorities[,]" alongside "refugees with disabilities who have special needs requiring attention."[69] Because of the intersection between disability and PLWDs, the discussion of the latter below amplifies and, in some sense, continues the definition of disability here.

Persons Living with Disabilities

Persons living with disabilities (PLWDs) are individuals with "long-term physical, mental, intellectual or sensory impairments which in interaction with various barriers may hinder their full and effective participation in society on an equal basis with others."[70] In the lingo of the United States' disability law, these are impairments that "substantially limit one or more major life activities, such as seeing, hearing, eating, sleeping, walking, standing, lifting, bending, speaking, breathing, learning, reading, concentrating, thinking, communicating, [. . .], caring for oneself, or performing manual tasks."[71] A cross-national tool for measuring disability is the International Classification of Functioning, Disability and Health (ICF).[72] The World Health Organization (WHO), a global health czar, approved the instrument on May 22, 2001, in place of an earlier model developed in 1980, "to provide a unifying framework for classifying the consequences of disease."[73] Many persons are born with disabilities, but many also will experience some form of disability, temporary or permanent, at some points in their lives.[74]

PLWDs are a huge community of individuals that, due to the deprivations they endure, the academic literature in disability studies, correctly analogize to the world's largest minority.[75] About 80 percent of these individuals live in developing countries.[76] A host of other distinctively dismal statistics mark out this community: 19 percent of less educated people have disabilities, compared to 11 percent among better educated persons; according to a United Nations Development Program study in 1998, the global literate rate for adults with disabilities is as low as 3 percent, and 1 percent for women with disabilities; and, based on information provided by the United Nations Educational, Scientific, and Cultural Organization (UNESCO), 90 percent of children with disabilities in developing countries do not attend school.[77] Other gloomy statistics are that, in some countries, about 80 percent of PLWDs are unemployed, with employers often assuming them to be unable to work; 20 percent of the world's poorest people have some kind of disability and tend to be classified in their own countries as a most disadvantaged group; according to a study in the United States in 2004, only 35 percent of working-age PLWDs worked, compared to 78 percent of those without disabilities; based on a WHO study, in some countries, up to a quarter of disabilities result from injuries and violence; and according to a study conducted in the UK in 2004, PLWDs are more likely to be victims of violence or rape, and less likely to obtain police intervention, legal protection or preventive care.[78]

Because of its view of disability as an "evolving concept,"[79] the CRPD does not include "persons living with disabilities" among the list of its defined terms. However, the Protocol of the African Charter on Human and Peoples' Rights on the Rights of Persons with Disabilities in Africa (hereinafter Protocol to the African Charter Related to Disabilities or PACRD), the African regional disability instrument patterned after the CRPD, includes the term among its list of defined terms.[80] Along with the CRPD, the PACRD is elaborated in Chapter 2 of this book.

THE CHANGING NATURE OF DISABILITY IN MODERN TIMES

A study jointly published in 2011 by the WHO and the World Bank provided an authoritative picture of the general conditions of disabled persons across the world, including the changing nature of disability in modern times.[81] The report originated from a World Health Assembly's Resolution in 2005, which mandated the WHO to produce a world study on disability that draws upon the best available scientific evidence.[82] The study enjoined all stakeholders, including governments, civil society, and non-governmental organizations (NGOs) who advocate for disabled persons "to create enabling environments, develop rehabilitation and support services, ensure adequate social protection, create inclusive policies and programs, and enforce new and existing standards and legislation, to the benefit of people with disabilities and the wider community."[83]

With respect to the general conditions of disabled persons, the report found that over one billion people, about 15 percent of the world's population, as indicated before, its largest minority,[84] "live with some form of disability, of whom nearly 200 million experience considerable difficulties in functioning,"[85] and that PLWDs experience barriers in accessing services like healthcare, education, employment, transportation, and information that many nondisabled persons, especially in developed countries, take for granted.[86] Take healthcare as example. PLWDs stand the risk of developing secondary or co-morbid conditions, greater vulnerability to age-related diseases, increased rates of health-risk behaviors, greater risk of being exposed to violence, higher risk of unintentional injuries, and higher risk of premature death.[87] PLWDs regularly lack access to needed healthcare for multiple reasons that, beside the reality that they are outrightly denied healthcare, include the facts that they cannot afford such care, compared to nondisabled people; that they find health-care providers' skills inadequate; and that they are treated badly than non-disabled people.[88] Other findings from the study are that children with disabilities have less access to education than non-disabled children, especially in developing countries, with many children not going to school at all; and that, compared to their nondisabled counterparts, PLWDs endure restricted participation in their societies as well as lack the help they need to engage in everyday activities.[89]

Next, to the changing nature of reality in the modern world, the report points out that: the prevalence of disability is high and growing, due to multiple factors, such as aging populations, increase in chronic conditions, road traffic crashes, violence, and disasters; disability disproportionately affects vulnerable populations like the elderly, women, and the poor; despite the stereotype of a disabled person as a wheelchair user, disability is diverse; PLWDs face barriers in accessing services, including education, healthcare, employment, and transportation; many of the barriers disabled persons face are avoidable; and the disadvantages associated with disability are overcome-able, not intractable.[90]

With its load of infections and deaths, COVID-19 has compounded these disparities.[91] Globally, the pandemic "has created a human crisis of unprecedented scale," requiring the global community to seize the "opportunity to reimagine disability inclusion."[92] In the United States, changes in daily lives of residents traceable to the pandemic have had a negative effect on mental health and created new barriers for persons seeking mental healthcare.[93] Anxieties about contracting the virus, job losses, loss of childcare, and death of loved ones from the pandemic are among the negative impacts on mental health.[94] These effects are not limited to the adult population of the country but instead include young people. In addition to the estimated 140,000 children who lost a parent or grandparent caregiver as a result of COVID-19, the pandemic led to an increase in anxiety, depression, and related mental health issues within this stratum of the US populace.[95] In a world marked by global interdependence,[96] these broad effects extend to Africa. In addition, for Africa, the pandemic is leading to what some perceptive observers assess as a "democratic decline," because of the greater leverage for anti-democratic practices, including enforcement of pandemic restrictions by security services, the pandemic has notoriously afforded Nigeria and other governments in Africa.[97]

ARGUMENT AND ANIMATING THEME

Argument

This book examines the performance of Nigeria's national government related to the global and regional regimes on disability. It argues that the Nigerian government has not done enough to remove numerous obstacles that impede the lives of PLWDs in the country,[98] thereby preventing them from achieving their full potentials on an equal basis with fellow citizens. Led by the national government, and working with PLWDs and their families, along with NGOs who advocate for disabled persons, Nigerian governments at all three levels have a special responsibility to take actions to remove those obstacles.[99] They have not fulfilled that obligation. Instead, the performance of the Nigerian national government, the level of government at the cynosure in this book, is lethargic at best.[100]

Nigeria is not a state party to the PACRD, adopted by the AU in January 2018.[101] The Protocol obligates state parties "to take appropriate and effective measures [. . .] to ensure, respect, promote, protect[,] and fulfill the rights and dignity of persons [living] with disabilities," on a non-discriminatory basis, using multiple means.[102] These means include making adequate budgetary provisions for disability services;[103] "modify[ing] or abolish[ing] existing policies, laws, regulations, customs and practices that constitute discrimination against persons with discrimination";[104] and "[m]odifying, outlawing, criminalizing or campaigning against [. . .] any harmful practices applied to persons [living] with disabilities."[105] Others are ensuring effective participation of PLWDs or their representatives in decision-making processes,[106] and "[t]aking measures to eliminate discrimination on the basis of disability by any person, organization[,] or private enterprise."[107] Moreover, passage of Nigerian Disabilities Act,[108] referenced in this introductory material and elaborated in Chapter 2, was possible only because of pressure on the government by PLWDs and their families, together with NGOs who advocate for disabled persons.[109]

Faced with these suboptimalities, "[t]here is an urgent need to improve the current socioeconomic situation of persons with disabilities in Nigeria."[110] Consequently, this book unearths and makes remedial proposals designed to help Nigeria fulfil its international obligations related to the welfare of PLWDs. This is consistent with the advice of the WHO and the World Bank for countries to adopt a national strategy on disability coupled with a plan of action, including the involvement of PLWDs in matters affecting their welfare, more adequate funding for disability-related services, improved public awareness of disability, better data collection on disability, and enhanced general research on disability.[111] Relegating PLWDs to the margins of society and leaving them dependent is costly for their families and society.[112] Conversely, empowering them "to live independently and contribute to society is socially and economically beneficial."[113] Moreover, because of its focus on Nigeria, this book meets the recommendation by perceptive disability scholars like James Staples and Nikita Mehrota to inject local context and experience in disability studies.[114]

Animating Theme

A notion animating this book is the conviction that addressing the barriers PLWDs face in Nigeria is within human reach. This proposition taps into the optimism of the English physicist and cosmologist Stephen W. Hawking (1942–2018) in his foreword to the *World Report on Disability.*[115] Hawkings opined that "the majority of people with disabilities in the world have an extremely difficult time with everyday survival, let alone productive employment and personal fulfilment"; they face numerous physical, attitudinal, and financial handicaps that deny them the opportunity to shine.[116] However, addressing these barriers is within human reach.[117] Going further, humanity "ha[s] a moral duty to remove the barriers to participation, and to invest sufficient funding and expertise to unlock the vast potential of people with disabilities."[118] He posited, and we concur, that governments globally "can no longer overlook the hundreds of millions of people with disabilities who are denied access to health, rehabilitation, support, education and employment, and never get the chance to shine."[119] Hawkings expressed the hope, which we also share, that the 21st century "will mark a turning point for inclusion of people with disabilities in the lives of their societies."[120]

These statements echo the thoughts of other perceptive observers. These observers include former U.S. First Lady Rosalynn Carter, who once stated, "[o]ur dream of the day when stigma no longer exists, when services are available to all and when every individual can look forward to a happy and fulfilling future is within [. . .] reach,"[121] and then US President Bill Clinton who posited that "[m]ental illness is nothing to be ashamed of, but stigma and bias shame us all."[122] All of these views converge around the proposition stated above to the effect that many of the barriers disabled persons face in our time can be minimized, if not completely avoided.[123]

RECENT DEVELOPMENTS THAT INSPIRED AND LENT IMPETUS TO THIS RESEARCH

On January 23, 2019, Nigeria's President, Muhammadu Buhari, signed into law the Nigerian Disabilities Act of 2018.[124] The signature came several days after a bout of protests by a group of PLWDs and their supporters following a claim by the president, on national television, that he had *not* received the bill.[125] Nigerian lawmakers, formally known as the National Assembly, passed the bill in November 2016 and sent it to General Buhari for assent in December 2018.[126] Altogether, the bill became law after nearly one long decade in the works.[127] Following Nigeria's ratification of the CRPD, along with the acceptance of the individual-complaint and inquiry procedures of its Optional Protocol, PLWDs and non-governmental organizations (NGOs) which advocate for them pressed the Nigerian government to incorporate the treaties into Nigerian law and implement them.[128] Chapter 2 of this book elaborates the twin instruments. Yielding to these pressures, in 2011 and

2015, the National Assembly passed a precursor of the Nigerian Disabilities Act that then President Goodluck Jonathan failed to sign into law.[129]

About 25 million, out of the estimated one billion PLWDs in the world,[130] live in Nigeria.[131] The number represents little over 12 percent of Nigeria's population in 2020 of over 208 million people.[132] About 7–8 percent of household members above the age of five (as well as 9 percent of those 60 or older) have some level of difficulty in functional domains like seeing, hearing, communication, cognition, walking, and self-care.[133] While in its seeming extraordinariness the share of population may be comparable to those of even developed countries like the United States,[134] many of Nigeria's PLWDs endure a range of human right abuses, such as stigma and other acts of discrimination, violence, as well as lack of access to healthcare, housing, and education, more severe than their counterparts in the developed world.[135]

Inadequate access to medical services complicates all forms of ailments in Nigeria, including mental illnesses.[136] Nigeria is an abjectly poor country in the world,[137] where, given their greater socioeconomic susceptibility and vulnerability, disabled persons are, imaginably, disproportionally represented.[138] In 2020, the World Bank undertook what it called a rapid social assessment to document the socioeconomic status of PLWDs in Nigeria.[139] Findings from the study showed that PLWDs lack access to basic services; that attitudinal barriers pose a major impediment to their socioeconomic inclusion; and that inclusive policies are either nonexistent, weak, or inadequately implemented.[140] Based on these findings, the study noted that there is an urgent need to improve the current socioeconomic situation of PLWDs in Nigeria.[141]

A cache of disability initiatives preceded the passage of the Nigerian Disabilities Act. These measures include ratification, on September 24, 2010, of the CRPD, and acceptance of the CRPD's Optional Protocol individual-complaint and inquiry procedures;[142] hosting of the Africa Regional Community-Based Rehabilitation Conference on October 7, 2010;[143] and the adoption in 2012 of a national policy on albinism, which guaranteed equal access to health, education, and other benefits for albinos.[144] All of these initiatives took place under the administration of Goodluck Jonathan (2010–2015). Under General Buhari, in 2016, the Federal Ministry of Education finalized the National Policy on Inclusive Education, after consultation with governmental and non-governmental organizations, including those advocating for PLWDs.[145] Most recently, in 2019, the ministry updated the policy on albinism.[146] Despite these positive developments, PLWDs continue to experience discrimination, exclusion, and barriers in accessing various services.[147] Due to a range of constraints that includes inadequate funding, the policies meant to implement the CRPD remain mostly unimplemented.

FOUR SUB-APPROACHES TO DISABILITY STUDIES AND THE LOCATION OF THIS BOOK WITHIN THESE APPROACHES

This book is propelled by the vision of an inclusive society, where we "are all able to live a life of health, comfort, and dignity."[148] It is imbued with a human-right approach embedded in the proposition that PLWDs should play a central role in initiatives designed to improve their living conditions. Table I.2 encapsulates the distinctions between the human-right and non-human-right approaches to disability studies, based on the degree of inclusiveness each embodies. Each approach embeds two sub-approaches: the non-human-right approach embodies the charity and medical sub-approaches, while the human-right approach encompasses the social and human-right sub-approaches. The main difference between the medical-charity sub-approaches on the one hand and the social-human rights sub-approaches to disability on the other lies in the difference between "special" and "inclusive" treatment.[149] The term "special" often arises in connection with PLWDs: children with special needs, special schools, special services, and special institutions.[150] However, the CRPD signifies a marked departure from specialness because that distinction is a notoriously negative one that, for PLWDs, spells a badge of marginalization, rather than holds reward.[151]

Table I.2. Differences between the non-human-right and human-right approaches in Disability Studies

Item No.	*Human-Right Approach*	*Non-Human-Right Approach*
1.	State obligation	Non-obligatory
2.	Personal autonomy	Lacking in personal autonomy
3.	Empowering	Non-empowering
4.	Fixing the environment	"Fixing" personal weakness
5.	State-facilitating activity	State-constraining activity
6.	Dignifying	Lacking in personal dignity
7.	Independence	Dependence
8.	Equality and nondiscrimination	Discrimination based on disability
9.	Inclusiveness	Institutionalization or non-inclusiveness
10.	Integration	Segregation

Source: Adapted from Table 1. "Understanding Disability as a Human Rights Issue" in *Monitoring the Convention on the Rights of Persons with Disabilities: Guidance for Human Rights Monitors,* Professional Training Series No. 17 (Geneva and New York: Office of the UN High Commissioner for Human Rights, 2010), 9 available at Disabilities_training_17EN.pdf (ohchr.org) (pg. 10).

The *charity* model is the least inclusive of the sub-approaches. The sub-approach treats PLWDs "as passive objects of kind acts or of welfare payments [. . .] not [. . .] able to provide for themselves because of their impairment[,]" with the result that the "society provides for them."[152] Consistent with this view, PLWDs depend for their wellbeing on "duty bearers," such as charity houses, foundations, and churches to whom society delegates responsibility for PLWD wellbeing.[153] In a word, the model considers disability as an individual problem and pays little or no attention to environmental conditions.[154] As a result, the model passes off as positive, attitudes that are, in actuality, harmful in that they relegate PLWDs "into a state of perpetual dependence [that] can prevent them from exercising their rights."[155]

The *medical* sub-approach is an outgrowth of the charity model and a sub-approach closely associated with the charity outlook. Under this model, PLWDs are treated as sick persons needing to be repaired through medicine and rehabilitation to reach the normality that they need to get back to society.[156] Given this "diagnosis," disability services which embrace this model focus on curing the disability in question or rendering the PLWD non-disabled, instead of adjusting the environment to promote accessibility.[157] For example, the PLWD may be provided wheelchair without reasonable accommodation that renders the streets accessible.[158] Consistent with this outlook, the disability experts implementing the vaunted cures are mostly medical professionals, such as physicians, therapists, and nurses.[159] Just as the charity model it is sometimes associated with, this sub-approach perceives disability "as a condition that is inherent in the person—for example, a medical condition that requires the person to be in a wheelchair or to take medication[,]"[160] with little or no attention paid to environmental conditions.[161] The Independent Living Movement (ILM) evolved out of the belief by many PLWD activists that physicians, therapists, and associated members of the medical model were not empowering PLWDs to live independently.[162] ILM builds its philosophy on three main propositions, namely: PLWDs know best what their needs are (consumer sovereignty), and must, therefore, rely on themselves to promote their own self-interests (self-reliance), and that they have the right to participate in the political and economic life of their own communities (political-economic rights).[163]

The connection between the social and human rights sub-approaches to disability is that both models "emphasize that disability-related problems stem from an inaccessible social structure, as opposed to the disability itself[;]" they stress "environmental and attitudinal barriers that prevent people [living] with disabilities from having equal opportunities in their societies."[164] For example, instead of asking, "What is wrong with persons with disabilities?," the more appropriate question is, "What is wrong with society? What social, economic, political and/or environmental conditions need to be changed to facilitate the full enjoyment of all rights by all persons with disabilities?"[165] Thus, under these forward-looking sub-approaches, PLWDs are "able to attend a school, go to work, participate in community activities alongside non-disabled people, perhaps using disability-related accommodations or modifications that make the environment more accessible to them."[166]

The *social* sub-approach to disability is so-called because it views impairment as a social construct. Rather than the impairment, this model "puts the person at the center," thereby "recognizing the values and rights of [the disabled] as part of society."[167] Under this model, the burden of disability is placed on society rather than PLWDs, thereby granting disabled persons the empowerment that puts them "in control of their lives and [enabling them to] enjoy full participation on an equal basis with others."[168] Current themes in disability studies "recognize[] the necessity of addressing both [. . .] individual needs [. . .] and the shortcomings of the society" indicated by "various obstacles for participation."[169]

The *human right* sub-approach represents a progressive deepening of the social sub-approach. It "builds on the social approach by acknowledging persons [living] with disabilities as subjects of rights and the State and others as having responsibilities to respect these persons" as well as "treats the barriers in society as discriminatory and provides avenues for persons with disabilities to complain when they are faced with such barriers."[170] It is an agreement nay commitment "by persons [living] with disabilities, States and the international human rights system to put into practice some primary aspects of the social approach."[171]

Understandably, the last two sub-approaches embedded in human rights are the models today that underpin the work of many disability rights activists. Our book embedded in human rights joins this progressive trend. Here is why. All four model continue till today. "In spite of the adoption of the [CRPD], the charity and medical models are still very prevalent—even among the human rights community."[172] PLWDs "have historically been invisible in the human rights system and have been overlooked in human rights work."[173] However, "[t]his is no longer acceptable[,]"[174] an outlook this book, consecrated in human rights, embodies.

ORGANIZATION OF THE BOOK

This book is divided into four chapters, plus this introduction and a conclusion. Chapter 1 sketches the history of disability in Nigeria, using the past to understand the present and to gauge the future. The sketch is organized around three interrelated features enshrined in equally three eras. The features are: sources (or drivers) of disabilities and prevalence, representative laws and policies, and societal attitudes toward disabilities and individuals living with these conditions. The three eras are: the precolonial, colonial, and postcolonial periods. A constant that runs through the three eras that the discussion unearths is an invariably negative attitude toward PLWDs.

Chapter 2 unpacks the global and regional disability regimes pertaining to Nigeria. Proper understanding of the response of the Nigerian government toward matters relating to the welfare of disabled persons must be predicated on an outline of the specific rules involved. Thus, the task of Chapter 2 is to pinpoint those international measures and the domestic laws meant to facilitate their implementation as Nigerian domestic law. Chapter 3 explores the record of the Nigerian government since 1999 under the Fourth Republic. To provide heuristic benchmarks for realistic assessment of the labor of the government, the chapter analyzes in some detail the Nigerian Disabilities Act of 2018, a signature legislative achievement of the Fourth Republic pertaining to disabilities, followed by a list of ten sectors of inaccessibility that impede the lives and prospects of PLWDs in Nigeria. The chapter also includes a statement related to the negative impact of sustained military rule in the country, spanning three decades until 1999, on disability rights.

Chapter 4 outlines workable measures for enhancing the capability of the Nigerian government under the Fourth Republic to implement disability laws. While Chapter 3 chronicles, arguably negatively, the failures of the national government relating to the welfare of PLWDs, this chapter looks, arguably positively, on what can be done to remediate or minimize the effect of those failures in the lives of PLWDs. Its highlights consist of a set of ten measured proposals, underlain by the predicate of improved civilian rule, that it proposes for advancing disability laws in Nigeria under the Fourth Republic. The Conclusion ties together the achievements of the book, with a look into the future, anchored on two recommendations: more robust provisions for disability rights in the Nigerian constitution, and the need for Nigeria to ratify the PACRD.

This book departs from similar or comparable works because of its increased emphasis on the human rights of PLWDs, and their untapped potentials to contribute to socioeconomic development that a progressive government must unlock and harness. Key highlights and achievements of the book include the set of ten sectors of inaccessibility that impedes the lives of PLWDs in Nigeria that it composes, and the set of ten targeted measures, predicated upon improved civilian rule, that it proposes, for advancing disability laws in Nigeria under the Fourth Republic. Since the 1990s, Nigeria and many other African countries embarked upon a journey to more democratic and participatory governing processes,[175] that will remain incomplete unless the governments of these countries change their policies toward PLWDs, in conformity with their obligations in international law.

Nigerian constitutionalism imposes on the government definite duties toward the citizenry,[176] that the national government has not extended to its disabled communities. Nigeria's ratification of the CRPD, its acceptance of the individual-complaint and inquiry procedures of the CRPD's Optional Protocol, and its enactment of the Nigerian Disabilities Act, which made these instruments part of its domestic legislation, afford an opportune moment this book seizes for a midrange examination of the country's implementation of its obligations related to the welfare of PLWDs. Concededly, the burgeoning scholarship on disability has been the scene of notable recent works.[177]However, until this book, none of these studies deal with Nigeria, particularly Nigeria under the Fourth Republic since 1999.[178]

NOTES

1. Discrimination Against Persons with Disabilities (Prohibition) Act (2018) [hereinafter DPDP or Nigerian Disabilities Act]. For a text of this law, see *Nigeria Health Watch*, https://nigeriahealthwatch.com/wp-content/uploads/bsk-pdf-manager/2019/02/1244-Discrimination-Against-Persons-with-Disabilities-Prohibition-ACT-2018.pdf.

2. Convention on the Rights of Persons with Disabilities, UN General Assembly Resolution No. A/RES/61/106, Annex I (December 13, 2006), https://www.refworld.org/docid/4680cd212.html [hereinafter CRPD].

3. See Chapter 2 for elaboration of these multilateral treaties.

4. The acronym PLWDs is used interchangeably with "persons with disabilities," and "disabled persons." The last is used descriptively and non-pejoratively to minimize monotony. On a note of style, an "s" is added to the acronym to pluralize it.

5. West Africa is one of six subregions in Africa; the remaining five are: Central Africa, Eastern Africa, Northern (Arab) Africa, Southern Africa, and the African Diaspora. See "Subregions," African Center for Strategic Progress, https://acstrap.org/subregions/. See also "The Six Regions of the African Union," West Africa Brief, http://www.west-africa-brief.org/content/en/six-regions-african-union (with map showing subregions). With its fifteen countries, all of which are members of the Economic Community of West African States (ECOWAS), West Africa is the subregion with the largest number of states. See Subregions. And with a population estimated at 350 million people, it is also the most populous subregion. See ibid. In 2003, the African Union created the African Diaspora as a sixth subregion in an attempt to encourage the participation of people of African descent living outside the continent, irrespective of their nationalities, to contribute to the development of Africa. Ibid.

6. "Nigeria Population (Live)," *Worldometers*, https://www.worldometers.info/world-population/nigeria-population/. This feature and its relative wealth make Nigeria by far a most important country in West Africa and a linchpin of ECOWAS, which it helped create in 1975. In 2015, Nigeria made up 53 percent of ECOWAS' population, 76 percent of its total GDP of US $652 billion, and contributed (and still contributes) nearly one-third of the community's annual budget. See Philip C. Aka, *Human Rights in Nigeria's External Relations: Building the Record of a Moral Superpower* (Lanham, Boulder, New York, and London: Lexington Books, 2017), 229–30,

including tbl. 10.1., p. 229, showing ECOWAS member-states with their distinctive characteristic as of 2015.

7. To the uninitiated, the name is confusedly similar to Nigeria. The two countries took their names after the River Niger which courses through their landscapes. See "Niger River," *New World Encyclopedia*, https://www.newworldencyclopedia.org/entry/Niger_River. The confusion is needlessly amplified by some other facts, including that one of Nigeria's 36 states also goes by the name Niger, and that the national flag of Niger Republic has a green bar, compared to two green bars in Nigeria's.

8. "Nigeria—Location, Size, and Extent," *Nations Encyclopedia*, https://www.nationsencyclopedia.com/Africa/Nigeria-LOCATION-SIZE-AND-EXTENT.html.

9. Ibid.

10. See Philip C. Aka, "The 'Dividend of Democracy': Analyzing U.S. Support for Nigerian Democratization," *Boston College Third World Law Journal*, 22(2) (2002), 225, 228–29; "History," in *Nigeria: A Country Study*, ed. Helen Chapin Metz (Washington, DC: GPO for the Library of Congress, 1991).

11. Aka, "The Dividend of Democracy," note 10.

12. See, for example, Adeyinka Samson Adeniyi and Michael Emeka Ofiwe, "The Impact of Ethnicity on Nigeria's Political Development: An Assessment, 1999–2011," *International Journal of Research and Development Organization,* 2(12) (December 2015), 71–99.

13. See "Nigeria Fact Sheet," United States Embassy in Nigeria (January 2012), https://photos.state.gov/libraries/nigeria/487468/pdfs/Nigeria%20overview%20Fact%20Sheet.pdf.

14. See Robert L. Tignor, *Capitalism and Nationalism at the End of Empire: State and Business in Decolonizing Egypt, Nigeria, and Kenya, 1945–1963* (Princeton, NJ: Princeton University Press, 1998), 195.

15. Ibid.

16. See Kathleen Sheetz, "Slave Coast," *Encyclopedia Britannica*, https://www.britannica.com/place/Slave-Coast.

17. See "Nigeria Independence Act[,] 1960," 1960 Ch. 55 8 & 9 Eliz. (July 29, 1960), 2, https://www.legislation.gov.uk/ukpga/1960/55/pdfs/ukpga_19600055_en.pdf ("An Act to make provision for, and in connection with, the attainment by Nigeria of fully responsible status within the Commonwealth").

18. "Nigeria Republic Act[,] 1963," 1963 Ch. 57 (December 18,1963), https://www.legislation.gov.uk/ukpga/1963/57/enacted ("An Act to make provision as to the operation of the law in relation to Nigeria as a Republic within the Commonwealth"). For example, § 2 of the Nigerian Independence Act stipulated that "[n]o Act of the Parliament of the United Kingdom passed on or after [October 1, 1960] shall extend, or be deemed to extend, to Nigeria or any part thereof as part of the law thereof, and as from that day." "Nigeria Independence Act[,] 1960," note 17. However, the same law also indicated in § 1 that from October 1, 1960, the supposedly independent country "shall [. . .] constitute part of Her Majesty's dominions under the name of Nigeria." Ibid. Republican status eliminated the seeming contradiction.

19. Constitution of the Federal Republic of Nigeria (1999), https://www.constituteproject.org/constitution/Nigeria_1999.pdf, schedule 1, Parts I-II.

20. "Brief Notes on Nigeria," *Online Nigeria,* http://www.onlinenigeria.com/history.asp.

21. The authors are indebted to the anonymous reviewer of the manuscript for this book for this insight.

22. See Aka, *Human Rights in Nigeria's External Relations,* note 6, p. 1.

23. See, for example, CRPD, note 2, art. 4(5) ("The provisions of the present Convention shall extend to all parts of federal states without any limitations or exceptions"). This seminal human right instrument, elaborated in Chapter 2, is referenced repeatedly in this book.

24. *New State Ice Co. v. Liebmann*, 285 U.S. 262 (1932), Louis Brandeis, J., dissenting ("It is one of the happy incidents of the federal system that a single courageous State may, if its citizens choose, serve as a laboratory; and try novel social and economic experiments without risk to the rest of the country"). Also, in its reports to treaty bodies, as part of the reporting requirements for multilateral treaties that Nigeria is party to, whether on disability or any other matter, the Nigerian national government typically includes progress within Nigerian states among its achievements, as it arguably should.

25. See Aka, *Human Rights in Nigeria's External Relations*, note 6, pp. 73 (tbl. 4.1), and 82–3.

26. See ibid., p. 72 (tbl. 4.1), 76–9, 79–81.

27. See ibid., pp. 75–6.

28. Ibid., pp. 79–80 (extending into the discussion on the "Second Round of Military Regimes, 1983–1999").

29. See Aka, *Human Rights in Nigeria's External Relations*, note 6, pp. 84–85, n.1; Philip C. Aka, "Judicial Independence under Nigeria's Fourth Republic: Problems and Prospects," *California Western Int'l Law Journal*, 45(1) (2014), 1, 3 n.2.

30. "The Rectification of Names," *Cultural China*, http://www.cultural-china.com/chinaWH/History/en/165History878.html.

31. Michael G. Maxfield and Earl R. Babbie, *Research Methods for Criminal Justice and Criminology,* 7th ed. (Stamford, CT: Cengage Learning, 2015), 110–11, 112. See also ibid., p. 239 (stating that "there are no ultimately true meanings for any of the concepts we typically study in social science").

32. See, for example, *International Regimes*, ed. Stephen D. Krasner (Ithaca, NY: Cornell University Press, 1983), 1–2; Andreas Hasenclever et al., *Theories of International Regimes* (New York: Cambridge University Press, 1997); and Charles Lipson, "Why are Some International Agreements Informal?" *International Organization*, 45 (1991), 495–538.

33. Carl I. Fertman et al., *Promoting Child and Adolescent Mental Health* (Burlington, MA: Jones & Bartlett Publishers, 2013), 260.

34. *Toolkit on Disability for Africa: Culture, Beliefs, and Disability*, UN Department of Economics & Social Affairs, Module 13, p. 6, https://www.un.org/esa/socdev/documents/disability/Toolkit/Cultures-Beliefs-Disability.pdf.

35. See Erving Goffman, *Stigma: Notes on the Management of Spoiled Identity* (New York: Simon and Schuster, 2009), 1.

36. Kathryn Jagoe, "The Disability Rights Movement: Its Development in South Africa," Independent Living Institute, https://www.independentliving.org/toolsforpower/tools6.html.

37. Ibid.

38. Ibid.

39. Brigitte Rohwerder, "Disability Stigma in Developing Countries," *K4D Helpdesk Report* (May 9, 2018), 4, 12–13, https://opendocs.ids.ac.uk/opendocs/bitstream/handle/20.500.12413/13795/Disability_stigma_in_developing_countries.pdf?sequence=1.

40. Ibid., p. 2.

41. Ibid.

42. Ibid.

43. Sarah G. Brouillard, "Disability Inequality in Developing African Countries: A Comparison of Disability Legislation and Social Rights in Mali and Niger," *Story Maps* (December 8, 2020), https://storymaps.arcgis.com/stories/e8f5bbadc9594b0da39cbaa7fa1bfbbb.

44. Rohwerder, "Disability Stigma in Developing Countries," note 39, p. 13

45. Ibid., pp. 4, 13.

46. Felix Silwimba, "Possibilities of Independent Living of Persons with Disabilities in Africa," Independent Living Institute, https://www.independentliving.org/toolsforpower/tools5.html.

47. Ibid.

48. Brenda Major and Laurie T. O'Brien, "The Social Psychology of Stigma," *Annual Review of Psychology,* 56 (1) (2005), 393–421, doi:10.1146/annurev.psych.56.091103.070137.

49. "Message from Donna E. Shalala," Secretary of Health and Human Services, in *Mental Health: A Report of the Surgeon General* (Rockville, MD: U.S. Department of Health and Human Services, 1999), https://collections.nlm.nih.gov/ext/document/101584932X120/PDF/101584932X120.pdf ("Mental illnesses are just as real as other illnesses, and they are like other illnesses in most ways. Yet fear and stigma persist, resulting in lost opportunities to seek treatment and improve or recover").

50. "Disability and Health Overview," CDC: Centers for Disease Control and Prevention, https://www.cdc.gov/ncbddd/disabilityandhealth/disability.html.

51. Standard Rules on the Equalization of Opportunities for Persons with Disabilities, UN General Assembly Resolution No. A/RES/48/96 (December 20, 1993), 15, item 17, https://www.refworld.org/docid/3b00f2e80.html [hereinafter Standard Rules].

52. CRPD, note 2, preamble, item (i).

53. See, for example, Kevin L. Crow, "Four Types of Disabilities: Their Impact on Online Learning," Tech Trends: Linking Research and Practice to Improve Learning, 52(1) (January 2008), 51–55, https://eric.ed.gov/?id=EJ798639.

54. See, for example, "What is a Physical Disability?" *Achieve Australia*, https://achieveaustralia.org.au/ndis-overview-and-faqs/physical-disability/#:~:text=A%20physical%20disability%20is%20a,and%20visual%20impairments%20and%20more."Physical Disability," Educ. to Employment, https://web.archive.org/web

/20130724013228/http://pubsites.uws.edu.au/ndco/employment/what/physical.htm; "Types of Physical Disabilities," Carehome.Co.UK, https://www.carehome.co.uk/advice/types-of-physical-disabilities.

55. See "What to Know about Intellectual Disability," *Medical News Today*, https://www.medicalnewstoday.com/articles/intellectual-disability.

56. See, for example., "What is a Sensory Disability?" *Achieve Australia*, https://achieveaustralia.org.au/ndis-overview-and-faqs/what-is-sensory-disability/; and "Types of Sensory Disabilities," *Aruma*, https://www.aruma.com.au/about-us/about-disability/types-of-disabilities/types-of-sensory-disabilities/.

57. See, for example, "Mental Disorders," *MedlinePlus*, https://medlineplus.gov/mentaldisorders.html; "Mental Illness," Mayo Clinic, https://www.mayoclinic.org/diseases-conditions/mental-illness/symptoms-causes/syc-20374968; "What Is Mental Illness?" American Psychiatric Association, https://www.psychiatry.org/patients-families/what-is-mental-illness. See also John Petrila and Thomas Brink, "Mental Illness and Changing Definitions of Disability Under the Americans with Disabilities Act," 52(5) *Psychiatric Services,* 52(5) (May 2001), 626.

58. CRPD, note 2.

59. Ibid., preamble, item (e).

60. CRPD, note 2, art. 2 ("Definitions") (defining discrimination based on disability to "mean any distinction, exclusion or restriction on the basis of disability which has the purpose or effect of impairing or nullifying the recognition, enjoyment or exercise, on an equal basis with others, of all human rights and fundamental freedoms in the political, economic, social, cultural, civil or any other field [. . .] including denial of reasonable accommodation").

61. *World Report on Disability* (Geneva Switzerland and Washington, DC: World Health Organization and the World Bank, 2011), xxi, https://www.who.int/disabilities/world_report/2011/report.pdf.

62. CRPD, note 2, preamble, item (h).

63. *World Report on Disability*, note 61, p. xxi.

64. Standard Rules, note 51.

65. See ibid. (Annex: "Background and Current Needs," 3). The General Assembly observed that present policy on disability "is the result of developments over the past 200 years" that "[i]n many ways [. . .] reflects the general living conditions and social and economic policies of different times." Ibid.

66. See Ngozi C. Umeh and Ramola Adeola, "Nigeria," in *African Disability Rights Yearbook* (2013), 277–290; and Timothy Ali Yohanna, *They Call Us Senseless Beggars* (Abuja: Grassroots Researchers Association, n.d.), 16–35, https://www.grassrootresearchers.org/wp-content/uploads/2019/01/disability_challenges.pdf.pdf.

67. Margaret Chan and Robert B. Zoellick, "Preface," in *World Report on Disability*, note 61, p. xi.

68. *World Report on Disability*, note 61, pp. 65–83.

69. Standard Rules, note 51, 15.

70. CRPD, note 2, art. 1 ("Purpose").

71. Americans with Disabilities Act (ADA), P.L. 101–336 (1990), including changes made by ADA Amendments Act, P.L. 110–325 (2008), effective January 1, 2009.

72. "International Classification of Functioning, Disability[,] and Health (ICF)," National Center for Health Statistics, US CDC (January 24, 2008), http://www.cdc.gov/NCHS/about/otheract/icd9/icfhome.htm. See also *Toward a Common Language for Functioning, Disability and Health ICF* (Geneva, Switzerland: World Health Organization, 2002), https://www.who.int/classifications/icf/icfbeginnersguide.pdf.

73. "International Classification of Functioning, Disability[,] and Health (ICF)," note 72.

74. See "Disability and Health," note 50; Toyin Falola and Nic Hamel, "Africanizing Disability: Toward an Articulation of African Disability Studies," in *Disability in Africa: Inclusion, Care, and the Ethics of Humanity,* eds. Toyin Falola and Nic Hamel (New York: University of Rochester Press, 2021), 1–46 (describing impairment as "an actual or potential condition of all living bodies in all places"); *From Exclusion to Equality: Realizing the Rights of Persons with Disabilities,* Handbook for Parliamentarians No. 14 (New York: Office of the UN High Commissioner for Human Rights, 2007), 7 ("Everyone is likely to experience disability at some point during his/her lifetime because of illness, accident or ageing").

75. "Fact Sheet on Persons with Disabilities," United Nations: Enable, https://www.un.org/disabilities/documents/toolaction/pwdfs.pdf.

76. Ibid.

77. Ibid.

78. Ibid.

79. See note 59 and accompanying text.

80. Protocol to the African Charter on Human and Peoples' Rights on the Rights of Persons with Disabilities in Africa (January 29, 2018), art. 1, https://au.int/sites/default/files/treaties/36440-treaty-protocol_to_the_achpr_on_the_rights_of_persons_with_disabilities_in_africa_e.pdf [hereinafter PACRD] ("Definitions") (defining almost word for word with the CRPD, "persons with disabilities" as "includ[ing] those who have physical, mental, psycho-social, intellectual, neurological, developmental[,] or other sensory impairments[,] which[,] in interaction with environmental, attitudinal[,] or other barriers[,] hinder their full and effective participation in society on an equal basis with others"). Like the CRPD, again almost word for word, the PACRD includes on its definition list, the term "[d]iscrimination on the basis of disability." Ibid.

81. See generally *World Report on Disability*, note 61.

82. *World Report on Disability*, note 61, p. xxi, referring to WHA 58.23, "Disability, Including Prevention, Management, and Rehabilitation," Fifty-Eighth World Health Assembly (May 25, 2005), https://apps.who.int/iris/bitstream/handle/10665/20373/WHA58_23-en.pdf?sequence=1&isAllowed=y.

83. Chan and Zoellick, note 67, p. xi.

84. See note 75 and accompanying text.

85. Chan and Zoellick, note 67, p. xi.

86. *World Report on Disability,* note 61, p. 57. See also Odirin Omiegbe, "Poverty and Persons Living with Disabilities in Nigeria," in *Africa's Radicalisms and Conservatisms: Politics, Poverty, Marginalization[,] and Education*, eds. Edwin Etieyibo et al. (Leiden, The Netherlands: Brill Publishing, 2021), 164–185.

87. *World Report on Disability,* note 61, pp. 58–60.

88. See *World Report on Disability*, note 61.

89. Ibid.

90. Ibid.

91. See Anita Powell, "Pandemic Takes Unique Toll on South Africa's Disabled," *VOA News* (March 10, 2021), https://www.voanews.com/a/covid-19-pandemic_pandemic-takes-unique-toll-south-africas-disabled/6203126.html (focusing on South Africa); and "A More Accessible and Sustainable World: A Disability-Inclusive Response to COVID-19," World Bank (December 1, 2020), https://www.worldbank.org/en/news/feature/2020/12/01/a-more-accessible-and-sustainable-world-a-disability-inclusive-response-to-covid-19.

92. "A More Accessible and Sustainable World," note 91.

93. Audrey Kearney et al., "Mental Health Impact of the COVID-19 Pandemic: An Update," *KFF* (April 14, 2021), https://www.kff.org/coronavirus-covid-19/poll-finding/mental-health-impact-of-the-covid-19-pandemic/. See also Pam Belluck, "Covid Patients May Have Increased Risk of Developing Mental Health Problems," *New York Times* (February 16, 2022), https://www.nytimes.com/2022/02/16/health/covid-depression-anxiety.html (reporting on a study based on the analysis of about 154,000 COVID patients in the Veterans Health Administration). The study found that one year after catching the disease, patients infected were significantly more likely to be diagnosed with psychiatric disorders they did not have before, compared to patients who were not infected. Ibid.

94. Kearney et al., note 93.

95. See Monique Beals, "Surgeon General Warns of Mental Health Challenges Confronting Youth," *The Hill* (December 7, 2021), https://thehill.com/policy/healthcare/mental-health/584656-surgeon-general-warns-of-mental-health-challenges-confronting.

96. See, for example, Mary E. Wilson, "Travel and the Emergence of Infectious Diseases," *Emerging Infectious Diseases*, 1(2) (1995), 39–46, doi:10.3201/eid0102.950201 (pointing out that "[w]hen they travel, humans carry their genetic makeup, immunologic sequelae of past infections, cultural preferences, customs, and behavioral patterns[,]" along with "[m]icrobes, animals, and other biologic life [. . .]"). See also William H. McNeill, *Plagues and Peoples* (Garden City, NY: Anchor Press/Doubleday, 1976).

97. See John Campbell and Nolan Smith, "What's Happening to Democracy in Africa," Council on Foreign Relations (May 26, 2021), https://www.cfr.org/article/whats-happening-democracy-africa.

98. See, for example, Augustine Edobor Arimoro, "Are They Not Nigerians? The Obligation of the State to End Discriminatory Practices against Persons with Disabilities," *International Journal of Discrimination and the Law,* 19(2) (2019), https://doi.org/10.1177/1358229119846764.

99. *World Report on Disability*, note 61, preamble (underscoring the point "that persons with disabilities, and their parents, guardians, advocates and organizations, must be active partners with States in the planning and implementation of all measures affecting" the "civil, political, economic, social and cultural rights" of persons living with disabilities).

100. See, for example, Arimoro, note 98; and Edwin Etieyibo, "Social Justice and Persons with Disabilities in Nigeria," in *Africa's Radicalisms and Conservatisms*, note 86, pp. 143–163.

101. As of June 17, 2020, 9 of the 55 countries in Africa, excluding Nigeria, were signatories to the Protocol. See "List of Countries Which Have Signed, Ratified/Acceded to the Protocol to the African Charter on Human and Peoples' Rights on the Rights of Persons with Disabilities in Africa," https://au.int/sites/default/files/treaties/36440-sl-PROTOCOL%20TO%20THE%20AFRICAN%20CHARTER%20ON%20HUMAN%20AND%20PEOPLES%E2%80%99%20RIGHTS%20ON%20THE%20RIGHTS%20OF%20PERSONS%20WITH%20DISABILITIES%20IN%20AFRICA.pdf. These countries are Angola (which appended its signature on June 17 2020), Burkina Faso, Cameroon, Central African Republic, Gabon, Mali, Rwanda, South Africa, and Togo. Ibid.

102. PACRD, note 80, art. 4.

103. Ibid., art. 4 (i).

104. Ibid., art. 4 (c).

105. Ibid., art. 4 (d).

106. Ibid., art. 4 (j).

107. Ibid., art. 4 (f).

108. Nigerian Disabilities Act, note 1.

109. Arimoro, note 98 (abstract).

110. See *Disability Inclusion in Nigeria: A Rapid Assessment* (Washington, DC: World Bank, 2020), https://doi.org/10.1596/34073 (abstract).

111. *World Report on Disability,* note 61, pp. 265–268.

112. *From Exclusion to Equality*, note 74, p. 7.

113. Ibid.

114. See James Staples and Nikita Mehrota. "Disability Studies: Developments in Anthropology," *Disability in the Global South: The Critical Handbook*, eds. Shaun Grech and Karen Soldatic (Cham, Switzerland: Springer, 2016), 40, 41, https://www.academia.edu/31965669/Disability_Studies_Developments_in_Anthropology (pleading for openness "to new perspectives" in disability studies, based on "people's everyday experiences in particular settings," including the wisdom that "[d]isability needs first to be understood in people's own terms and in relation to their particular experiences[,]" and the need to utilize "local, on the ground realities" in constructing models, bearing in mind the different contexts involved in the development of disability studies). See also Nora Ellen Groce, "Guest Editorial: Framing Disability Issues in Local Concepts and Beliefs," *Asia Pacific Disability Rehabilitation Journal*, 10(1) (1999), 1–6, https://discovery.ucl.ac.uk/id/eprint/15160/1/15160.pdf ("Culturally imbedded conceptual frameworks of disability affect the way in which individuals with disability see themselves and the world around them"). As Groce points out,

"[w]hen specific cultures have positive practices[,] these may provide models for more universal approaches to disability." Ibid., p. 1. But "[w]hen specific cultures have negative practices[,] change may be more effectively advocated when local people come to understand that their particular opinions and practices are not found world-wide." Ibid.

115. Stephen W. Hawking, "Foreword," *in World Report on Disability*, note 61, p. ix.

116. Ibid.

117. Ibid.

118. Ibid.

119. Ibid.

120. Ibid.

121. Rosaylnn Carter, Susan K. Golant, and Kathryn E. Cade, *Within Our Reach: Ending the Mental Health Crisis* (Emmaus, PA: Rodale, 2010), p. xxvi.

122. President [Bill] Clinton and Mrs. [Tipper] Gore, "Combating the Stigma of Mental Illness," Clinton White House (June 5, 1999), https://clintonwhitehouse4.archives.gov/textonly/WH/Work/060599.html.

123. See notes 117 and 121 and accompanying texts.

124. Nigerian Disabilities Act, note 1. For a sample of the numerous news stories on the law, see, for example, Terhemba Daka, "President Buhari Signs Disability Bill into Law," *Guardian* (Lagos) (January 24, 2019), https://guardian.ng/news/president-buhari-signs-disability-bill-into-law/24; Ayo Aluko-Olokun, "President Buhari Signs Long[-]Awaited Disability Bill into Law," *Nigeria Democratic Report* (January 24, 2019), https://www.ndr.org.ng/president-buhari-signs-long-awaited-disability-bill-into-law/; and Samuel Ogundipe, "Buhari Signs Law Banning Discrimination Against Persons with Disability," *Premium Times* (Abuja) (January 23, 2019), https://www.premiumtimesng.com/news/headlines/307474-buhari-signs-law-banning-discrimination-against-persons-with-disability.html.

125. See Oluwatobi Enitan, "Physically Challenged Protest Buhari's Non-Assent to Disability Bill," *Roots TV* (Nigeria) (January 18, 2019), https://www.youtube.com/watch?v=8jQhcIEMVG8. See also Anietie Ewang, "Nigeria Passes Disability Rights Law: Offers Hope of Inclusion, Improved Access," *Human Rights Watch* (January 25, 2019), https://www.hrw.org/news/2019/01/25/nigeria-passes-disability-rights-law. Buhari was the military dictator who gained notoriety for overthrowing a democratic government in 1983 and bringing to an end the country's Second Republic (from 1979 until 1983). See David Smith, "Muhammadu Buhari: Reformed Dictator Returns to Power in Democratic Nigeria," *Guardian* (London) (March 31, 2015), https://www.theguardian.com/world/2015/mar/31/muhammadu-buhari-military-dictator-nigeria-new-democratic-president. Buhari ruled repressively until August 1985 when he was himself overthrown in a counter-coup. Ibid. Buhari became president in 2015 after running for the office three times, packaging himself as a "converted democrat." Ibid. He was reelected to a second term in office in an election some independent observers assessed as "marred by consistent irregularities." See "Nigeria," Freedom in the World 2020: Country Report (Washington, DC: Freedom House, 2020), https://freedomhouse.org/country/nigeria/freedom-world/2020 ("Overview").

126. Ewang, note 125. Under the Nigerian presidential system of government, modelled on the United States', a bill becomes law only when the president gives his complementary assent, that he could also choose to withhold by a veto. Like in the US, the bill still becomes law if two-thirds of the legislature overrides the veto.

127. Aluko-Olokun, note 124.

128. Ewang, note 125.

129. Ibid.

130. See note 85 and accompanying text.

131. See "[Twenty-Five] Million Lives at Stake: Nigerians with Disabilities During the Pandemic," International Disability Alliance (December 4, 2020), https://www.internationaldisabilityalliance.org/blog/25-million-lives-stake-nigerians-disabilities-during-pandemic; Ewang, note 125. This does not include about 3.5 million persons in the country with significant social and physical functioning impairment. See Precious Sango, "Visible but Invisible: People Living with Disability in Nigeria," *Books2Africa* (November 13, 2013), https://books2africa.org/visible-but-invisible-people-living-with-disability-in-nigeria/; and C. Jonah Eleweke and Jannine Ebenso, "Barriers to Accessing Services by People with Disabilities in Nigeria: Insights from a Qualitative Study," *Journal of Educational & Social Research,* 6(2), 113–24. World Health Organization data for 2018 put the number at about 29 million. See *Disability Inclusion in Nigeria*, note 110 (quoting the WHO).

132.See "Nigeria Population (Live)," note 6; "Countries in the World by Population (2020)," Worldometers, https://www.worldometers.info/world-population/population-by-country/ (placing the number at about 206 million). To put the matter in comparative perspective, this number equates the population of Cameroon (26.5 million), Côte d'Ivoire (26 million) or Niger Republic (24 million). "Countries in the World by Population (2020)."

133. *Disability Inclusion in Nigeria*, note 110 (referencing data from the 2018 Nigeria Demographic and Health Survey in 2018). The World Bank speculates that the numbers are probably even higher because currently available data likely underestimate the prevalence. Ibid. Nigeria lacks reliable statistics on disability, meaning that there is a significant knowledge gap that needs to be bridged. See N. Amusat, "Disability Care in Nigeria: The Need for Professional Advocacy," *AJPARS,* 1(1) (2009), 3036.

134. In the US, the percentage of persons living with disability was 11.9% in 2010 and 12.8% in 2016. See "2017 Disability Status Report," Cornell University (2019), https://www.disabilitystatistics.org/StatusReports/2017-PDF/2017-StatusReport_US.pdf. In the US, the population of disabled persons varies by state, in employment, poverty, earnings, and health behaviors. Ibid. There are approximately 40.7 million disabled Americans. See "A Brief History of the Disability Rights Movement," ADL, https://www.adl.org/education/resources/backgrounders/disability-rights-movement. The acronym ADL stands for Anti-Defamation League, headquartered in New York. Founded in September 1913, the ADL is a Jewish organization that works for justice by fighting to combat antisemitism, extremism, and hate, among other strands of its mission.

135. *See* Ewang, note 125.

136. See generally Philip C. Aka and Joseph A. Balogun, *Healthcare Reform and Economic Restructuring in Nigeria* (Gateway East, Singapore: Palgrave Macmillan, 2022), 79–111.

137. Bukola Adebayo, "Nigeria Overtakes India in Extreme Poverty Ranking," *CNN* (June 26, 2018), https://www.cnn.com/2018/06/26/africa/nigeria-overtakes-india-extreme-poverty-intl (reporting that "Nigeria has overtaken India as the country with the largest number of people living in extreme poverty, with an estimated 87 million Nigerians, or around half of the country's population, thought to be living on less than $1.90 a day"). As this news story observed, "[d]espite being the largest oil producer in Africa, Nigeria has struggled to translate its resource wealth into rising living standards." Ibid.

138. Looking beyond Nigeria, about 80 percent of the overall number of disabled persons in the world, live in developing countries. See "Factsheet on Persons with Disabilities," UN Department of Economic and Social Affairs, https://www.un.org/development/desa/disabilities/resources/factsheet-on-persons-with-disabilities.html; and Jackie Marchildon, "[Five] Facts About Living with a Disability in the Developing World," *Global Citizen* (November 23, 2018), https://www.globalcitizen.org/en/content/disability-in-the-developing-world/#:~:text=1)%2080%25%20of%20people%20living,people%20live%20in%20developing%20countries.

139. See generally *Disability Inclusion in Nigeria,* note 110.

140. Ibid.

141. Ibid. (abstract).

142. See "Ratification Status for Nigeria," UN Treaty Body Database, Office of the High Commissioner for Human Rights, https://tbinternet.ohchr.org/_layouts/15/TreatyBodyExternal/Treaty.aspx?CountryID=127&Lang=EN.

143. See Grace Musoke and Priscille Geiser, eds., "Linking CRB, Disability, and Rehabilitation," CRB Africa Network (2013), 5, http://www.fatoafrique.org/site/IMG/pdf/cbr_africa_final.pdf ("Foreword").

144. See Federal Ministry of Education, *National Policy on Albinism in Nigeria* (Abuja: Federal Ministry of Education, 2012), https://albinofoundation.org/wp-content/uploads/2017/04/National-Policy-on-Albinism-Implementatio-Guideline.pdf. See also Marika Toumi et al., *Report: Regional Action Plan on Ending Attacks and Human Rights Violations Against Persons with Albanism in Africa, 2017–2021: Action on Albinism* (July 1, 2021), 19–21, https://www.ohchr.org/Documents/Issues/Albinism/RAP_Report_01-07_21_EN.pdf.

145. "FG Unveils National Draft Policy on Inclusive Education," *Vanguard* (Lagos) (February 22, 2016), https://guardian.ng/news/fg-unveils-national-draft-policy-on-inclusive-education/.

146. Federal Ministry of Education, *National Policy on Albinism in Nigeria* (Abuja: Federal Ministry of Education, 2019), https://albinofoundation.org/wp-content/uploads/2021/09/REVIEWED-NATIONAL-POLICY-ON-ALBINISM-DESIGNED-1.pdf.

147. See Arimoro, note 98.

148. Chan and Zoellick, note 67, p. xi.

149. *The Convention on the Rights of Persons with Disabilities Training Guide,* Professional Training Series No. 19 (New York and Geneva: Office of the UN High Commissioner for Human Rights, 2014), 11, [hereinafter CRPD Training Guide], https://www.ohchr.org/Documents/Publications/CRPD_TrainingGuide_PTS19_EN%20Accessible.pdf.

150. Ibid.

151. Ibid.

152. Ibid. pp. 8–9.

153. Ibid.

154. Ibid.

155. *Disability Inclusion in Nigeria*, note 110, p. 16.

156. CRPD Training Guide, note 149, p. 9.

157. Ibid.

158. The CRPD defines "reasonable accommodation" as "necessary and appropriate modification and adjustments not imposing a disproportionate or undue burden, where needed in a particular case, to ensure to persons with disabilities the enjoyment or exercise on an equal basis with others of all human rights and fundamental freedoms." CRPD, note 2, art. 2 ("Definitions").

159. CRPD Training Guide, note 149, p. 9.

160. Ibid., p. 1.

161. Ibid., p. 9.

162. Irmo Marini et al., *Psychosocial Aspects of Disability: Insider Perspectives and Strategies for Counselors, Second Edition* (New York: Springer Publishing, 2011), 17.

163. Ibid., p. 18.

164. "Models of Disability: An Overview," MIUSA: Mobility Int'l USA, https://www.miusa.org/resource/tipsheet/disabilitymodels.

165. *Monitoring the Convention on the Rights of Persons with Disabilities: Guidance for Human Rights Monitors,* Professional Training Series No. 17 (Geneva and New York: Office of the UN High Commissioner for Human Rights, 2010), p. 9.

166. "Models of Disability," note 164.

167. CRPD Training Guide, note 149, p. 9.

168. Ibid., p. 10.

169. Standard Rules, note 51, item 3, 21 ("Background and Current Needs").

170. CRPD Training Guide, note 149, p. 10.

171. Ibid.

172. Ibid., p. 11.

173. Navanethem Pillay, United Nations High Commissioner for Human Rights, "Foreword," in *Monitoring the Convention on the Rights of Persons with Disabilities,* note 165.

174. Ibid.

175. For a sample of the extensive literature on this topic, see Michael Bratton and Nicolas van de Walle, *Democratic Experiments in Africa: Regime Transitions in Comparative Perspective* (New York: Cambridge University Press, 1997); and John A. Wiseman, *The New Struggle for Democracy in Africa* (Aldershot, Brookfield,

Singapore, and Sydney: Ashgate, 1996). See also Marina Ottaway, *Africa's New Leaders: Democracy or State Reconstruction?* (Washington, DC: Carnegie Endowment for International Peace, 1999); and *Democracy in Africa: The Hard Road Ahead*, ed. Marina Ottaway, SAIS African Studies Library (Boulder and London: Lynne Rienner Publishers, 1997). For more recent commentaries, see Gabrielle Lynch and Gordon Crawford, "Democratization in Africa 1990–2010: An Assessment," *Democratization* 18(2) (2011), 275–331; Jeffrey Herbst, "Political Liberalization in Africa after Ten Years," *Comparative Politics* 33(3) (2001), 357–375.

176. See Christopher C. Mojekwu, "Nigerian Constitutionalism," in J. Roland Pennock and John W. Chapman, eds., *Constitutionalism* (New York: New York University Press, 1979), 163, 174.

177. For a sample, see *Disability in Africa*, eds. Falola and Hamel (2021), note 74; *Rethinking Disability: World Perspectives in Culture and Society, 2nd Edition*, eds. Patrick Devlieger et al. (Antwerp, Belgium: Maklu, Garant, and Cyclus, 2016); *Searching for Dignity: Conversations on Human Dignity, Theology[,] and Disability: Conference Proceedings*, eds. Julie Claasssens et al. (Stellenbosch, South Africa: Sun Media Corp., 2013); *Disability, Society[,] and Theology: Voices from Africa*, eds. Samuel Kabue et al. (Eldoret, Kenya: Zapf Chancery Publishers, 2012); Irmo Marini et al., note 162; *Disability and Poverty: A Global Challenge*, eds. Arne Eide, and Benedicte Ingstad (Bristol, UK: Policy Press, University of Bristol, 2011); and Mirey Ovadiya, and Giuseppe Zampaglione, *Escaping Stigma and Neglect: People with Disabilities in Sierra Leone*, Working Paper No. 164 (Washington, DC: World Bank, 2009).

178. The closest competitors to this book are: Halim Doma, *Human Rights and Persons with Disabilities in Nigeria: Laws, Policies, and Institutions* (London and Abuja: Adonis & Abbey, 2020); and Edwin Etieyibo and Odirin Omiegbe, *Disabilities in Nigeria: Attitudes, Reactions, and Remediation* (Lanham, MD: Hamilton Books, 2017). With respect to the first, the book here is more recent. Also, although like that book, focused on laws, policies, and institutions, its accent on the human right of disabled persons is greater. Compared to the Etieyibo and Omiegbe book, the work here is more recent, more focused on laws and public policies, with equally more emphasis on human rights.

Chapter 1

Background History of Disability in Nigeria

INTRODUCTION

Every study has a proverbial beginning that a historical background account chronicles. This wisdom informs the presentation in this chapter. It is a truism reflected in the notion that to explain current events, the researcher needs a good grasp of activities from the past that shape those events.[1] For, as the Igbo say, persons drenched by rain will have difficulty drying from their wetness, unless they can establish where the rain started beating them.[2] Table 1.1 encapsulates the gist of this chapter.

The history this chapter sketches is, as the table shows, organized around three interrelated features enshrined in equally three eras. The features are sources (or drivers) of disabilities and prevalence, representative laws and policies, and societal attitudes toward PLWDs. The three eras are the precolonial, colonial, and postcolonial periods. In the scheme of things, both eras and characteristic features are interrelated. For example, a constant that runs through the three eras is an invariably negative attitude toward disabilities and individuals living with these conditions.

First, the eras. Consistent with the focus in this book on the Fourth Republic, the postcolonial era is subdivided into two subperiods separated by 1999 as defining date: the time frames before and after 1999. The three periods overlap, more so the colonial and postcolonial eras. Back to the bequeathal of English from British colonial rule as official language, until the present day, Nigeria's history is replete with influences from its colonial past, positive and negative alike.[3] Thus, there is little surprise that the Lunacy Ordinance of 1916, elaborated later in this chapter, created during the colonial period, crossed over into the postcolonial period. In other words, rather

Table 1.1. Three eras and three characteristic features of disabilities in Nigeria

		Eras			
Item No.	*Characteristic feature*	*Precolonial*	*Colonial*	*Postcolonial*	
				Pre-1999	*Fourth Republic since 1999*
1.	Sources (or drivers) of disabilities, and	Intertribal wars, and work injuries	"Pacification" campaigns, and injuries from World Wars I and II	Multiple, including conflicts, road accidents, and impairments from infectious and non-infectious diseases (e.g., HIV/AIDS)	Multiple, including conflicts, road accidents, impairments from infectious and non-infectious diseases (e.g., HIV/AIDS), and impairments from implementation of Sharia laws
	Prevalence	Low	Medium	High	High
2.	Representative laws and policies	Not applicable	Lunacy Ordinance (1916), Lunacy Act (1958)	Nigerians with Disabilities Decree (1993)	Nigerian Disabilities Act (2018)
3.	Societal attitude toward PLWDs	Negatively high	Negatively high	Negatively high	Negatively high

Source: Created by the authors

than limited to any one period, government policies toward disabilities and persons living with these conditions run across periods.

Of the three eras under review, by far the longest period, based on duration, is the precolonial. We begin, counterclockwise, with the postcolonial period. The era numbers over sixty-two years from Nigeria's independence on October 1, 1960, up until the date of this book. Next, the colonial period. The era numbers more than forty-six years from the UK's amalgamation of three administrative units on January 1, 1914, to create modern-day Nigeria.[4] As recited in the primer on Nigeria in the introductory portion of this book, these three units are the Colony of Lagos, the Northern Protectorate, and the Southern Protectorate.[5] In actuality, British colonization of what today is known as Nigeria dates back nearly 100 years before independence to the declaration of Lagos as a British colony on March 5,1962, following London's annexation of the territory on August 6, 1861.[6] British presence in the Northern and Southern Protectorates dates back in each case to January 1, 1900, when the British government established these protectorates.[7] Although, as we see the longest, the precolonial era is also the least definitive period. Historians postmark it as 1500–1800.[8] However, the era dates back at least to the eighth century, based on archaeological finds from Igbo Ukwu in what became Eastern Nigeria.[9]

Now to the three characteristic features embedded in the three eras, the one feature that calls for some comment at this point is attitudes toward PLWDs. Many of the discriminations PLWDs in Nigeria experience emanate from this source. Accordingly, instructively, across the three eras, as earlier indicated, attitudes toward disabilities and people living with these conditions remained invariably high. In other words, negative attitudes toward disabilities and PLWDs is a characteristic that, to certain degrees, these three eras share. This is a proposition that the results from the assessment of the records of the Nigerian national government in Chapter 3 points up. The discussion that follows is a presentation on the three eras, beginning with the precolonial period, along with the events or activities, formalized as characteristic features, that mark each era. For reasons made obvious in the text of the conversation, the bulk of the activities covered in the discussion took place during the postcolonial period. However, the extensiveness does not lend that era more importance than its co-eras, given that all three eras, without exception, are equally momentous.

PRECOLONIAL ERA

Sources of Disabilities and Prevalence

During this era, in communities in what became Nigeria, as well as many other societies in Africa, intertribal wars and work injuries, within and outside farm lands, formed the main sources of disabilities.[10] Consistent with these sources and drivers of disability, during this period, as available sources reveal, the population of PLWDs consisted of individuals with amputated hands, severed earlobes, and plucked-out eyes as a form of punishment for wrongdoings,[11] among other forms of disabilities. As indicated in Table 1.1, prevalence of disabilities in this period was low. First, due to lack of medical services in the sense we understand them today, there were relatively few PLWDs: children born with impairments died early, as was the case with individuals who developed life-threatening diseases.[12] In sheer volume, disability was less vast than in the colonial and postcolonial eras. This had to do with the fact that the demography of many traditional societies lacked the sprawling urbanization and populous-ness of many African countries today, including Nigeria. A typical example is Lagos whose population jumped from over 60,000 residents to 9 million within 100 years.[13] Moreover, given the salience of physical strength to agricultural production, during this period, intellectual disability not tied to physical ability went largely unrecognized.[14]

Representative Laws and Policies

During the precolonial era, there were few such laws and policies we can point to in the sense we understand these phenomena today. Whether civil law or common law, regardless of the legal tradition in question, representative laws and policies spell certain degree of written documentation.[15] In contrast, much of traditional Africa were oral cultures with little written materials in the sense we understand them in the contemporary period. Oral tradition is a mode of human communication not based on documents, but, instead on "the recall and transmission of a specific, preserved textual and cultural knowledge through vocal utterance."[16] Moreover, much of Nigeria, as we know it today, came into being only in the second decade of the twentieth century.[17] The Treaty of Westphalia, signed in 1648, laid the ground for the modern-state system.[18] However, the state concept for organizing societies reached Africa only in the last quarter of the nineteenth century. That was in 1884–85 at the Berlin Conference, which legitimized the "scramble for Africa" and partitioned the continent among the contending major European powers.[19]

Societal Attitudes toward Disabilities

Given that they can, for example, impede employment opportunities for PLWDs, concern about these attitudes is not an abstract preoccupation. During the precolonial period, societal attitudes toward disabilities and persons afflicted with these conditions were negative. These attitudes emanate from inaccurate beliefs about disabilities and PLWDs, together with the sense that these individuals look different or behave differently from the norm.[20] PLWDs who survived into adulthood were often ridiculed and excluded from society.[21] However, this was not universal, as disabled persons from high-status families, were treated with some degree of respect—even where society viewed their contributions to community development as nominal.[22] Thus, in parts of present-day Republic of Benin, formerly Dahomey, in West Africa, infants born with disabilities were believed to be the result of supernatural forces and, in some instances, embodiment of good luck.[23] Similarly, among the Chagga of East Africa, children living with disabilities were viewed as positive forces who pacified evil spirits, thereby preventing some unnamed misfortune from visiting the larger community.[24]

There were some attitudes that were hard to classify, whether as negative or positive. In many societies in precolonial Africa, a disabled man is considered as a sick man needing to be provided for by the other family members and the extended family system.[25] This is due to the superstition that letting a disabled family member suffer offends ancestral spirits, especially if the individual died unhappily from his or her impairment.[26] Consequently, many families held PLWDs with reverence, over-emphasizing their impairment and allowing these individuals little opportunity to explore the environment.[27] Such practice harks back to the charity model in disability studies commented upon in the introduction of this book.[28]

COLONIAL ERA

Sources of Disabilities and Prevalence

Although the process of "pacification" remained violent and problematic, colonization brought some measure of peace and stability because of the cessation of intertribal wars that took place during this period.[29] Therefore, during this era, disabilities from this source ceased a bit. "This meant that a severely traumatized person or one suffering from a chronic disease, [such as] tuberculosis, had a chance to survive. Consequently, conditions which may have caused death now lead to disablement."[30] But with peace relatively on the ascent, strong men looked for jobs and found them in likely places, such as mines of mineral resources, to feed the engines of the economies of the colonial powers.[31]

This era coincided with the introduction of medical services and improvement in community hygiene, which, in turn, led to major improvements in infant mortality and maternal morbidity.[32] It was also a period when Western missionary societies in Nigeria used primordial health care for "native" Africans, persons living with various kinds of disabilities, as a tool of proselytization. Thus, the Methodist Missionary Society established the Provincial Leprosy Settlement at Uzuakoli in August 1932, with one Dr. J. A. Kinnear Brown as founding Superintendent.[33] From 1932 and 1936, under his leadership, the Settlement cared for 800 patients.[34] By 1938, that number had grown to about 1,000 people, with about five times the number turned away due to inadequate resources for care.[35] Prevalence of this disease was high in the Owerri Province, the administrative unit under which the Settlement came; a survey of one division in the province turned up an incidence of thirty-three sufferers out of every 1,000 residents.[36] Other leprosy centers created by the missionaries included the Oji River Leprosy Settlement, also in Eastern Nigeria, founded in 1956.[37]

But disabilities came from new sources, such as "work-related accidents, inhumane treatment from colonists, and injuries resulting from the two world wars."[38] The First World War (1914–1918) and Second World War (1939–1945) involved recruitment of African soldiers who fought for the contending colonial powers,[39] many of which fighters came home with more or less permanent injuries. The First World War "produced a lot of military activities in Nigeria, leading to the establishment of several military health care facilities,"[40] to facilitate the treatment of thousands of disabled servicemen who faced challenges to their masculine identities.[41] These men were referred to innocuously in British archives as "amputated men."[42] Testament to the spike in disabilities was the fact that during World War II, the colonial authorities set up the Nigerian Forces Comforts Fund, 1940–1947, which tasked the colonial administration to provide funds for the welfare of returning soldiers, many of them obviously disabled.[43]

Another notable source of disability during this period was polio, short(hand) for poliomyelitis, a foremost cause of disability for many youths and adults, especially in northern Nigeria.[44] Testament to the spike, but also as well a preview of negative attitudes toward disabilities among Nigerian cultures that we elaborate upon subsequently in this conversation, is the name that the major ethnic groups in the country give to the condition, based supposedly on the causes of the disease.[45] The Igbo in the East call it *öriá ngwulö*, translatable into English as lameness or paralysis of the limbs; the Yoruba in the West call it *arun aromolapa romolese*, translatable into English as a disease that cripples a child's hands and legs; and the Hausa in the North call it *cuta Shan Inna*, meaning drinking of Inna [*Inna* standing for paralysis].[46] These characterizations of polio victims gave a sense that, within this period, societal understanding of disability and views regarding PLWDs, were steeped within the charity model, distinctly removed from human right.

Table 1.1 ranked the prevalence of disabilities during this period as "medium." Here is why. This was a markedly different era from the precolonial era marked by relatively low-volume disability. Moreover, the absence of intertribal conflicts that marked the precolonial era was in little order replaced by new and deadlier drivers like the two world wars that came almost back-to-back. This is in spite of improvements in modern medicine and hygiene arguably traceable to colonial rule, including the important contributions by Western missionaries in their proselytization campaigns in search of converts.[47]

Representative Laws and Policies

There are three episodes that, for illustration's sake, we cite here as representative laws and policies, during the era here in question. The first is the

Lunacy Ordinance of 1916, the first law ever in Nigeria's mental history.[48] In 1958, close to the eve of the country's independence in 1960, the law became the Lunacy Act.[49] It was amended to permit the arrest and detention of persons suspected to be mentally ill. As we write this book, the Act remains the governing law on mental health in Nigeria.[50] Here are some insights on how the law managed to crisscross two of the three eras here under review. In 2003, a Mental Health Bill was presented to the National Assembly of Nigeria for deliberation and passage. It received no attention until April 2009, more than six years later, when it was withdrawn, due to inadequate support to make it through passage.[51] The bill was presented again in 2013, yet still unsuccessfully, within the context of a national policy for delivery of mental health treatment for people with disorders related to mental, neurological, and substance abuse.[52]

The failure of legislative initiative occurred despite the burden of mental health issues that Nigeria confronted, matched against limited resources. For "[u]nderpinned by poor societal attitudes toward mental illness and inadequate resources, facilities, and mental health staff, figures suggest that approximately 80 [percent] of individuals with serious mental health needs in Nigeria cannot access care."[53] Moreover, "[w]ith fewer than 300 psychiatrists for a population of more than 200 million, most of whom are based in urban areas, and in view of poor knowledge of mental disorders at the primary health-care level, caring for people with mental illness is typically left to family members."[54] Reflective of a period when mental health was severely misunderstood and when treatment of people living with mental illness was inhumane, this law is today "outdated and archaic."[55]

Given these negative statistics, some perceptive commentators posit that Nigeria urgently needs to reform its mental health law to bring it at par with international standards. This is a progressive position that this book shares. In February 2020, the Nigerian Senate held a public hearing for the Mental Health and Substance Abuse Bill. If passed, the bill will increase budgetary allocations for mental health facilities and providers.[56] As it should, the absence of an updated legislation on mental health care is also an issue that troubles organizations advocating for mental health patients in Nigeria.[57]

Institutionalization of mental patients is another practice during the colonial era that we analogize as policy. Like the Lunacy Ordinance, this one also carried over into the postcolonial period. Institutionalization of persons adjudged insane into large asylums was introduced in Nigeria in 1906 in which year British colonial authorities constructed two institutions in southwestern Nigeria, the Yaba Lunatic Asylum (later Mental Hospital) in Lagos, and the Aro Mental Hospital in Abeokuta.[58] The introduction tracked British precedents that go back to the nineteenth century, but ran contrary to African way of life.[59] The institutionalization still occurred despite the fact that many

British government officials then felt persons living with mental disabilities "were better cared for in their own communities."[60] This is how, "introduced diffidently in the early colonial period," by the country's independence in 1960, lunatic asylums "bec[a]me an established [. . .] feature of the Nigerian [disability] landscape."[61]

A third and last episode here that we use to illustrate prevailing policy was the practice of giving disabled persons from the North free train rides into southern Nigeria and at times even to locations outside Nigeria like Ghana. During the colonial period until 1960, when Nigeria became independent from the UK, British officials created transportation routes designed to facilitate shipment of primary commodities, such as cotton, to the UK.[62] Thus, the railroad from Lagos to Kano, completed in 1912, not only filled this bill and function, it was the mode of transportation for Northern Nigerians to travel to the south.[63] This was beneficial for disabled people who were allowed to travel free of charge.[64] Some of these disabled persons traveled this route to Ghana where they worked as beggars.[65] The practice was commented upon in the *Report on the Enquiry into Begging and Destitution in the Gold Coast 1954*, conducted by Ghanaian sociologists employed by the colonial government.[66] Bear in mind that there is no suggestion here that allowing these individuals living with disability to travel free to different destinations within and outside Nigeria amounted to expressed government policy. If per adventure it was, it belongs in the category of pity that comes under the charity model of disability, contrasted with the human right approach, which animates this book.[67]

The preceding examples focused heavily on health care. This could leave the impression that British colonial policy was more progressive in other areas. However, such interpretation would be erroneous or incorrect. Take education, another key area, for example. One extensive study found that British colonial policy in Nigeria attached low priority to the education of disabled people.[68] The study blamed the failure of the Nigerian educational system to provide equal educational opportunity for PLWDs to a range of factors that includes occurrences or lack thereof during British rule and tutelage.[69]

Negative Attitudes Toward Disabilities

Like in the precolonial period, societal attitudes toward disabilities and persons living with these conditions remained unyieldingly negative, as indicated in Table 1.1. Among the Igbo of Eastern Nigeria, wholesomeness plays an important role in community worldview.[70] The importance makes congenital disability a stigma.[71] In Igbo folklore, a disabled person is considered unable "to pray for progress that would reach God. It is only a complete person that can call on God the maker of heaven and the earth."[72] Among the Igbo, stereotypes extend to "courtesy stigma," prejudice that "extends to other family members and proximal loved ones."[73] Thus, "before a man is to marry a woman, he is to seek out the lineage of her family that must be approved by the family and God [. . .]. Evidence that there are family members with mental illness or disabilities would be a red flag in this process."[74] Among the Yoruba of Western Nigeria, no less than other groups, disability was viewed as payback or punishment for a wrongdoing by the disabled person or a parent or family member.[75] This superstition explains, but does not justify, the use of derogatory names to describe and label PLWDs, based on the perceived sin or offence committed.[76] Thus, names like *Abirun* (handicap), *Abami* (strange person), *Didinrin* (imbecile), and *Alawoku* (mentally retarded) were among the many insults perpetrated against PLWDs.[77] In addition to the pains they caused, these gratuitous labels also created barriers that limit the involvement of PLWDs in their own communities and societies.[78] Similarly, among the Hausa in Northern Nigeria, Islamic religious beliefs shaped attitudes toward PLWDs, most of which also remained negative.[79]

In sum, misconceptions about the causes of disability shaped by erroneous beliefs include that disability arises from a curse resulting from transgressions by an ancestor; "bad" acts of a parent; "bad" acts of the disabled; "bad" spirits, such as demonic possession; witchcraft and magic, and "bad" fate or supposed curse from God.[80] Severe consequences potentially detrimental to the welfare of PLWDs attend these misconceptions. These include surreptitious infanticide of children living with disabilities; parental abandonment of a disabled child, often by a father; violence and abuse of children living with disability, such as mocking, bullying and maltreatment in the form of neglect or malnutrition; rejection or ostracization of PLWDs and, sometimes, with their whole family, especially when the disability in question is associated with punishment for previous immorality; restricted participation in community events that happens when caregivers of children living with disabilities hide them away or forbid them from taking part in social activities due to stigma and shame, or to putatively protect them from stigmatization; and low registration or complete un-reporting in national censuses or related official statistics of children living with disabilities, due to stigmatization.[81]

Formed during the precolonial period, these negative attitudes toward disabilities and people living with impairments took firm hold during the colonial era. This was in an era of low awareness and sensitization on disability issues in Africa, given the relative infancy of the disability movement, a fledgling-ness indicated by the fewness of organizations advocating for the welfare of PLWDs. The prevailing orientation both in disability studies and the popular culture remained confined to the charity model, joined soon by its kindred spirit, the medical model.[82] In short, the concept of disability as human rights did not take root. Instead, the orientation evolved only after

World War II in 1945 and with it, the disbandment of the League of Nations and its replacement with the United Nations, together with the option for human rights the new system emblematized.

POSTCOLONIAL ERA

Sources of Disabilities and Prevalence

To much relief, the end of colonial rule and the advent of postcolonial governance removed factors like "the inhumane treatment from colonists and the injuries resulting from the two world wars"[83] as sources or drivers of disabilities. But work-related injuries remained. So too did intractable diseases from the preceding period like leprosy and polio[84]—although not as before because of the eradication campaigns to the present day mounted against these scourges.[85] Otherwise, as the French saying goes, the more things change, the more they seem to remain the same. More formally speaking, during this era, the sources of disability became multiple and include conflicts of every kind and description, road accidents, impairments from infectious and non-infectious diseases, and impairments from the implementation of Sharia law. As Table 1.1 shows, these sources straddle the time frames before and since the Fourth Republic in 1999.

We begin with the conflicts. Two illustrative clashes, one from the pre-1999 subperiod and the other from the subperiod since 1999, are victims of the Nigeria-Biafra war from 1967–1970,[86] and Boko Haram.[87] The victims of the civil war in question are Biafran veterans who survived the conflict with various forms of physical and psychological injuries, including trauma, lost or impaired vision, amputated limbs, and injuries in other parts of the body.[88] These wounded veterans are quartered in rundown homes in Oji River in southeastern Nigeria, near a leprosy settlement center referenced above,[89] where they depend mostly for their rehabilitation on private charity with little governmental support.[90] Boko Haram is a terrorist group, with an operational nerve center located in northeastern Nigeria, bent on creating a "pure" Islamic state based on Sharia law.[91] Driven by an ideology that brands Western education as evil, the group targets all emblems of Western institution within its operational range, including police stations, army barracks, at one point the United Nations office in Abuja, churches, and recreation centers, among other whimsical symbols.[92] The group is said to be responsible for the death of about 350,000 people, many of whom are children, as well as for the dislocation and homelessness of about 2 million people.[93]

Many roads in Nigeria are ill-maintained or lack any maintenance at all.[94] In 2018, Nigeria ranked among countries with the worst roads in Africa, placing 127 out of 140 countries in the world surveyed, with a score of 2.5 out of a possible 7 points.[95] With respect to road accidents, with a road casualty average of 33.7 accidents per 100,000 people, Nigeria is one of the countries with the highest number of fatalities in Africa.[96] The number breaks down to about 426 deaths every month, 15 daily, and 4 persons every six hours.[97] To restate, these figures dubiously place Nigeria among countries with the highest number of road fatalities in Africa, despite its vast natural resources.[98] More to our purpose in this book, in their frequency and fatality, road accidents result in serious injuries that, in the perceptive observation of one analyst, if not timely addressed, can lead to disabilities like "stroke, paralysis, and [even] mental illness."[99] Like road accidents, infectious and non-infectious diseases are a source of disability in Nigeria. To use HIV/AIDS as example,[100] the disease is widespread in Nigeria. As of 2020, about 49,000 people, including adults and children, died from AIDS in the country, with an estimated 1.7 million people living with HIV.[101] As of 2019, the national HIV prevalence in the country was 1.4 percent among adults aged 15 to49, down from estimates of 2.8 percent before.[102] More to our purpose here, many persons living with HIV/AIDS develop different types of impairments and functional limitations.[103]

Last but not least are disabilities emanating from the implementation of Sharia laws as legal code in twelve Northern states in Nigeria. The twelve states, in no particular order, are: Zamfara, Kano, Sokoto, Katsina, Bauchi, Borno, Jigawa, Kebbi, Yobe, Kaduna, Niger, and Gombe.[104] As Table 1.1 shows, the upgrade of Sharia into legal code in these states fell into the subperiod since 1999.[105] The most visible symbols from the implementation of Sharia laws in the country's Sharia States are amputation of arms for stealing and related offenses under the guise of enforcing Islamic law.[106] In these Sharia states, amputation could occur for a crime as bland or pedestrian as stealing a goat or grocery in a marketplace.[107] In these states, enforcers of Sharia law include judges known as Alkalis and police that goes by the name Hisbah.[108]

Unlike the colonial era, the prevalence of disabilities in this era is unequivocally high. The era is a period marked by drivers of disabilities quite unlike any other, matched against a relative fewness of representative laws and policies. The illustrative governing law identified for this era took place more than thirty years into the country's independence during the period of repressive military rule. In the specific area of mental health, the governing law was the Lunacy Law, updated in 1958, toward the end of British colonial rule. As if this combination of occurrences were not bad enough, disability activism came late into the picture. As Table 1.2 shows, the two most senior organizations advocating for disabled persons, the Joint National Association

Table 1.2. Disability activism in Nigeria: List of organizations advocating for PLWDs

Item No.	*Name of organization*	*Date Founded*	*Head-office*	*Mission*
1.	Joint National Association of Persons with Disabilities (JONAPWD)	1992	Abuja	Umbrella organization of six groups that aims to promote the rights and development of Nigerians with disabilities. The six are the blind, physically disabled, deaf, intellectually impaired, persons living with spinal cord injuries, and persons living with leprosy.
2.	Nigeria National Association of the Deaf (NNAD)	1992	Abuja	Umbrella organization of deaf people
3.	Center for Citizens with Disabilities (CCD)	2002	Lagos	Charity organization that works to promote the well-being of PLWDs in Nigeria
4.	Association for the Comprehensive Empowerment of Nigerians with Disabilities (ASCEND)	2006	None indicated	A grassroots-oriented movement that, just as its name connotes, ASCEND works for the participation of PLWDs in all spheres of life, including politics
5.	Deaf Women Association of Nigeria (DWAN)	2012	Lagos	Umbrella group of deaf women and girls

Sources: Created by the authors from multiple sources, including Audrey L. Comstock, *Committed to Rights: Volume 1: UN Human Rights Treaties and Legal Paths for Commitment and Compliance* (New York: Cambridge University Press, 2021), 16; Olusola Ogundola, "Disability Narratives in the News Media: A Spotlight on Africa," in eds. *The Routledge Companion to Disability and Media,* Katie Ellis et al. (New York and London: Routledge, 2020), 169–176; and Ngozi C. Umeh and Ramola Adeola, "Nigeria," *African Disability Rights Yearbook* (2013), 1, 277–290.

of Persons with Disabilities (JONAPWD), and the Nigerian National Association of the Deaf (NNAD) did not come into being until 1992, one short year before the promulgation of the Nigerians with Disability Decree of 1993. The three other organizations on the list did not make their debut until the Fourth Republic. And though too early to say, so far, the impact of these groups on the Nigerian disability scene has been minimal and negligible.[109]

Representative Laws and Policies

For an era outside the precolonial period, a most noticeable aspect of the disability landscape in the postcolonial age is the paucity of government law and policies that marks the era. Given this confounding lack, a representative law that comes to mind is the Nigerians with Disability Decree, a law adopted on January 1, 1993,[110] during the regime of General Ibrahim Babangida, military ruler from August 27, 1985, until August 26, 1993.[111] The law made it "the duty and responsibility" of all organs of government in the country to "adopt and promote policies that will ensure full integration [of PLWDs] into the mainstream of the [Nigerian] society," the idea being to guarantee for these persons equal treatment with the rest of Nigerians.[112] It defined "disabled persons" as individuals certified as having a condition, temporary or permanent, which limits their "functional ability substantially, but not limited to seeing, hearing, thinking, ambulating, climbing, descending, lifting, grasping, rising, any related function or any limitation due to weakness or significantly decreased endurance so that [they] cannot perform [their] everyday routine, living and working without significantly increased hardship and vulnerability to everyday obstacles and hazards."[113]

"Rights and privileges" created for PLWDs under the law were health services, education, vocational rehabilitation and employment, housing, and "access and adequate mobility within" public institutions.[114] Others were transportation, such as bus and rail services designed for general public needs; supportive social services, such as prosthetic devises; access to public and private sport facilities; access to telecommunication facilities, such as telephones and postal services; and access to voting.[115] The law created a fourteen-member National Commission for People with Disabilities tasked with responsibility for enforcing the law and advancing the welfare of PLWDs.[116] These duties include promoting: the full utilization of PLWDs in the development of human resources, their "acceptance as full participants in every phase of [the] national economy [. . .] with equal rights and corresponding obligations[,]" and "total elimination of" harmful cultural practices that discriminate against and dehumanize" PLWDs.[117] Others were serving as a link between the government and PLWDs and coordinating the work of the states aimed at integrating PLWDs into the society, enforcing the rights of PLWDs in any existing legislation, monitoring the response of various governmental agencies charged with the welfare of the PLWDs, and publishing an annual report on its activities.[118] The members serve for a two-year term with possibility of renewal for another term.[119]

The decree spoke in terms of the antiquated "rights-privileges" dichotomy. Accordingly, it falls belong the standard of human rights that animates this book.[120] Also, guarantees like voting rights that it provides are scarce commodities in military regime, given the abridgment of basic rights, including disbandment of the legislature, a known tool of popular representation, that characterizes military dictatorships of the type Nigerians lived under from 1966 until 1999.[121]

Societal Attitudes toward Disabilities

(i) Overview

Like with the other eras, societal attitudes remain stubbornly negative in this period. As Table 1.1 shows, societal attitudes toward PLWDs is a feature that crisscrosses all three eras. The occurrence calls for more probing. Much of the discrimination PLWDs face in Nigeria "stems from the negative public perceptions due to misinformed cultural beliefs."[122] These negative attitudes emanate from inaccurate beliefs about disabilities and PLWDs, such as that they display behaviors outside the "norm" of conventional societal dictations.[123]

Negative attitudes toward PLWDs invoke the concept of stigma, one of the key terms of this study set off and defined in the introduction of this book. These negative attitudes converge around the *nature* and *causes* of disability, resulting in two categories related to these attitudes: misconceptions about the nature of disability, and misconceptions about the causes of disability embedded in cultural and religious beliefs.[124] Misconceptions about the nature of disability include that: disabled persons are a burden less able to contribute to the good of the family and the community; they and their families will, wittingly or unwittingly, spread their supposed bad luck to others; the bodies of PLWDs have magical properties, for their assailants, supposedly justifying abuses that at times include mutilating or killing them to harvest part of their bodies for use in rituals, potions or amulets that would make these assailants wealthy, socially prominent, or grant them sucess in love, or victory over their rivals; children living with disabilities are witches; girls living with disabilities, especially those with intellectual, communicational, or visual impairments, will be unable to report sexual abuses, supposedly because they will be unable to narrate to others such abuses; and PLWDs cannot have normal relationships or are sexually inactive.[125] On this last misconception, myths run the gamut, some of them contradictory, such as that girls living with disabilities are virgins free of sexually transmitted diseases that, to their assailants, make them safe sexual partners; having sex with girls living with disability brings good luck; women with disabilities lack feminine attractiveness, which for their assailants, justify abuse of these women; and females living with disability are hypersexual, an occurrence that makes them unfit to participate in discussions on sexual and reproductive issues, since such conversations could trigger sexual feelings these disabled persons would be unable to control.[126]

Three impairments that feature a great deal in the academic literature, going by the weight of stigma attached to them, are intellectual disability, albinism, and leprosy.[127] Leprosy has already been touched upon earlier in this chapter.[128] Throughout history and across cultures, people living with intellectual disability have faced ostracization and, as an entity, rank among the most marginalized and excluded social groups in the world.[129] Derogatory terms, such as "retarded," "moron," and "fool," used in many countries to refer to these individuals reflect the vast disrespect this community of disabled persons endure.[130]

Many albinos live with some kind or degree of visual impairment.[131] In some parts of Africa, albinism is viewed as a curse on the family, with the health issues these albinos sometimes face perceived as a result of the curse.[132] Other superstitions related to albinism include that the mother of a child with this condition had an affair with a white person or spirit, an albino is a ghost rather than human, or a witch or other "omens of disaster."[133] Families often reject marriages to albinos out of fear of the birth of another albino child.[134]

Because they avoid the sun to protect their vulnerable skins, some people regard albinos as lazy.[135] Some other people believe that albinism is caused by physical interactions, such as shaking hands, or sharing meals with an albino.[136] The body parts of albinos are believed to bring good luck, wealth and medical cures, as well as electoral victory.[137] Marginalization and exclusion of albinos made them easier targets of mutilation and killing.[138] The apparentness of these abuses have forced some parents to escort their children to school, hide them at home or send them to supposed safer areas, such as boarding schools.[139]

A common experience reported by persons with albinism in particular is being called derogatory names, as one respondent, an albino, who lived in Abuja, recounts:[140]

> There are many other names like "anyare," [. . .] in the Onitsha area. There are all kinds of names, you go to the Yorubas, [they say] "Afin," *afin oriran osan* (afin does not see in daylight). [. . .] it is derogatory, you know. You go to the north, they call us "baturen tuda," which is "fake white man." Then, you go to Benin, they call us *ebo, ebo, ebo*. All those names are not complimentary, they are very derogatory, and we have to live with that.[141]

As the quote shows, negative attitudes toward albinos is an orientation different ethnic groups in the country share. PLWDs respond to these negative attitudes with a range of emotions that includes low self-esteem, isolation, depression, rejection, withdrawal from society, and even suicide.[142] Prejudice and social isolation are the greatest barriers PLWDs face; because of their ability to "contribute to other barriers" they are the mother of all barriers that PLWDs face.[143]

(ii) Putting the Matter in Broader Analytical Perspective

Stigmatization of PLWDs is a universal phenomenon not limited to Nigeria. Therefore, not that it justifies it, Nigerian ethnic groups are not unique when it comes to stigmas related to PLWDs. Commenting on narratives related to women intellectual disability in ancient Greece, the disability scholar M. Lynn Rose argued that the criteria for intellectual impairment had ancient meaning and status with little to do with modern definitions.[144] She showed how comparing ancient and modern attitudes about taking a person with an intellectual disability as spouse provides an instructive window through which to view change over time.[145] Among the Chinese community in Hong Kong, families believed birthing a child with disability brought disgrace to their households and that disabled persons created an imbalance.[146] And although the killing of children with disabilities in Nazi Germany was an extreme example of eugenics, across cultures and at many points in human history, children with disabilities were among communities left to die by abandonment or exposure or deliberately killed, presumably because some people, usually people in authority, had determined that their lives were not worth living.[147]

Another force is the influence of external factors, for good or bad. One study of disability in the Netherlands indicated that developments in the country related to disability mirrored occurrences in neighboring countries.[148] Thus, among the Dutch, the notion that people with mental disabilities were a danger to society became "common sense" only after the First World War, the result of external events arguably traceable or ascribable to that conflict.[149]

Discriminatory laws and policies reinforce prejudice and discrimination, while the segregation of people with disabilities perpetuates negative stereotypes. Yet, to every rule, even tragic ones, there are exceptions and there were, of course, variations to the general pattern. For example, Judaism had a practical approach to intellectual disability reflected in a flexible outlook on the complex issues pertaining to disability.[150] Thus, under Jewish law, the blind person was regarded as full normal, such that most of the legal and religious restrictions placed on him were due to physical disability.[151]

The upshot is that, although false perceptions and beliefs about disability are often difficult to overcome, they can change over time, especially when interventions aimed at addressing disability stigma are implemented. The insights of Nelson Mandel relating to racism is relevant and instructive:

> I always knew that deep down in every human heart, there is mercy and generosity. No one is born hating another person because of the color of his skin, or his background, or his religion. People must learn to hate, and if they can learn to hate, they can be taught to love, for love comes more naturally to the human heart than its opposite.[152]

Negative attitude toward disability and individuals afflicted with these conditions can be unlearned. For sure, attitude determines altitude,[153] but though not easy, attitudes can change too. This is where increased awareness on disability issues, covered in Chapter 4, comes in. The non-viable alternative is that a country unwittingly deprives itself of the material contributions of a key section of society, in the case of Nigeria not insubstantial, given the sizable number of disabled persons in the country.[154]

CONCLUSION

Although our main focus in this book is the period since 1999, in the lexicon of Nigeria's constitutional history denominated the Fourth Republic, we must look back to understand the present and gauge the future. Herein lies the essence of this chapter. It is a tale of three eras where progress in the welfare of PLWDs in each period is a function of three interrelated variables: sources of disabilities and prevalence (widespread-ness), representative laws and policies governing disabilities, and societal attitudes toward PLWDs. Although interrelated, equally each era embodies attributes that sets it apart from co-eras. For the precolonial period, it was the absence of representative laws and policies in the sense we understand these phenomena today. For the colonial period, it was a major change in the sources-cum-drivers of disability, underscored by injuries from two world wars, with immense significance for prevalence of disabilities. For good or bad, the colonial era also laid the foundation and set the tone for representative laws and policies.

The postcolonial period is confoundingly notable for its relative paucity of representative laws, especially given the spike in the range and proportion of disability sources-cum-drivers, with immense significance for prevalence of disabilities. In no issue is this lacuna more obvious than in mental health on which the Lunacy Act, initially enacted in 1916 as an ordinance—steeped in the usages of "lunatics," "idiots," and "asylums," characteristic of the antiquated charity and medical models, discussed in the introduction of the book before this chapter—remains national law. Given the option for human rights that the formation of the UN made possible, beginning in 1945, another intriguing feature was the recentness of disability activism dating back only to 1992. This could be explained by the experience of repressive military rule in the country spanning one whole generation until the advent of the Fourth Republic in 1999. Paradoxically, the first set of interest groups advocating for disability rights made their emergence during military rule.

A major constant across all three eras was societal attitudes toward PLWDs which remained invariably negative. Such is the lack of progress on this variable all the way to the present era that, in its only report on the CRPD,

Nigerian officials responded to a question regarding contemporary challenges related to PLWDs that the country faces to the effect that "[t]here are deep-seated negative social attitudes and perceptions of persons [living] with disabilities" all the way to "ritual killings" of albinos.[155] The lesson from the history of disabilities in Nigeria this chapter chronicles is "complexity" across space and time in "the relationship between disabled and nondisabled persons," testament to the virus of "systemic ableism," signified by the reality that "attitudes, stigma and practices are so deeply entrenched in history and societal norms that most people do not recognize their own role in perpetuating" discrimination against PLWDs.[156] It is an occurrence that calls for an alliance between nondisabled people and PLWDs in all societies to "develop progressive theories for examining and teaching disability theories," as well as "work[ing] together toward greater societal change."[157] To critically assess the performance of the Nigerian national government under the Fourth Republic in its international obligations toward PLWDs, as we do in this book, we must first lay out the applicable regimes of disability pertaining to those obligations. That is the object of Chapter 2, to which topic this book turns next.

NOTES

1. Frank L. Wilson, *Concepts and Issues in Comparative Politics: An Introduction to Comparative Analysis* (Upper Saddle River, NJ: Prentice Hall, 1996), 17.
2. See Kyle Minor, "*There Was a Country*, Chinua Achebe's Long-Awaited Memoir of Biafra," *Salon* (November 8, 2012), https://www.salon.com/2012/11/08/there_was_a_country_chinua_achebes_long_awaited_memoir_of_biafra/ (citing the venerated Nigerian writer Chinua Achebe (1930–2013), who was Igbo, to the effect that "a man who does not know where the rain began to beat him cannot say where he dried his body")
3. See, for example, Jackline Wangare, "Colonialism in Nigeria: Positive and Negative Impacts of Nigerian Colonization," *Legit* (October 25, 2021), https://www.legit.ng/1131998-colonialism-nigeria-positive-negative-impacts.html.
4. See Book's Introduction, note 10 and accompanying text.
5. Ibid.
6. See Toyin Falola and Matthew M. Heaton, *A History of Nigeria* (New York: Cambridge University Press, 2012), 85–109.
7. See ibid.; and Jack McCaslin, "Lord Lugard Created Nigeria 104 Years Ago," Council on Foreign Relations (January 2, 2018), https://www.cfr.org/blog/lord-lugard-created-nigeria-104-years-ago.
8. See Falola and Heaton, note 6, pp. 39–60.
9. See ibid., pp. 16–38 ("Early States and Societies, 9000 BCE-1500 CE"). See also G.I. Jones, *The Trading States of the Oil Rivers: A Study of Political Development in*

Eastern Nigeria, Classics in African Anthropology (Münster, Germany: LIT Verlag, 2000); and Major Arthur Glyn Leonard, *The Lower Niger and Its Tribes* (London: Macmillan & Co. Ltd., 1906).

10. Felix Silwimba, "Possibilities of Independent Living of Persons with Disabilities in Africa," Independent Living Institute, https://www.independentliving.org/toolsforpower/tools5.html.

11. Ibid.

12. See ibid.

13. Patrick Enaholo, "Colonial Footprints: Lagos, Then and Now," Centenary Project, Arts and Culture (n.d.), https://artsandculture.google.com/story/LAUBxuvCARsA8A. See also Alastair Leithead, "The City That Won't Stop Growing: How Can Lagos Cope with Its Spiraling Population," *BBC News* (August 21, 2017), https://www.bbc.co.uk/news/resources/idt-sh/lagos.

14. Filwimba, note 10.

15. "What is the Difference Between Common Law and Civil Law," Washington University in St. Louis School of Law (January 28, 2014), https://onlinelaw.wustl.edu/blog/common-law-vs-civil-law/#:~:text=The%20main%20difference%20between%20the,law%20systems%2C%20codified%20statutes%20predominate (explaining that though, on the surface, the divisions are less clear-cut because, in real life, some countries straddle them, the main difference between the two legal traditions is that in common-law countries, case law, signified by "published judicial opinions, is of primary importance, whereas in civil law systems, codified statutes predominate").

16. See John Miles Foley, "Oral Tradition," *Encyclopedia Britannica*, https://www.britannica.com/topic/oral-tradition.

17. See Book's Introduction ("Primer on Nigeria").

18. See, for example, Steven Patton, "The Peace of Westphalia and it[s] [E]ffects on International Relations, Diplomacy and Foreign Policy," *Histories,* 10(1) (2019), 91–99 https://digitalcommons.lasalle.edu/cgi/viewcontent.cgi?article=1146&context=the_histories; and Richard Cavendish, "The Treaty of Westphalia," *History Today*, 48(1) (October 1998), https://www.historytoday.com/archive/months-past/treaty-westphalia.

19. Courtney Faal, "The Partition of Africa," *Black Past* (February 21, 2009), https://www.blackpast.org/global-african-history/partition-africa/.

20. *Nigeria: Children and Young People with Disabilities* (London: Asylos and ARC Foundation, October 2021), 19, https://www.ecoi.net/en/file/local/2061263/AsylosARC-Foundation_Nigeria-disability-report_October-2021.pdf. Asylos is a global network of volunteers providing free-of-charge Country of Origin Information (COI) research for legal representatives and NGOs helping asylum seekers with their claim. Asylos works to ensure that asylum seekers and their legal counsel have access to crucial sources and data to substantiate their claim. Ibid., p. 10. ARC, in full Asylum Research Centre, is a charity based in London. The group undertakes research, advocacy, and training, avowedly designed to improve the quality of determination of refugee status. LinkedIn, linkedin.com/in/asylum-research-centre-arc-arc-foundation-070665165/?OriginalSubdomain=uk.

21. Sarah G. Brouillard, "Disability Inequality in Developing African Countries: A Comparison of Disability Legislation and Social Rights in Mali and Niger," *Story Maps* (December 8, 2020), https://storymaps.arcgis.com/stories/e8f5bbadc9594b0da39cbaa7fa1bfbbb.

22. Silwimba, note 10.

23. Irmo Marini et al., *Psychosocial Aspects of Disability: Insider Perspectives and Strategies for Counselors,* 2nd Edition (New York: Springer Publishing, 2011), 3.

24. Ibid.

25. Silwimba, note 10.

26. Ibid.

27. Ibid.

28. See Book's introduction, notes 152–155, and accompanying texts.

29. Silwimba, note 10. For a statement on the violence that came with the pacification process in Africa, see Philip C. Aka, "The Military, Globalization, and Human Rights in Africa" *New York Law School Journal of Human Rights*, 18(3), 361, 380 (Summer 2002), https://digitalcommons.nyls.edu/cgi/viewcontent.cgi?article=1493&context=journal_of_human_rights ("Notwithstanding its deceptive peaceable sounding name, pacification was a violent military process that was [. . .] very destructive of African law and order"). In the apt assessment from this source, "[t]he entire architecture of colonial rule, like that of military rule down the road in the continent, was built and maintained solely and completely on naked force designed to crush any and every 'native' resistance to external domination." Ibid., p. 379.

30. Silwimba, note 10.

31. See ibid.

32. See Deanne van Tol, "Mothers, Babies, and the Colonial State: The Introduction of Maternal and Infant Welfare Services in Nigeria, 1925–1945," *Spontaneous Generations* 1(1) (2007), 110–131.

33. "Uzuakoli (Nigeria)," International Leprosy Association—History of Leprosy, https://leprosyhistory.org/geographical_region/site/uzuakoli. See also C.N. Ubah, "Hope for the Despondent: A Colonial Health Care Scheme at Uzuakoli, Eastern Nigeria," *Transafrican Journal of History*, 21(1992), 51–68.

34. "Uzuakoli (Nigeria)," note 33.

35. Ibid.

36. Ibid. For an update on the Settlement, including progress against the disease it was set up in 1932 to combat, see Linus Unah, "Leprosy Lives on in Nigeria, 20 Years after Its 'Elimination' as a Public Health Problem," *Devex* (January 15, 2020), https://www.devex.com/news/leprosy-lives-on-in-nigeria-20-years-after-its-elimination-as-a-public-health-problem-96345.

37. "Oji River Leprosy Settlement: Chapel of the Transfiguration, Built Largely by Patients, 1956," ArchiveSearch, https://archivesearch.lib.cam.ac.uk/repositories/2/archival_objects/171271.

38. Brouillard, note 21.

39. Sharika Crawford, "Beyond the Scramble: African Veterans, the Second World War and Decolonization in the World History Classroom," *World History Connected*, https://worldhistoryconnected.press.uillinois.edu/12.1/

crawford.html ("African Colonial Soldiers in the First and Second World War"). A memorandum from the British Colonial Office in 1945 summarized the African contributions to those wars thus: "African soldiers beat Italians out of Somaliland and Abyssinia, defeating the best Blackshirt battalions. [. . .] They defended British West Africa from attack from the Vichy territory, helped take Madagascar, and went to the Middle East as Pioneers and to the Far East to fight Japan." Ashley Jackson, *The British Empire and the Second World War* (London: Hambledon Continuum, 2006), 171.

40. Ajovi Scott-Emuakpor, "The Evolution of Health Care Systems in Nigeria: Which Way Forward in the Twenty-First Century," *Nigerian Medical Journal*, 51(2) (2010), 53–65, https://www.nigeriamedj.com/article.asp?issn=0300-1652;year=2010;volume=51;issue=2;spage=53;epage=65;aulast=Scott-Em ("The Emergence of Organized Health Care Services").

41. George N. Njung, "Amputated Men, Colonial Bureaucracy, and Masculinity in Post-World War I Colonial Nigeria," *Journal of Social History*, 53(3) (Spring 2020), 620–643; George Njung, "Amputated Men: The British Nigerian Disabled Men of the First World War and Their Crisis of Masculinity," Lecture at the University of Nottingham, UK (December 10, 2019) [hereinafter Njung Lecture], https://www.nottingham.ac.uk/home/featureevents/2019/amputated-men-the-british-nigerian-disabled-men-of-the-first-world-war.aspx. See also "The First World War and Its Consequences in Africa," *UNESCO Courier*, https://en.unesco.org/courier/news-views-online/first-world-war-and-its-consequences-africa.

42. See Njung, "Amputated Men, Colonial Bureaucracy, and Masculinity in Post-World War I Colonial Nigeria, note 41; and Njung Lecture, note 41.

43. Emmanuel Nwafor Mordi, "Nigerian Forces Comforts Fund, 1940–1947: 'The Responsibility of the Nigerian Government to Provide Funds for the Welfare of Its Soldiers,'" *Itinerario: Journal of Imperial and Global Interactions*, 43(3) (December 2019), 516–542, https://doi.org/10.1017/S0165115319000585.

44. See, for example, Elisha P. Renne, "Polio in Nigeria," *History Compass*, 10(7) (2012), 496–511, https://citeseerx.ist.psu.edu/viewdoc/download?doi=10.1.1.818.5571&rep=rep1&type=pdf ("Early Documented Experiences of Polio in Nigeria").

45. See ibid., pp. 496–497.

46. Ibid.

47. See, for example, Adedamola Adetiba and Enocent Msindo, "Chiefs and Rural Health Services in South-Western Nigeria, c. 1920—c. 1950s," *Social History of Medicine* (2022), https://doi.org/10.1093/shm/hkab116; and "Health Care Services in Colonial Nigeria," *Wefinder* (July 7, 2021), wefinder24.com/2021/07/health-care-services-in-colonial-nigeria.html. See also van Tol, note 32.

48. See Adegboyega O. Ogunlesi and Adegboyega Ogunwale, "Mental Health Legislation in Nigeria: Current Leanings and Future Years," *International Psychiatry*, 9(3), 62–64 (August 2012).

49. Ibid.; Obianuju Ugochukwu et al., "The Time is Now: Reforming Nigeria's Outdated Mental Health Laws," *Lancet*, 8(8)E989-990 (August 2020), https://doi.org/10.1016/S2214-109X(20)30302-8.

50. Ugochukwu et al., note 49. See also Yusuf Hassan Wada et al., “Mental Health in Nigeria: A Neglected Issue in Public Health,” *Public Health in Practice*, 2 (2021), 1–3.

51. Ugochukwu et al., note 49.

52. Ibid.

53. Ibid.

54. Ibid.

55. Ibid.

56. Ibid.

57. See *Consequences of Exclusion: A Situation Report on Organizations of People with Disabilities and COVID-19 in Bangladesh, Nigeria, and Zimbabwe* (London, UK: Inclusive Futures, September 2021), p. 35, https://www.sddirect.org.uk/media/2268/english-situation-report-opds-covid-19-report-final.pdf (“Case Study 1”).

58. Jonathan Sadowsky, *Imperial Bedlam: Institutions of Madness in Colonial Southwest Nigeria* (Berkeley, Los Angeles, and London: University of California Press, 1999), 1–2, back cover.

59. Ibid., p. 2.

60. Ibid.

61. Ibid.

62. Elisha P. Renne, *The Politics of Polio in Northern Nigeria* (Bloomington and Indianapolis: Indiana University Press, 2010), 73.

63. See ibid.; and John Stocker, *Nigerian Railway Jubilee, 1901–1951: An Illustrated and Descriptive History of the Nigerian Railway* (Lagos: Railway Printer, 1951) [digitized August 8, 2006, by the University of Michigan].

64. Renne, note 62, p. 73.

65. Ibid., pp. 86–101 (“Polio in Northern Nigeria and Northeastern Ghana”).

66. Gold Coast Government, *Report on the Enquiry into Begging and Destitution in the Gold Coast 1954* (Accra, Ghana: Government Printer, 1955).

67. Book’s Introduction (discussion commenting on the location of the book within four sub-approaches to Disability Studies).

68. See, for example, Helen Senu-Oke, *A Genealogy of Disability and Special Education in Nigeria: From the Pre-Colonial Era to the Present*, Ed.D. Dissertation in Educational Leadership, Miami University (2011) (abstract).

69. Ibid.

70. Okechukwu V. Nwokorie and Patrick J. Devlieger, “‘We Only Got Coca-Cola’: Disability and the Paradox of (Dis)empowerment in Southeast Nigeria,” *African Journal of Disability*, 8(444) (2019), doi: 10:4102/ajod.v8i0.444.

71. Ibid.

72. Ibid. (comments of the respondent Ifeanyi Nwosu, February 17, 2016).

73. See Gabrielle Udoka Robertson, *Explanatory Models of Autism in Nigeria: Exploring Sociocultural Beliefs to Inform Systems of Care*, Honor Thesis, University of Mississippi (April 2021), 24, https://egrove.olemiss.edu/cgi/viewcontent.cgi?article=2862&context=hon_thesis.

74. Ibid.

75. Adejumoke Adeworan, *The Realities of Living with Disability in Ibadan, Nigeria: An Ethnographic Study*, MA thesis, Department of Disability Studies, University of Manitoba, Canada (2019), i.

76. Ibid.

77. Ibid.

78. Ibid.

79. See "Nigeria Situational Analysis Version II–June 2020," *Inclusive Futures: Promoting Disability Inclusion* (Brighton, UK: Institute of Development Studies, July 2020), 16–17, https://opendocs.ids.ac.uk/opendocs/bitstream/handle/20.500.12413/15561/DID%20SITAN%20Nigeria%20V2%20July%202020.pdf?sequence=1&isAllowed=y

80. Ibid., pp. 4–5.

81. Ibid., pp. 6–8.

82. Book's Introduction (discussion commenting on the location of the book within four sub-approaches to Disability Studies).

83. See note 38 and accompanying text.

84. For leprosy, see, for example, Unah, note 36; for polio, see, for example, Renne, note 62, pp. 33–50 ("Politics and Polio in Nigeria"); pp. 51–67 ("Islam and Immunization in Northern Nigeria"); and pp. 68–87 ("Polio Disability and Begging").

85. Unah, note 36 (leprosy); and Renne, note 62, pp. 102–118 ("The Ethics of Eradication") (polio).

86. For a more or less recent book on the Nigeria-Biafra War, see Chinua Achebe, *There Was a Country: A Personal History of Biafra* (London, UK: Penguin, 2012).

87. "Boko Haram in Nigeria," Global Conflict Tracker, Council on Foreign Relations (last updated February 24, 2022), https://www.cfr.org/global-conflict-tracker/conflict/boko-haram-nigeria.

88. See Arinze Chijioke, "Wounded in Battle, Abandoned at Home: Pains of Being a Biafran Soldier," *International Policy Digest* (February 27, 2020), https://intpolicydigest.org/wounded-in-battle-abandoned-at-home-pains-of-being-a-biafran-soldier/.

89. See "Oji River Leprosy Settlement," note 37.

90. See Chijioke, "Wounded in Battle, Abandoned at Home," note 88; Jude Chinedu, "Plight of Forgotten Biafran Heroes," *Sun* (Abuja and Lagos) (January 17, 2020), https://www.sunnewsonline.com/plight-of-forgotten-biafra-heroes/; and "Disabled Biafran Veterans Cry Out for Help," *Vanguard* (Lagos) (June 27, 2015), https://www.vanguardngr.com/2015/06/disabled-biafran-veterans-cry-out-for-help/.

91. See Madiha Afzal, "From 'Western Education is Forbidden' to the World's Deadliest Terrorist Group: Education and Boko Haram in Nigeria," *Foreign Policy at Brookings* (April 2020), https://www.brookings.edu/wp-content/uploads/2020/04/FP_20200507_nigeria_boko_haram_afzal.pdf; Andrew Walker, "What Is Boko Haram?" United States Institute of Peace, Special Report No. 308 (June 2012), https://www.usip.org/sites/default/files/resources/SR308.pdf.

92. Philip C. Aka, *Human Rights in Nigeria's External Relations: Building the Record of a Moral Superpower* (Lanham, Boulder, New York, and London: Lexington Books, 2017), 83.

93. Will Ross, "Boko Haram War Has Led to 350,000 Deaths—UN," BBC World Service (June 24, 2021), https://www.bbc.com/news/topics/c50znx8v435t/boko-haram.

94. Mukhtar Ya'U Madobi, "Nigerian Roads: Death Traps for Commuters," *Cable* (November 24, 2021), https://www.thecable.ng/nigerian-roads-death-traps-commuters#:~:text=It%20was%20estimated%20that%20about,really%20indicated%20a%20terrifying%20situation (labelling Nigerian roads "death traps for commuters").

95. Inemesit Udodiong, "Here Are the Countries with the Best and Worst Roads in Africa," *Pulse* (December 10, 2018), https://www.pulse.ng/bi/lifestyle/lifestyle-here-are-the-countries-with-the-best-and-worst-roads-in-africa/3d6jeng.

96. Madobi, note 94. commuters#:~:text=It%20was%20estimated%20that%20about,really%20indicated%20a%20terrifying%20situation.

97. Ibid.

98. Ibid.

99. Mohammed Awaisu Haruna, "The Problems of Living with Disability in Nigeria," *Journal of Law, Policy, and Globalization*, 65 (2017), 103–113, https://www.iiste.org/Journals/index.php/JLPG/article/viewFile/39027/40128.

100. HIV stands for Human Immunodeficiency Virus, the virus epidemiologists believe is responsible for HIV infections. The acronym can refer either to the virus itself or to the infection. For its part, AIDS stands for Acquired Immuno-Deficiency Syndrome, believed by epidemiologist to be the most advanced stage of HIV infection. The nature of the connection between the two diseases is that "HIV attacks and destroys the infection-fighting CD4 cells (CD4 T lymphocyte) of the immune system. The loss of CD4 cells makes it difficult for the body to fight off infections and certain cancers. Without treatment, HIV can gradually destroy the immune system and HIV infection advances to AIDS." HIV and AIDS: The Basics, National Institute of Health (last reviewed August 16, 2021), https://hivinfo.nih.gov/understanding-hiv/fact-sheets/hiv-and-aids-basics.

101. "Number of Deaths Due to AIDS in Nigeria as of 2020," *Statista* (February 1, 2022), https://www.statista.com/statistics/1262130/deaths-due-to-aids-in-nigeria/#:~:text=As%20of%202020%2C%201.7%20million,adults%2C%20with%2020%20thousand%20deaths.

102. "New Survey Results Indicate that Nigeria Has an HIV Prevalence of 1.4%," Press Release, UNAIDS (March 14, 2019), https://www.unaids.org/en/resources/presscentre/pressreleaseandstatementarchive/2019/march/20190314_nigeria#:~:text=New%20survey%20results%20indicate%20that%20Nigeria%20has%20an%20HIV%20prevalence%20of%201.4%25,-14%20March%202019&text=ABUJA%2FGENEVA%2C%2014%20March%202019,national%20HIV%20prevalence%20of%202.8%25.

103. Debra L. Cameron et al., "Children with Disabilities in Low-Income Countries," *Pediatric Child Health*, 10(5) (May-June 2005), 269–272, doi: 10.1093/pch/10.5.269 (abstract).

104. See Jude Egbas, "[Four] Things You Should Know about Sharia Law in Nigeria," *Pulse* (August 12, 2020), https://www.pulse.ng/news/metro/sharia-in-nigeria-4-things-you-should-know-about-islamic-law/y29g15v.

105. See, for example, Katrin Gänsler, "Nigeria Looks Back on 20 Years of Sharia Law in the North," *DW* (October 27, 2019), https://www.dw.com/en/nigeria-looks-back-on-20-years-of-sharia-law-in-the-north/a-51010292.

106. See, for example, John Campbell, "Sharia Punishments Embarrass Nigeria," Council on Foreign Relations (September 30, 2020), https://www.cfr.org/blog/sharia-punishments-embarrass-nigeria (opining that "Inhumane sharia punishments, including flogging, amputations, and stoning, have long embarrassed the federal government of Nigeria"); Egbas, note 104; and Human Rights Watch, "Political Sharia"?: Human Rights and Islamic Law in Northern Nigeria (New York: Human Rights Watch, September 21, 2004), https://www.hrw.org/report/2004/09/21/political-sharia/human-rights-and-islamic-law-northern-nigeria#.

107. Egbas, note 104.

108. Ibid.

109. See Ngozi C. Umeh and Ramola Adeola, "Nigeria," *African Disability Rights Yearbook* (2013), 1, 288 (portraying the disability movement in the country as "non-homogenous").

110. Nigerians with Disability Decree, 1993, GLADNET Collection, Paper 133, http://digitalcommons.ilr.cornell.edu/gladnetcollect/133. In Nigeria, a decree refers to a law made by a military dictator without need for a legislative process since under military regimes in the country, the constitution is abrogated and the legislative branch is disbanded. In effect, under a military regime, there are only two branches of government—the executive and judicial—other than the traditional three branches. Moreover, the judicial branch is dependent, rather than free from executive interference, and their rulings are not usually enforced. The media, the unofficial fourth branch of the government, is also repressed under the military. So are civil society or the non-governmental sectors of society. See, for example, Robert Longley, "What Is a Military Dictatorship? Definition and Examples," *ThoughtCo* (January 29, 2021), https://www.thoughtco.com/military-dictatorship-definition-and-examples-5091896. See also Daniel Sutter, "Legitimacy and Military Intervention in a Democracy: Civilian Government as a Public Good," *American Journal of Economics and Sociology*, 58(1) (1999), 129–143.

111. See "The Babangida Government," in Helen Chapin Metz, ed., *Nigeria: A Country Study* (Washington, DC: GPO for the Library of Congress, 1991), http://countrystudies.us/nigeria/73.htm.

112. Nigerians with Disability Decree, note 110, § 2 ("Declaration of Policy").

113. Ibid., § 3 ("Interpretation").

114. Ibid., §§ 4–13.

115. Ibid.

116. Nigerians with Disability Decree, note 110, (§ 14, "Establishment of the National Commission for People with Disabilities"; and § 14, "Membership of the Commission").

117. Ibid. (§ 14, "Objectives of the Commission"; and § 14, "Special Functions of the Commission").

118. Ibid. (§ 14, "Objectives of the Commission"; and § 14, "Annual Reports").

119. Ibid. (§ 4, "Tenure of Office").

120. See "Difference Between Right and Privilege," *Difference Between* (July 14, 2012), https://www.differencebetween.com/difference-between-right-and-vs-privilege ("Privileges are conditional and can be withdrawn[,] while rights are inherent and cannot be withdrawn"). For a description of the distinction between these two doctrines in US constitutional history, see Dennis J. Mahoney and Kenneth L Karst, "Right-Privilege Distinction," *Encyclopedia of the American Constitution* (1986), https://www.encyclopedia.com/politics/encyclopedias-almabacs-transcripts-and-maps/right-privilege-distinction.

121. See generally Sutter, note 110.

122. Audrey L. Comstock, *Committed to Rights: Volume 1: UN Human Rights Treaties and Legal Paths for Commitment and Compliance* (New York: Cambridge University Press, 2021), 16.

123. See ibid.

124. Brigitte Rohwerder, *Disability Stigma in Developing Countries*, K4D Helpdesk Report (London: Institute of Development Studies, May 9, 2018), 4–11, https://assets.publishing.service.gov.uk/media/5b18fe3240f0b634aec30791/Disability_stigma_in_developing_countries.pdf.

125. Ibid., pp. 8–11.

126. Ibid., p. 9.

127. See ibid., 13–15 (discussing stigma specific to different types of impairment).

128. See notes 33–37 and accompanying texts.

129. See Rohwerder, note 124, p. 14.

130. Ibid.

131. Ibid., p. 13.

132. Ibid., p. 14.

133. Ibid.

134. See Akinwale Akinyoade, "Strength Beyond All Odds: Living with Albinism in Nigeria," *Guardian* (Lagos) (June 13, 2021), https://guardian.ng/life/strength-beyond-all-odds-living-with-albinism-in-nigeria/.

135. Ibid.

136. Ibid., p. 13.

137. Ibid.

138. Ibid.

139. Ibid., pp. 13–14.

140. *Disability Inclusion in Nigeria: A Rapid Assessment* (Washington, DC: World Bank, 2020), p. 16.

141. Ibid. (views of a respondent in the survey, a man suffering from albinism who lived in Abuja).

142. *Nigeria: Children and Young People with Disabilities*, note 20, pp. 19–20.

143. "Common Barriers to Participation Experienced by People with Disabilities," CDC: Centers for Disease Control and Prevention (USA), https://www.cdc.gov/ncbddd/disabilityandhealth/disability-barriers.html.

144. M. Lynn Rose, "The Courage of Subordination: Women and Intellectual Disability in the Ancient Greek World," in *The Routledge History of Disability,* eds. Roy Hanes et al. (London and New York: Routledge, 2018), 35–47. For her earlier work along this line, see Martha L. Rose, *The Staff of Oedipus: Transforming Disability in Ancient Greece* (Ann Arbor: University of Michigan Press, 2013) (unearthing centuries-old myths on disability going back to ancient Greece that still survive today). Working within the framework of ancient social history, the book examined not only ancient literature, but also evidence from papyri, skeletal remains, inscriptions, sculpture, and painting, as well as modern sources, including disability autobiographies, medical research, and related sources in the field of disability studies. Ibid.

145. Rose, "The Courage of Subordination," 144.

146. Karen K.H. Ngai et al., "A Journey of Change—History of Disability in Hong Kong[,] 1841–2014," in *The Routledge History of Disability,* eds. Roy Hanes et al. (London and New York: Routledge, 2018), 163–203.

147. Ivan Brown, "When is Life Unworthy of Living? Lessons from the Systematic Killing of Children with Disabilities in Nazi Germany," *The Routledge History of Disability,* eds. Roy Hanes et al. (London and New York: Routledge, 2018), 421–433.

148. Luc Brants et al., "A Short History of Approaches to Disability in the Netherlands," *The Routledge History of Disability,* eds. Roy Hanes et al. (London and New York: Routledge, 2018), pp. 151–162.

149. Ibid.

150. Joav Merrick et al., "A Short History of Disability Aspects from Israel," in *The Routledge History of Disability,* eds. Roy Hanes et al. (London and New York: Routledge, 2018), 94–114.

151. Ibid.

152. Nelson Mandela (1918–2013), quoted in Sherman D. Manning, *American Dream, A Search for Justice* (American Dream Online Books, 2016).

153. The inspiration for this thought came from the American author, salesman, and motivational speaker Hilary Hinton Ziglar (1926–2012) who is given credit for the quote that "[y]our attitude, not your aptitude, will determine your altitude."

154. Katharine Hanifen, "Living with Disabilities in Nigeria," Borgen Project, https://borgenproject.org/disabilities-in-nigeria/ (quoting Cobhams Asuquo, a blind Nigerian singer, songwriter, and producer, to the effect that "[a]s a nation [Nigeria is] missing out on the value [people with disabilities] can add, just because [it is] not creating an enabling environment for [PLWDs] to thrive").

155. Umeh and Adeola, note 109, p. 288.

156. Ilija Tomanić Trivundža et al., "Concluding Remarks," in *The Routledge History of Disability,* eds. Roy Hanes et al. (London and New York: Routledge, 2018), 500–501.

157. Ibid.

Chapter 2

Survey of the Global and Regional Regimes on Disability Pertaining to Nigeria

INTRODUCTION

Assessing the response of the Nigerian national government toward matters bearing on the welfare of disabled persons within its own country, as this book does, requires that the assessor set forth the governing rules that form the basis for assessment. Herein lies the essence of this chapter. The governing rules here involved, echoing the definition of key terms laid out in this book's introduction, are the global regime on disability anchored on the United Nations (UN) human rights system, and the regional regime on disability tied to the African human rights system. Although separate, the two disability regimes are complementary. African delegations, made up of governmental and civil society organizations, participated actively in the negotiations leading to the adoption of the Convention on the Rights of People with Disabilities (CRPD) and its Optional Protocol in 2006.[1] Unsurprisingly, the African disability instrument, discussed later in this chapter, in important respects, tracked the CRPD.

The following discussion describes the two regimes. Overall, there are three parts to the analysis in this chapter. The first, focused on the global disability regime, includes separate comments on the CRPD and its Optional Protocol, antecedents of the two instruments, and some placement of the two instruments along with the global regime they embody into analytical perspectives. The second part, focused on the African regional disability regime, encompasses the African Charter on Human and Peoples' Rights on the Rights of Persons with Disabilities in Africa (PACRD) and its antecedents.

The third is an analysis of *Purohit and Moore v. The Gambia* (2003), a decision of the African Commission on Human and Peoples' Rights, the group charged with responsibility for monitoring the implementation of the African Charter on Human and Peoples' Rights, that we portray as a foretaste and harbinger of positive future developments with respect to all three instruments under review in this chapter: the CRPD, its Optional Protocol, and the PACRD.

THE GLOBAL DISABILITY REGIME UNDER THE UNITED NATIONS

The global disability regime under the UN comprises the CRPD,[2] and its Optional Protocol.[3] The twin instruments were adopted by general consensus on December 13, 2006, by the UN General Assembly,[4] opened for signature on March 30, 2007, and entered into force on May 3, 2008.[5] Consistent with the grundnorm governing each treaty, the CRPD came into force on the thirtieth day after the deposit of the twentieth instrument of ratification or accession,[6] while its Optional Protocol entered into force on the thirtieth day after the deposit of the tenth instrument of ratification or accession.[7]

The history of the twin instruments dates back to December 19, 2001, when an *ad hoc* Committee drafted the CRPD.[8] The Committee was set up under UN General Assembly Resolution No. 56/168 of 2001.[9] The Resolution mandated the Committee "to consider proposals for a comprehensive and integral international convention to promote and protect the rights and dignity of persons [living] with disabilities, based on the holistic approach in the work done in the fields of social development, human rights and non-discrimination."[10] Negotiations next occurred in eight sessions before the General Assembly's adoption of the instruments in December 2006.[11] Nigeria is a state party of the both the CRPD and its Optional Protocol. Nigeria signed the CRPD on March 30, 2007, the very date the instrument was opened for signature, and ratified it on September 24, 2010,[12] over two years after it came into force.[13] Similarly, it accepted the competence of the OPCRPD on September 24, 2010,[14] the same day that it ratified the CRPD.

The Convention on the Rights of Persons with Disabilities (CRPD)

The CRPD consists of a preamble and 50 articles. Its preamble is distinctively long and comprises 25 clauses, numbered (a) to (y). While, constitutionally speaking, a preamble by itself does not confer rights, something the substantive provisions in the main body of the treaty does, the purposes, motivations, and related considerations for concluding the treaty, embedded in a preamble, can assist in understanding, interpreting, and applying the specific powers listed in the articles, if nothing else, for the reason that the treaty may not be interpreted in a manner that defeats its purposes.[15] Table 2.1 summarizes the clauses that, in our assessment, stand out in the CRPD preamble.

Article 1 sets forth the purpose of the multilateral treaty, namely, "to promote, protect and ensure the full and equal enjoyment of all human rights and fundamental freedoms by all persons [living] with disabilities, and to promote respect for their inherent dignity."[16] The article also provides a definition of sort for "persons [living] with disability." Article 2 outlines key terms the treaty defines. Terms that stand out are "discrimination on the basis of disability," referenced in the introduction of this book,[17] "reasonable accommodation," and "universal design." The treaty defines "reasonable accommodation" to mean "necessary and appropriate modification and adjustments[,]" free of "undue burden" for the implementer, designed to ensure that PLWDs enjoy or exercise their human rights, free of any discrimination based on disability.[18] The treaty defines "universal design" to mean "the design of products, environments, programs and services to be usable by all people, to the greatest extent possible, without the need for adaptation or specialized design."[19] Instructively, the CRPD points out, "usable by all people" does "not exclude assistive devices for particular groups of persons [living] with disabilities where this is needed."[20] The term that should be on the list but is not included is "persons [living] with disability," but rather instead added, as stated above, in Article 1 on the purpose of the treaty. As we explained in the introduction of this book, the non-inclusion of the term is due to the CRPD's view of disability as an "evolving concept," even though, as we observed, "discrimination on the basis of disability," for which the CRPD provides a formal definition, comes close to being a formal definition of "persons [living] with disability."[21]

Article 3 lays down the general principles applicable to all human beings, PLWDs and non-disabled persons alike, that underpin the adoption of the treaty, namely: respect for inherent dignity and individual autonomy of all humans, emblematized by the freedom to make their own choices; non-discrimination; full and effective participation and inclusion in society; respect for difference[s] and acceptance of PLWDs as part of humanity and human diversity; equal opportunity; accessibility; equality between men and women; as well as respect for the evolving capacities of children with disabilities and respect for the right of these children to preserve their identities.[22] Some of these principles, such as respect for inherent dignity and personal autonomy, are reiterations of ideas that appeared initially in the preamble.

Table 2.1. Key clauses in the CRPD preamble

Item No.	*Clause*	*Location in Preamble*
1.	"]T]he inherent dignity and worth" of all human beings.	(a)
2.	PLWDs possess "individual autonomy and independence, including the freedom to make their own choices."	(n)
3.	"[T]he need to promote and protect the human rights of all persons with disabilities, including those who require more intensive support"	(j)
4.	Opportunity for PLWDs "to be actively involved in decision-making processes about policies and programs," particularly in matters that affect them	(o)
5.	Disappointment that various past instruments and undertakings failed to eliminate barriers against PLWD participation in society and violations of their human rights in all parts of the world	(k)
6.	"[I]mportance of international cooperation for improving the living conditions of persons [living] with disabilities [. . .], particularly in developing countries"	(l)
7.	Recognition of PLWDs' current and potential contributions to the well-being and diversity of their communities	(m)
8.	Notion of disability as an evolving concept and a condition that results from the interaction between persons with impairments on the one hand and attitudinal and environmental barriers on the other hand that impede PLWDs' full and effective participation in society on an equal basis with others	(e)
9.	Recognition of the diversity of PLWDs	(i)
10.	Awareness of the reality that PLWDs are subject to multiple and at times aggravated discrimination, based on grounds like race, gender, language, religion, political or other opinion, national, ethnic, indigenous or social origin, property, birth, or age	(p)
11.	Recognition that females living with disabilities are often at greater risk of violence, injury, neglect, exploitation and related mistreatments	(q)
12.	Recognition that children with disabilities should have full enjoyment of all human rights on an equal basis with other children, consistent with treaties like the Convention on the Rights of the Child	(r)
13.	The need to incorporate a gender perspective in all efforts to promote the full enjoyment of the human rights and fundamental freedoms of PLWDs	(s)
14.	The reality that the majority of PLWDs live in conditions of poverty, thus recognizing the critical need to address the negative impact of poverty on PLWDs	(t)
15.	Recognition of the importance of accessibility to the physical, social, economic and cultural environment, to health and education, and to information and communication, in enabling PLWDs to fully enjoy all human rights and fundamental freedoms	(v)
16.	Persuaded that the key to redressing the social disadvantage PLWDs face and promotion of their participation in all spheres of society is a comprehensive and integral international convention	(y)

Source: Created by the authors.

Table 2.2. General obligations of state parties under the CRPD

Item No.	*Provision*	*Location in Article*
1.	Adopting measures that will facilitate effective implementation of the rights in the treaty	1.a.
2.	Taking steps "to modify or abolish existing laws, regulations, customs and practices that constitute discrimination against" PLWDs	1.b.
3.	Close consultation and active involvement of PLWDs, or organizations which represent these individuals, in the formulation and implementation of laws and policies relating to disability	4.3
4.	Integration of protection and promotion of PLWD human rights in all governmental policies and programs	1.c.
5.	Taking measures to eliminate discrimination based on disability by any person, organization, or private enterprise	1.e.
6.	State parties' promoting research and development, availability and use of new technologies at affordable costs for PLWDs, including Information and Communications Technologies (ICT), mobility aids, and assistive devices	1.g.
7.	Providing accessible information to PLWDs regarding mobility aids, devices and assistive technologies, new technologies, and other forms of assistance, support services, and facilities	1.h
8.	Promoting the training of professionals and staff working with PLWDs related to the rights recognized in the CRPD so as to better provide the assistance and services guaranteed by those rights.	1.i.
9.	State parties adopting measures within their economic means to progressively realize the rights of PLWDs, taking into account available governmental resources	4.2

Source: Created by the authors

Article 4 spells out the "general obligations" of state parties related to the treaty. Table 2.2 assembles the provisions that stand out among these general obligations.

Articles 5–9 contain specific obligations of state parties, additional to the general obligations in Article 3, complete with practical steps state parties need to facilitate implementation. Article 5 relates to equality and non-discrimination, Article 6 to women with disabilities, Article 7 to children with disabilities, Article 8 to raising awareness regarding persons living with disability, and Article 9 to accessibility.

With respect to non-discrimination, Article 5 requires state parties to take steps to ensure the provision of reasonable accommodation.[23] Instructively, it also indicated that preferential programs designed to promote equality for PLWDs may not be considered discriminatory against nondisabled persons.[24] In light of the multiple discriminations that women and girls are subject to, Article 6 mandates state parties to take steps to ensure "the full and equal enjoyment by them of all human rights and fundamental freedoms."[25] Article

7 mandates states parties to "take all necessary measures to ensure the full enjoyment by children with disabilities of all human rights and fundamental freedoms on an equal basis with other children."[26] Moreover, all their actions related to children living with disabilities should be guided by "the best interests of the child" as "a primary consideration[,]"[27] and they should ensure that children living with disabilities "have the right to express their views freely on all matters affecting them, their views being given due weight in accordance with their age and maturity, on an equal basis with other children[.]"[28]

Article 8 mandates state parties "[t]o raise awareness throughout society" regarding PLWDs, "[t]o combat stereotypes, prejudices[,] and harmful practices" related to them, and to promote awareness of their capabilities and potential contributions to society.[29] Article 9 mandates state parties to take necessary steps to provide PLWDs "access, on an equal basis with others, to the physical environment, to transportation, [and] to information and communications."[30] In both urban and rural areas alike, access to these facilities and services is necessary to enable PLWDs "to live independently and participate fully in all aspects of life[.]"[31]

Articles 10–30 set forth the rights that state parties are obligated to protect and promote for PLWDs. Table 2.3 encapsulates these rights. Article 31 relates to undertaking by state parties to collect appropriate information, including statistical and research data, to facilitate formulation and implementation of the provisions of the treaty. Article 32 deals with recognition of the importance of international cooperation, complementary to national initiatives, in protecting and ensuring the human rights of PLWDs. Article 33 focuses on implementing and monitoring the CRPD by state parties and organizations representing PLWDs.

Still on the critical topic of monitoring implementation, Articles 34–40 deal with a range of issues centered around the Committee on the Rights of Persons with Disabilities (hereinafter CRPD Committee), a body of independent experts, tasked with responsibility for reviewing implementation of the treaty by state parties. The Committee approaches its duties through review of periodic reports, prepared by state parties, on the steps they have taken designed to implement the treaty. Article 34 established this all-important Committee. For states that are also party to the Optional Protocol, the Committee also has authority to receive complaints from individuals who allege violation of their rights, a process referred to as *individual communications procedure*, and to undertake inquiries in cases of wholesale or systematic violations of the treaty, a process referred to as *inquiry procedure*.[32] In choosing the members of the CRPD Committee, state parties must take into consideration the competence of the members they select in human rights and the field of disability, as well as factors like geographic representation, different legal systems, and gender balance. Today, the CRPD Committee has

Table 2.3. Human rights of persons living with disabilities in the CRPD

Item No.	Right	Article
1.	Right to life	10
2.	Right to protection and safety in situations of risk, such as armed conflict, humanitarian emergencies, and natural disasters	11
3.	Right to health	25
4.	Right to habilitation and rehabilitation	26
5.	Right to personal mobility	20
6.	Right to education	24
7.	Right to work and employment	27
8.	Right to freedom from exploitation, violence, and abuse	16
9.	Right to an adequate standard of living and social protection	28
10.	Right to respect physical and mental integrity	17
11.	Right to liberty and security of the person	14
12.	Right to freedom from torture or related persecutions or treatments	15
13.	Right to freedom of movement and nationality	18
14.	Right of equal recognition before the law and legal capacity	12
15.	Right of access to justice	13
16.	Right to freedom of expression, opinion, and access to information	21
17.	Right to respect for privacy	22
18.	Right to freedom from discrimination on "all matters relating to marriage, family, parenthood, and relationship"	23
19.	Right of freedom to live independently within a community of their choice	19
20.	Right to participate in political and public life	29
21.	Right to participate in the cultural lives of their own societies	30

Source: Created by the authors

18 members, elected for a four-year term with possibility of reelection for another term.[33] These members serve in their individual capacities, rather than as representatives of their governments.[34] The Committee meets two times a year in Geneva.[35]

Article 35 deals with reports by states parties to the CRPD Committee. Each state party must submit to the Committee, within two years after the treaty enters into force for that state, an initial comprehensive report on measures it has taken to implement the treaty. The initial report should: establish the constitutional, legal and administrative framework for implementing the treaty; explain the policies and programs adopted to implement each of the treaty's provisions; and identify any progress made in realizing the rights of PLWDs since ratification.[36] Subsequently, the state party must submit reports at least every four years or whenever the Committee requests one. Such quadrennial reports should respond to the concerns highlighted by the Committee in its concluding observations to previous reports; indicate progress made in realizing the rights of PLWDs over the reporting period; and highlight any obstacles that the state party faced in implementing the treaty over the reporting period.[37]

Article 36 deals with the CRPD Committee's consideration of those reports. The article requires states parties to publicize their reports to their own citizens and receive feedback relating to these reports.[38] Article 37 requires state parties to cooperate with the Committee and to assist it to fulfil its mandate. Article 38 deals with the relationship between the CRPD Committee and other bodies, such as UN specialized agencies. Article 39 requires the Committee to update the UN General Assembly and the Economic and Social Council every two years on its activities, including suggestions and general recommendations, based on the examination of reports and information received from state parties.[39] Article 40 mandates states parties to "meet regularly in a Conference of States Parties," convened by the UN Secretary General, to consider any matter related to the CRPD Committee's implementation of the treaty.[40] Articles 41–50 deal with miscellaneous issues, immaterial to this discussion, such as depositary, entry into force, reservations, amendments, denunciation, and languages deemed authentic when applying the treaty.

The Optional Protocol to the UN Convention on the Rights of Persons with Disabilities (OPCRPD)

The Optional Protocol has 18 articles with no preamble. Article 1 of the Optional Protocol establishes the competence of the CRPD Committee to receive and consider complaints, denominated "communications," from individuals or groups who allege breaches of their rights under the treaty. The competence of the Committee does not, unsurprisingly, extend to countries who are not state parties of the Optional Protocol. Article 2 spells out the types of complaints or petitions that are inadmissible to the Committee. These include anonymous petitions, instances where domestic remedies have not been exhausted, except where application of remedies is unduly prolonged or exhausting remedies is futile, or where the petition is "manifestly ill-founded or not sufficiently substantiated."[41] Article 3 requires the Committee to bring any petition submitted to it confidentially to the attention of the affected state party. Article 4 permits the Committee to submit to a state party a request for interim measures as may be necessary to avoid possible irreparable damage to the victims of an alleged violation before it reaches a decision on a petition. Article 5 mandates the Committee to hold closed meetings when examining a petition, following which it makes recommendations to the state party in question and the petitioners.

Articles 6–8 relate to applicable procedures that apply in situations where the Committee received petitions involving egregious and systematic violations by a state party of rights set forth in the treaty. In a nutshell, the Optional

Protocol established two procedures, referred to before, designed to facilitate implementation and monitoring of the CRPD. The first is an *individual-complaint procedure*, under Article 1, allowing individuals to bring petitions to the Committee claiming breaches of their rights; the second is an *inquiry procedure*, under Articles 6 and 7, authorizing the Committee to undertake inquiries of wholesale or systematic violations of the Convention.[42] Under Article 8, a state party may decide not to recognize the competence of the Committee. Article 9 makes the UN Secretary General depositary of the Protocol, just like the CRPD did in its Article 41. Article 10 stipulates March 20, 2007, as the date the Protocol is open for signature by the states and regional integration organizations that the instrument recognizes as parties to the agreement. Article 11 stipulates that only state parties and regional integration organizations who ratify the CRPD may accept the competence of the Optional Protocol. Article 12 defines the regional integration organizations that, alongside with states, qualify as parties under the Protocol. They are organizations "constituted by sovereign States of a given region, to which its member States have transferred competence in respect of matters governed by the Convention and the present Protocol."[43]

Article 13 deals with the date for entry into force of the instrument, while Article 14 focuses on reservations. Reservations not compatible with the purpose of the Protocol are impermissible and reservations may be withdrawn at any time. Article 15 deals with techniques for proposing amendments to the Protocol, while Article 16 focuses on denunciation. Articles 17 and 18 deal with matters immaterial in this discussion, such as accessibility of the text of the Protocol, and languages deemed authentic (Arabic, Chinese, English, French, Russia, and Spanish) when applying the treaty.

Antecedents of the CRPD and Its Optional Protocol

Numerous instruments preceded the adoption of the CRPD and its Optional Protocol in 2006 with respect to global concern for the welfare of PLWDs. These instruments date back to the Declaration on the Rights of Disabled Persons in 1975. Table 2.4 pulls together these global instruments, twelve of them altogether, legally-binding and-non-binding alike. The CRPD preamble references many of these instruments.[44] The list here is not meant to be exhaustive.[45]

The Declaration on the Rights of Disabled Persons (DRDP) was proclaimed by the UN General Assembly "as a common basis and frame of reference" for protecting the rights of disabled persons.[46] Multiple considerations that animated the adoption of the Declaration include an understanding that disabled persons "have the same fundamental rights" as non-disabled persons, including "the right to enjoy a decent life, as normal and full as possible";[47] and a

Table 2.4. Recap on the antecedents of the CRPD and its Optional Protocol

Item No.	*Instrument*
	Legally non-binding pronouncements
1.	Declaration on the Rights of Disabled Persons (1975)
2.	World Program of Action concerning Disabled Persons (1982)
3.	Principles for the Protection of Persons with Mental Illness and The Improvement of Mental Health Care (1991)
4.	Standard Rules on the Equalization of Opportunities for Persons with Disabilities (1993)
	The International Bill of Human Rights
5.	Universal Declaration of Human Rights (1948)
6.	International Covenant on Civil and Political Rights (1966)
7.	International Covenant on Economic, Social and Cultural Rights (1966)
	Group-based human rights instruments
8.	International Convention on the Elimination of All Forms of Racial Discrimination (1965)
9.	Convention on the Elimination of All Forms of Discrimination against Women (1979)
10.	Convention Against Torture (1984)
11.	Convention on the Rights of the Child (1989)
12.	Convention on the Protection of the Rights of All Migrant Workers and Members of Their Families (1990)
13.	Convention for the Protection of All Persons from Enforced Disappearance (2006)

Source: Created by the authors

recognition of the need to "assist disabled persons to develop their abilities in the most varied fields of activities" in a bid to "promot[e] their integration as far as possible in normal life."[48]

The World Program of Action concerning Disabled Persons (WPA) aimed to enhance the prevention of disability while promoting rehabilitation and equal opportunities, leading to full participation in social life and national development of PLWDs.[49] Formulation of the document was a key result of the proclamation by the UN General Assembly in 1976 of the year 1981 as the International Year of Disabled Persons.[50] Taking as starting point, the proposition that "[a]ll persons have the right to the best available mental health care," the Principles for the Protection of Persons with Mental Illness and the Improvement of Mental Health Care (PPPMI) forbids discrimination based on mental illness.[51] Under the principles, "[a] determination that a person has a mental illness shall be made in accordance with internationally accepted medical standards[,]"[52] not on factors not directly connected to mental health status.[53] Nor may anybody "be compelled to undergo medical examination [. . .] to determin[e] whether or not he or she has a mental illness[,] except in accordance with a procedure authorized by domestic law."[54]

The Principles specify that persons with mental illnesses "have the right to live and work, as far as possible, [with]in the[ir] communit[ies],"[55] as well as "the right to be treated and cared for, as far as possible" within the same communities.[56] Similarly, persons with mental illnesses "have the right to receive such health and social care as is appropriate to [their] health needs, and [. . .] entitled to care and treatment[,] in accordance with the same standard as other ill persons."[57] To the extent it is possible, the Principles requires that treatments for mental patients should take place under conditions of informed consent,[58] consistent with the mental patient's right of personal autonomy.[59]

Moving forward, "[a]ny decision" relating to a mental patient, such as question about legal capacity or appointment of a personal representative, "shall be made only after a fair hearing by an independent and impartial tribunal established by domestic law[,]" at which hearing the patient must be represented by counsel.[60] And "[w]here a court or other competent tribunal finds that a person with mental illness is unable to manage his or her own affairs," the court must take necessary and appropriate measures to protect the interest of the party involved.[61] Some provisions of the PPPMI have been criticized,[62] but the CRPD supersedes these standards to the extent that there is any conflict between the two instruments.[63]

Standard Rules on the Equalization of Opportunities for Persons with Disabilities (hereinafter Standard Rules) were designed by the UN General Assembly as a tool to guide UN member states, and nongovernmental organizations that advocate for disabled persons, in the development of national disability programs.[64] Specifically, they were meant to provide a model that policymakers in these member states need to promote equal opportunity between disabled and non-disabled members in their societies, taking into account factors, such as differences in economic systems, and cultural contexts.[65] Equalizing opportunities between disabled and nondisabled persons means that, as members of society, PLWDs "have the right to remain within their local communities[,]" where they "receive the support they need within the ordinary structures of education, health, employment and social services."[66] And because rights go hand in hand with obligations, PLWDs have equal obligations in society with nondisabled individuals, with some degree of graduation, consistent with their condition. As the General Assembly put it, "[a]s persons [living] with disabilities achieve equal rights, they should also have equal obligations. As those rights are being achieved, societies should raise their expectations of persons [living] with disabilities."[67] This is where the rehabilitation and accommodation services of the government kick in. Such interventions are driven by the truism that equal opportunity for

PLWDs is facilitated only when provision is made to assist these individuals "to assume their full responsibility as members of society."[68]

The Standard Rules comprised four parts: preconditions for equal participation, target areas, measures for implementation, and mechanism for monitoring implementation of the rules.[69] The means for equal participation the Rules set forth as preconditions are raising awareness about PLWDs, including their rights, needs, potential, and contributions; effective medical care for this community; provision of rehabilitation services to enable PLWDs "reach and sustain their optim[al] level of independence and functioning"; as well as development and supply of support services and assistive devices to enable them "to increase their level of independence in their daily living and to exercise their rights."[70] Target areas for equal participation the Rules highlight include accessibility (such as to physical infrastructure and transportation), education, employment, social protections, family life and personal integrity, culture, recreation and sports, and religion.[71]

Less specialized human rights instruments relevant to PLWDs are the International Covenant on Economic, Social, and Cultural Rights (ICESCR); and the International Covenant on Civil and Political Rights (ICCPR). Along with the Universal Declaration of Human Rights, these two human rights instruments laid down "international standards on human rights" that should be afforded equally to all persons without discrimination. In other words, they shield against discrimination on any basis, including disability. Other human rights instruments, targeted on discrimination against specific issues or groups, such as women, children, or migrant workers, are the International Convention on the Elimination of All Forms of Racial Discrimination (ICERD); the Convention on the Elimination of All Forms of Discrimination against Women (CEDAW); the Convention on the Rights of the Child (CRC); the International Convention on the Protection of the Rights of All Migrant Workers and Members of Their Families (CRMW); the Convention Against Torture and other Cruel, Inhuman or Degrading Treatment or Punishment (CAT); and the International Convention for the Protection of All Persons from Enforced Disappearance (ICPPED).

Although it does not specifically mention disability, the ICERD has a broad definition of discrimination. It defines the term as "any distinction, exclusion, restriction or preference based on race, color, descent, or national or ethnic origin that has the purpose or effect of nullifying or impairing the recognition, enjoyment or exercise, on an equal footing, of human rights and fundamental freedoms in the political, economic, social, cultural or any other field of public life."[72] The definition implicitly includes disability. The CEDAW protects the rights of girls and women with disabilities. Similarly, the CRC prohibits discrimination based on disability and as well mandates special measures to protect the rights of children with disabilities. By the same token, the CRMW provides for some protective measures against disability. Conversely, by their structure, it is difficult to infer even an implicit coverage of disability in the CAT, and ICPPED.[73] Nevertheless, if nothing else, all of these instruments reaffirm the "commitment to human rights and fundamental freedoms, social justice and the dignity and worth of the human person proclaimed in the [UN] Charter."[74] Adding to the instruments enumerated above, certain conventions and recommendations of the International Labor Organization (ILO) urge participation in employment, free of discrimination against any group, including PLWDs.[75]

For the sake of a complete story, we find it necessary to recite these instruments. However, it is important to keep in mind that this is an old generation of instruments that the CRPD and its Optional Protocol have replaced. In the words of a UN manual, these twin treaties "supersede[] these [antecedents] as the most recent, specialized and comprehensive [instruments] to recognize the human rights of persons [living] with disabilities and to clarify the obligations of States to respect, protect and fulfil those rights."[76] Their adoption was borne out of the conclusion that prior to the adoption of the CRPD and its Protocol, UN treaty bodies and civil society did not use existing human rights instruments and monitoring mechanisms to their full potential to protect and promote the rights of PLWDs.[77]

The CRPD and Its Optional Protocol in Analytical Perspective

The CRPD and its Optional Protocol represent the most recent attempt made to "reinforce [global] understanding of disability as a human rights and development priority[,]"[78] as well as to comprehensively protect the rights of persons living with disabilities.[79] Although they do not per se create new human rights, the two instruments set forth "with much greater clarity[,] the obligations on States to promote, protect[,] and ensure the rights of persons with disabilities."[80] Their central message:

> is that persons with disabilities are entitled to the full spectrum of human rights and fundamental freedoms without discrimination. [. . .] In prohibiting discrimination on the basis of disability and establishing that reasonable accommodation shall be provided to persons with disabilities with a view to ensuring equality, the Convention promotes the full participation of persons with disabilities in all spheres of life. In establishing the obligation to promote positive perceptions and greater social awareness toward persons with disabilities, it challenges customs and behavior based on stereotypes, prejudices, harmful practices and stigma relating to persons with disabilities. In establishing a mechanism for complaints, the Convention's Optional Protocol ensures that persons with disabilities have an equal right to redress for violations of the rights enshrined in the Convention.[81]

In place of the charity and medical sub-approaches to disability studies referenced in the introduction of this book, the twin instruments "establish[ed] an empowering human rights-based approach to disability[,]"[82] one that views disability as a "pathology of society," specifically a result of the failure of society to generate an inclusiveness amenable to individual differences.[83] The crux of the matter is that society, rather than the individual, "need[s] to change, [. . .] and the [two instruments] provide a road map for such change."[84]

The twin instruments "came into existence through a forceful call from persons [living] with disabilities around the world to have their human rights respected, protected and fulfilled on an equal basis with others."[85] Their adoption "follow[ed] decades of work by the United Nations to change attitudes and approaches to persons with disabilities"—from perception of PLWDs as objects of charity to individuals with rights capable of vindicating those rights as active members of society.[86] Their adoption also underscored the frustration that, despite various human right instruments and initiatives by the international community before the adoption of the CRPD in 2006, "persons [living] with disabilities continue[d] to face barriers in their participation as equal members of society and violations of their human rights in all parts of the world."[87]

Adoption of the CRPD became necessary to achieve a clear reaffirmation that the rights of PLWDs are human rights and to strengthen respect for these rights. Although existing human rights conventions offer considerable potential to protect, promote, and ensure the rights of PLWDs, it was not hard to see that this potential was not being tapped. Instead, PLWDs continued to endure denial of their basic human rights that relegated them to the margins of their own society in all parts of the world.[88]

In a nutshell, five reasons that made the CRPD and its Optional Protocol important are that: they clarified the rights of PLWDs; set out in more detail the responsibilities of state parties to respect, protect and fulfil the rights of PLWDs; pinpointed disability as a social construct needing to be recognized for what it is to dismantle the barriers impeding full participation of PLWDs in society; promoted inclusive and accessible development; and ensured national and international monitoring of rights, not the same as ensuring legal enforceability, but still important.[89] In the light of these momentous achievements, the CRPD and its Optional Protocol may be analogized to be the gold standard of the global regime on disability. As of November 11, 2016, the tenth anniversary since its adoption, 168 countries, and the European Union as an entity, constituting 87 percent of UN membership, ratified the CRPD.[90] And as of November 11, 2020, fourteen years after, 182 countries, including Nigeria, were state parties to the CRPD.[91]

Testament to the importance of the CRPD and its Optional Protocol to the global disability regime is the secretariat under the UN that has evolved to facilitate their implementation. The UN established a joint secretariat for these instruments, comprising staff of both the UN Department of Economic and Social Affairs (DESA), based in New York, and the Office of the High Commissioner for Human Rights (OHCHR), based in Geneva.[92] DESA supports the Conference of State Parties, while OHCHR supports the CRPD Committee.[93] DESA and OHCHR work together to support states, civil society and national human rights institutions to implement and monitor the Convention and its Optional Protocol.[94]

REGIONAL DISABILITY INSTRUMENTS UNDER THE AFRICAN HUMAN RIGHTS SYSTEM

Protocol to the African Charter on Human and Peoples' Rights on the Rights of Persons with Disabilities in Africa

The instrument that forms the face of the regional disability instrument under the African human rights system is the Protocol to the African Charter on Human and Peoples' Rights on the Rights of Persons with Disabilities in Africa (hereinafter PACRD or the Protocol), adopted by the African Union (AU) in January 2018.[95] The Protocol comprises a preamble and forty-four articles. Like that of the CRPD, the preamble is long and embodies twenty-four clauses. Table 2.5 encapsulates the clauses that stand out in that preamble. Some of the clauses, such as items 3, 7, 9, 11, and 14, track the ones in the CRPD preamble.

Article 1 spells out the definition of key terms in the Protocol. The terms that stand out are: "discrimination on the basis of disability," "persons [living] with disabilities," "harmful practices," "reasonable accommodation," and "universal design." Except for "harmful practices," which did not feature in the CRPD, these terms were defined almost verbatim as the same terms in the CRPD. The PACRD defines "harmful practices" to "include behavior, attitudes[,] and practices based on tradition, culture, religion, superstition[,] or other reasons, which negatively affect the human rights and fundamental freedoms of persons [living] with disabilities or perpetuate discrimination."[96]

Article 2 spells out the purpose of the instrument, namely, "to promote, protect[,] and ensure the full and equal enjoyment of all human and people's rights by all persons [living] with disabilities and to ensure respect for their inherent dignity." Except for the expression "human and peoples' right," the language parallels the words of the CRPD, which, instead, read "human

Table 2.5. Key clauses in the African Protocol preamble

Item No.	*Clause*	*Location in preamble*
1.	Provision in Article 18(4) of the African Charter on Human and Peoples' Rights (1981) to the effect that PLWDs shall have the right to special measures of protection in keeping with their physical or moral needs	2nd item or paragraph
2.	The rights of PLWDs are affirmed in the CRPD (2006)	7th item or paragraph
3.	Acknowledgment that PLWDs have "inherent dignity and individual autonomy[,] including the freedom to make [their] own choices"	11th item or paragraph
4.	Recalling various AU human rights instruments, such as the African Charter on the Rights and Welfare of the Child (1990), the Protocol to the African Charter on Human and Peoples' Rights on the Rights of Women in Africa (2003), and the African Youth Charter (2006), which embody provisions for the rights of PLWDs	8th item or paragraph
5.	Reference to the Kigali Declaration on Human Rights (2003) which "call[ed] upon State Parties to develop a Protocol on the protection of the rights of the elderly and persons [living] with disabilities"	9th item or paragraph
6.	Reference to an Executive Council Decision of the AU in January 2013 which endorsed the African Union Disability Architecture (AUDA), of which a Protocol on the Rights of PLWDs to the African Charter is a central legal pillar	10th item or paragraph
7.	Concern that PLWDs continue to experience human rights violations, systemic discrimination, as well as political and socio-economic exclusions	16th item or paragraph
8.	Concern regarding the harmful practices that PLWDs often experience	17th item or paragraph
9.	Reality that PLWDs experience extreme levels of poverty	15th item or paragraph
10.	Appreciation of the value of PLWDs as full members of society	14th item or paragraph
11.	Recognition of the diversity of PLWDs	13th item or paragraph
12.	Cognizance of the importance of full and effective participation and inclusion of PLWDs in society.	12th item or paragraph
13.	Alarm regarding the "maiming or killing [of persons living] with albinism in many parts" of Africa	18th item or paragraph
14.	Concern regarding the multiple forms of discrimination, high levels of poverty, and the increased risk of violence, exploitation, neglect, and abuse, that women and girls living with disabilities face.	19th item or paragraph
15.	Recognition of the "essential roles" families, guardians, caregivers, and the community play in the lives of PLWDs	20th item or paragraph

16.	Concern that "adequate effective measures have not been taken" to ensure that PLWDs may exercise their rights on a full and legal basis with others.	21st item or paragraph
17.	Sensitive to the lack of a substantive binding African institutional and normative framework for protecting, promoting, and ensuring the rights of PLWDs	22nd item or paragraph
18.	Conscious of the need to establish firm AU legal framework as basis for laws, policies, and resources for ensuring the rights of PLWDs	23rd item or paragraph
19.	Determined that the rights of dignity of PLWDs should be protected and promoted to enable them to enjoy fully and equally all their human rights and fundamental freedoms	24th item or paragraph

Source: Created by the authors

rights and fundamental freedoms." Article 3 specifies the general principles that underpin and inform the Protocol. There are 10 of those principles, 8 of which are the values spelled out in the CRPD.[97] The only exception is the "best interest of the child." The CRPD embodies the same standard, as indicated earlier in this chapter,[98] but in a different context. Subsequent provisions elaborated some of these principles. These include the principle of non-discrimination expounded in Article 5, and equal opportunity (as "right to equality") in Article 6.

Article 4 specifies the "general obligations" of state parties under the Protocol. These obligations, which track those in the CRPD (see Table 2.2), in no particular order, include: mainstreaming disability in all spheres of national activities, including laws, policies, and development plans;[99] adequate budgetary allocations to facilitate full implementation of the Protocol;[100] ensuring effective participation of PLWDs in all national decision-making processes;[101] taking steps to eliminate discrimination based on disability "by any person, organization[,] or private enterprise";[102] and discontinuing, through modifying and outlawing or related means, "any harmful practice applied to" PLWDs.[103] Articles 7–26 spell out the rights of PLWDs. Table 2.6 enumerates and highlights these rights. Articles 27–30 specify the rights of diverse groups living with disabilities: Article 27 on women and girls, Article 28 on children, Article 29 on youth, and Article 30 on older persons. Consistent with the emphasis of the African human rights system on duties, Article 31 provides that state parties "recognize that [PLWDs] have duties on an equal basis with other person[s]."[104] This article makes it incumbent upon states parties to ensure that PLWDs receive "the forms of assistance and support, including reasonable accommodation," necessary for performance of these duties.[105] To facilitate the protection and promotion of PLWD rights, Article 32 mandates state parties "to ensure the systematic collection, analysis, storage[,] and dissemination of national statistics and data covering disability[.]"[106] To facilitate implementation of the Protocol, Article 33 enjoins state parties to cooperate at all levels—bilaterally, regionally, and internationally—to build capacity and cultivate good practices on issues pertaining to the welfare of PLWDs, including sharing research, as well as resources pertaining to technical, human and financial matters.[107] Article 34 requires state parties to submit periodic reports to the African Commission regarding the steps they have taken designed to fully realize the rights recognized in the Protocol.[108]

Article 35 mandates state parties to vigorously "ensure the widest possible dissemination of the [document]."[109] Article 36 embodies a "safeguard clause" which specifies that no provision in the document may be interpreted as derogating from the principles and values in other relevant instruments for realizing the rights of PLWDs.[110] Article 37 comments on signatures, ratifications and accession as they apply to the instrument.[111] Article 38 deals with entry into force. Under this article, the document enters into force 30 days after deposit of the instrument by the 15th state party to ratify. This condition is yet to occur as only 9 state parties have ratified the document.[112] This does *not* include Nigeria.[113] Article 39 focuses on reservations and withdrawal

Table 2.6. Human rights protected by the African Protocol on disabilities

Item No.	*Right*	*Article*
1.	Right to life	8
2.	Right to health	17
3.	Right to protection and safety in situations of risk	12
4.	Right to habilitation and rehabilitation	18
5.	Right to education	16
6.	Right to work	19
7.	Right to adequate standard of living	20
8.	Right of equal recognition before the law	7
9.	Right to access justice	13
10.	Right of freedom from harmful practices	11
11.	Right to integrity and security of the person	9
12.	Right of freedom from torture and related persecutions or treatments	10
13.	Right of freedom of expression and opinion	23
14.	Right of access to information	24
15.	Right to barrier-free access to facilities and services open or provided to the public	15
16.	Right to represent themselves in all spheres of life (self-representation)	22
17.	Right to family	26
18.	Right to live in the community	14
19.	Right to participate in political and public life	21
20.	Right to participate in sports, recreation, and culture	25

Source: Created by the authors

of any reservation, both of which must be in writing. Article 40 deals with depositary denominated as the chairperson of the AU Commission who then transmits a certified true copy of the instrument to the government of each signatory state. Article 41 deals with registration of the Protocol with the UN Secretary General. Article 42 relates to withdrawal from the treaty by a state party. This can take place any date three years from the date of entry into force by the affected state party upon written notice to the depositary of the instrument, in this case the chairperson of the AU Commission. Article 43 deals with amendments and revisions. Article 44 is on languages that will form the authentic texts for presenting the instrument, indicated as Arabic, English, French, and Portuguese. In addition to the stress on duties referenced before,[114] other distinctive features of the African human rights system are collective rights, and the right to development.[115] The PACRD is an integral component of the African human rights system.

Antecedents of the PACRD

Just like the CRPD, numerous instruments, more or less related to disability, preceded the adoption of the PACRD in 2018. These include the African Charter on Human and Peoples' Rights (ACHPR), adopted in June 1981, and the African Charter on the Rights and Welfare of the Child (ACRWC), adopted in 1990. The ACHPR affords disabled persons the right to special measures of protection in keeping with their physical or moral needs.[116] This is consistent with its stipulation to the effect that every individual shall have the right to enjoy the best attainable state of physical and mental health.[117] Like the ACHPR, the ACRWC provides for special measures of protection for disabled persons, together with principles of self-reliance, participation and access.[118] With the exception of the emphasis on duties, a distinctive characteristic of the ACHPR and the African human rights system, many of the provisions of the ACRWC are modelled after the Convention on the Rights of the Child (CRC), adopted by the UN General Assembly in 1989.[119]

Various activities pertaining to disability are associated with the two instruments referenced above. The first is the proclamation and set-aside by the then Organization of African Unity (OAU) in July 2000 of the period 2000–2009 as "Decade of Disabled People."[120] The OAU was succeeded by the AU from July 2002. The proclamation aimed to promote awareness and commitment to full participation, equality and empowerment of PLWDs in Africa.[121] It is recognized as a subprogram of the New Partnership for Africa's Development (NEPAD), designed to promote accelerated growth and sustainable development and minimize extreme poverty in Africa.[122] The Decade of Disabled People is accompanied with an action plan, Plan of Action for the

Decade, adopted by the OAU in February 2002, designed to provide guidance to OAU member states in furthering the goals of full participation, equality, and empowerment of PLWDs in Africa.[123] Other objectives include an appeal to African leaders to prevent disability by promoting peace and paying attention to other causes of disability; and to apply all African regional and global human right instruments to promote and monitor the rights of PLWDs.[124]

PUROHIT AND MOORE V. GAMBIA (2003) AS HARBINGER TEST CASE OF THE TWO DISABILITY REGIMES

On May 29, 2003, the African Commission of Human and Peoples' Rights (hereinafter the African Commission), gave its judgment in a complaint which challenged the legality of a Gambian law permitting the indefinite detention of mental patients in a psychiatric healthcare facility in the country.[125] The law in question was the Lunatics Detention Act (LDA), enacted in 1917 and last amended in 1964. The law defined a "lunatic" to include "an idiot or person of unsound mind,"[126] and subjected these individuals to automatic and indefinite detention. The African Commission is a quasi-judicial body, rather than a regular court, tasked with monitoring implementation of the ACHPR, including through consideration of individual complaints.[127] Established on October 21, 1986, the Commission has its head office in Banjul, Gambia.

Although decided before the CRPD and PACRD, this case amplifies and puts in perspective key provisions of the CRPD and its Protocol along with the PACRD that track these instruments of the global disability regime. Handed down three years before the CRPD and its Protocol and 15 years before the PACRD, the case arguably anticipated the human-right approach to disability exemplified in these three instruments. At the same time, it points up mixed messages on key issues, two of which were the right to participate in government, and the right to personal integrity under the ACHPR.

In *Purohit and Moore v. Gambia*, two mental health advocates, Ms. H. Purohit and Mr. P. Moore, filed a complaint before the African Commission on behalf of mental patients held involuntarily at Campama, the psychiatric unit of the Royal Victoria Hospital at Banjul in The Gambia.[128] The complaint alleged that the law governing mental health in the Gambia is "outdated," with sketchy definition of a lunatic, and no provisions for safeguards during the diagnosis, certification, and detention of mental patients.[129] Not only that, the psychiatric health facility at Campama was overcrowded, with no requirement of consent to treatment or subsequent review of continued treatment; and no independent examination of administration, management, and living conditions within the unit itself.[130] To compound these problems, the LDA did not provide for legal aid to enable the mental patients access the legal system; no provision for aggrieved patients to seek compensation when their rights are violated; and no right to participate in government, given that these patients were not allowed to vote.[131]

The gravamen of the petitioners' argument revolved around the notion that the practice under the LDA of detaining persons regarded as mentally ill indefinitely and without due process amounted to discrimination based on disability, and violated their right to personal liberty and freedom from arbitrary arrest and detention, inconsistent with the African Charter on Human and Peoples' Rights (ACHPR), of which Gambia was a state party. The provisions of the Charter that the petitioners claimed were violated were Articles 2, 3, 5, 6, 7(1) (a) and (c), 13(1), 16 and 18(4).[132] Article 2 provides that

> Every individual shall be entitled to the enjoyment of the rights and freedoms recognized and guaranteed in the present Charter without distinction of any kind[,] such as race, ethnic group, color, sex, language, religion, political or any other opinion, national and social origin, fortune, birth or any status.

Article 3 stipulates that:

1. Every individual shall be equal before the law
2. Every individual shall be entitled to equal protection of the law

Article 5 provides that:

> Every individual shall have the right to the respect of the dignity inherent in a human being and to the recognition of his legal status. All forms of exploitation and degradation of man, particularly slavery, slave trade, torture, cruel, inhuman or degrading punishment and treatment shall be prohibited.

Articles 6 stipulates that:

> Every individual shall have the right to liberty and to the security of his person. No one may be deprived of his freedom except for reasons and conditions previously laid down by law. In particular, no one may be arbitrarily arrested or detained.

Article 7 (1) stipulates that:

1. Every individual shall have the right to have his cause heard. This comprises:

a. The right to an appeal to competent national organs against acts of violating his fundamental rights as recognized and guaranteed by conventions, laws, regulations and customs in force;
b. [. . .]
c. The right to defense, including the right to be defended by counsel of his choice.

Article 13 (1) provides that:

> Every citizen shall have the right to participate freely in the government of his country, either directly or through freely chosen representatives, in accordance with the provisions of the law.

Article 16 stipulates that:

1. Every individual shall have the right to enjoy the best attainable state of physical and mental health.
2. State Parties to the present Charter shall take the necessary measures to protect the health of their people and to ensure that they receive medical attention when they are sick.

Article 18(4) provides that:

> The aged and the disabled shall also have the right to special measures of protection in keeping with their physical or moral needs.

In *Purohit and Moore v. The Gambia,* the legal question presented before the African Commission was whether or not domestic remedies were available to the complainants. The African Charter requires complainants to first exhaust domestic remedies, unless the process for such exhaustion was unduly prolonged.[133] The Gambian government posited that those remedies existed. "In practice," it said, "patients found to be insane are informed that they have a right to ask for a review of their assessment."[134] They could seek remedies through an action in tort for false imprisonment or negligence, consistent with the common law tradition of The Gambia, where a patient held at Campama Psychiatric Unit is wrongly diagnosed.[135] Mental patients detained under the LDA could also challenge their detention on constitutional grounds under the theory that the law deprived them of their right to freedom of movement and association under the Gambian constitution.[136]

The African Commission disagreed with the Gambian government. It ruled that the law and practices of the Gambian government constituted discrimination against the patients on grounds of their disability, in violation of Article 2 of the African Charter.[137] Considering that persons detained under the LDA were individuals from poor economic backgrounds likely to be picked up from the streets, there was a failure to meet the standards of non-discrimination and equal protection of the law in relation to review of detention under the LDA. Similarly, the government violated Article 3 on equality before the law.[138] Because mental patients certified under the LDA had no legal right to challenge the Medical Certificates that formed the basis for their detention, their right to equal access to the law under Article 3 of the African Charter was denied. Not only this, the denial was discriminatory because mental illness is analogous to a disability, a prohibited ground of discrimination under Article 2. In the same vein, the government violated Article 5 relating to inherent dignity of these patients.[139] Mentally disabled persons have the equal right to dignity and a life as full and normal as possible. Branding them lunatics and idiots, as Gambian law did, dehumanizes and denies these patients dignity.[140] "[M]entally disabled persons would like to share the same hopes, dreams and goals and have the same rights to pursue those hopes, dreams[,] and goals like any other human beings."[141] Moreover, the conditions of the units where the patients were detained constituted cruel, inhumane and degrading treatment.[142]

On Article 6 related to the right to personal integrity of the human being, emblematized by freedom from arbitrary arrest and detention, the African Commission indicated it found no violation.[143] The LDA authorized detention of persons believed to be mentally ill or disabled based on the opinions of general medical practitioners, some of whom may not be psychiatrists, leaving the possibility of a wrong diagnosis leading to institutionalization.[144] Worse still, because the LDA does not provide for review or appeal procedures, persons institutionalized under such circumstances are not able to challenge their institutionalization, where an error or wrong diagnosis is made.[145] The Commission considered the average length of detention, which was variable according to mental illness and family situation. The fact that any qualified medical practitioner could issue a certificate under the LDA, not just qualified psychiatrics, combined with the lack of review procedures led the Commission to conclude that the LDA fell short of international norms.[146] Nonetheless, it did not violate the provisions of Article 6 because the provision was not intended to cater for situations involving the institutionalization of persons in need of medical assistance.[147]

Next to the right to have their case heard, including the right of appeal and adequate defense under Article 7(1) (a) and (c), the Commission found clear violation.[148] This is because, it said, the LDA does not contain any provisions for the review or appeal against an order of detention or any remedy for detention made in error, wrong diagnosis, or treatment.[149] Moreover, patients did not have the legal right to challenge the two separate medical certificates, which constitute the legal basis for their detention.[150] And because the LDA lacks provision for legal aid necessary to pursue the tort case or constitutional challenge the Gambian government defended existed under the LDA (such assistance existed with respect to capital offenses), in practice, the right of legal redress was available only to rich persons with the wherewithal to pursue a suit without government legal assistance.[151] With respect to Article 13 on the right to participate freely in the government of one's own country, the Commission found no violation.[152] "Besides the view held by the respondent state questioning the mental ability of mentally disabled patients to make informed choices in relation to their civic duties and obligations," it said, there is no indication that the Gambian government meant to impede the political participation of PLWDs.[153]

The African Commission devoted the most extensive of its analysis ever in this case to Article 16 on the human right to health, and Article 18(4) on the right to special measures of protection for the disabled (along with the aged), consistent with their physical and moral needs, both of which guarantees it joined together.[154] Its finding here is measured as it is momentous, in due cognizance of the importance of the subject matter at hand. It first observed that "[e]njoyment of the human right to health [. . .] is vital to all aspects of a person's life and well-being, and is crucial to the realization of all the other fundamental human rights and freedoms. This right includes the right to health facilities, access to goods and services to be guaranteed to all without discrimination of any kind."[155] Next, it creatively tied Article 16 to Article 18(4), noting that "as a result of their condition and by virtue of their disabilities, mental health patients should be accorded special treatment which would enable them not only attain but also sustain their optimum level of independence and performance."[156]

Applying these joint standards to the case at hand, "it is clear that the scheme of the LDA is lacking in terms of therapeutic objectives as well as provision of matching resources and programs of treatment of persons with mental disabilities, a situation that [. . .] falls short of satisfying the requirements laid down in articles 16 and 18(4) of the African Charter."[157] The African Commission put on record its awareness of the impediment to the right of enjoyment of good health of millions of Africans due to inadequate resources, signified in "the problem of poverty," which makes it difficult for many governments in Africa "to provide the necessary amenities, infrastructure and resources that facilitate the full enjoyment of this right."[158] In a statement that harks back to the doctrine of "progressive realization" in the International Covenant on Economic, Social, and Cultural Rights, adopted by the UN General Assembly in 1966,[159] of which many countries, including Nigeria and The Gambia, are state parties,[160] the African Commission read the obligations of state parties embodied in the language of Article 16 into its ruling.[161]

> Therefore, having due regard to this depressing but real state of affairs [meaning "the problem of poverty" in Africa], the African Commission would like to read into article 16 the obligation on part of states party to the African Charter to take concrete and targeted steps, while taking full advantage of its available resources, to ensure that the right to health is fully realised in all its aspects without discrimination of any kind.[162]

In the light of these rulings, the African Commission advised the Gambian government to repeal the LDA and replace it with a more progressive disability law, sensitive to the human-right imperatives of the African Charter.[163] The law here in question was enacted in 1917 with the most recent amendment then in 1964.[164] "There is no doubt that since 1964, there have been many developments in the field of human rights, particularly addressing the rights of persons with disabilities. As such, the LDA should have long been amended to bring it in line with the changed circumstances."[165]

In the meantime, the Gambian government should create an expert body to review all cases of persons detained, while providing adequate medical and material care for persons suffering from mental health illnesses in the country.[166] Despite these admonitions, it took 18 long years before Gambia reformed its law related to PLWDs. The change took place with the passage of the Persons with Disabilities Bill by the Gambian National Assembly on July 6, 2021.[167] The law provides for "the health care, social support, accessibility, rehabilitation, education and vocational training, communication, employment and work protection and promotion of basic rights for persons with disabilities and for connected matters."[168]

Lingering Ramifications of Article 6

The African Commission's finding relating to Article 6 of the ACHPR on the right to personal integrity is criticized as endorsing the practice in Africa that allows people suffering from mental illness or disability to be forcefully detained if their detention is viewed as necessary for their treatment.[169] The implications of the decision were wide-ranging, given that in Africa cultural and traditional practices toward people living with mental disabilities are rife with human rights abuses.[170] In The Gambia and many other African countries, disability is perceived more as a curse than an illness.[171] In these countries, persons living with mental illnesses are often hidden from public view, in an attempt to shield them from harm, or to protect their families from shame.[172] They are pitied, protected from society, frequently detained in traditional healing facilities and religious institutions like prayer camps, supposedly for their own good, and subject to a host of other human rights abuses like chaining, beating, forced seclusion, denial of food, prolonged detention, oftentimes in unsanitary environments, forced treatment, as well as verbal and physical abuses.[173] Similarly, within medical facilities, the treatment of people living with mental disability also lacks a human rights approach. As the Gambian case showed, mental patients can be detained in medical or psychiatric units without appropriate diagnosis.

Unlike the ACHPR, going by the finding of the African Commission relating to Article 6 of the African Charter, certain regional and international human rights instruments, such as the ICCPR, the European Convention on Human Rights, and the American Convention on Human Rights, protect the personal liberty of people with mental disabilities. These human right instruments view detaining people on ground of mental illness as arbitrary. As we saw in our analysis earlier in this chapter, the CRPD and PACRD have similar provisions. If and when the PACRD goes into effect, it will be illegal to detain or institutionalize mentally ill or disabled people simply on the basis of their illness. Ratification of the Protocol will afford PLWDs an alternative avenue to ventilate their grievances and seek redress when their rights are not effectively protected domestically. In The Gambia for instance, people detained arbitrarily based on their disability would be able to seek protection from the African Commission, if domestic courts failed to afford them remedies.

CONCLUSION

To assess the performance of the Nigerian government in its obligations toward PLWDs in Nigeria, it is critical that we first set forth the applicable disability instruments related to its obligations. This chapter identifies and highlights the applicable instruments: the CRPD and its Optional Protocol under the aegis of the UN, at the global level, and the PACRD, an integral part of the African human rights regime, regionally. The chapter also analyzed in some detail the case *Purohit and Moore v. The Gambia* emanating from The Gambia related to the treatment of PLWDs as herald of the two regimes with their three emblematic disability instruments. The problems related to the decision, mostly its finding pertaining to the right to personal integrity under Article 6 of the ACHPR, have been resolved under the global and regional disability regimes signified by the CRPD, its Protocol, and PACRD. However, while Nigeria is a state party to the CRPD and its Optional, Abuja has not ratified the PACRD. The PACRD is still short by six countries out of the 15 ratifications necessary to bring it into force, as indicated before in this chapter.[174] The many benefits of the PACRD makes its adoption more imperative. It is therefore critical that Nigeria and some five-odd countries ratify to bring the instrument into operation. With discussion of the global and regional regimes on disability finalized, the searchlight moves next to Chapter 3, which assesses the Nigerian national government's performance on its treaty obligations pertaining to disability, followed by an examination in Chapter 4 of possible remedial steps it must timely implement.

NOTES

1. See Janet Lord and Michael Ashley Stein, "Prospects and Practices for CRPD Implementation in Africa," *African Disability Rights Yearbook,* 1 (2013), 97–113 (abstract). As Lord and Stein elaborated, the Working Group that developed the foundational text of the treaty included delegations from seven African nations, the lone seat allocated within the Working Group to represent national human rights institutions was held by a South African Human Rights Commissioner, the Committee on the Rights of Persons with Disabilities included experts from Africa, and the then Special Rapporteur on Disability was South African, among other indicators. Ibid.

2. Convention on the Rights of Persons with Disabilities, UN General Assembly Resolution No. A/RES/61/106, Annex I (December 13, 2006), https://www.refworld.org/docid/4680cd212.html [hereinafter CRPD].

3. Optional Protocol to the Convention on the Rights of Persons with Disabilities, UN General Assembly Resolution No. A/RES/61/106, Annex II (December 13, 2006), https://www.refworld.org/docid/4680d0982.html [hereinafter OPCRPD].

4. Lord and Stein, note 1, p. 97.

5. See CRPD, note 2, preamble, item (i).

6. See ibid., art. 45(1).

7. See OPCRPD, note 3, art. 13(1).

8. Audiovisual Library of International Law, https://legal.un.org/avl/ha/crpd/crpd.html.

9. Ibid.

10. Ibid.

11. "Frequently Asked Questions regarding the Convention on the Rights of Persons with Disabilities," UN Department of Economic and Social Affairs [hereinafter "Frequently Asked Questions regarding the CRPD"], https://www.un.org/development/desa/disabilities/convention-on-the-rights-of-persons-with-disabilities/frequently-asked-questions-regarding-the-convention-on-the-rights-of-persons-with-disabilities.html#neg1 ("How Was the Convention Negotiated?"). The following are the eight sessions that the *ad hoc* Committee held before it finalized the text of the Convention on August 26, 2006. At its first two sessions, in 2002 and 2003, the Committee considered the possibility of drafting an international instrument on the rights of persons with disabilities, and discussed the type of instrument and possible elements to be included. At its second session, the Committee established a working group to prepare a draft text of a convention. Composed of national governments

and representatives of non-governmental organizations (NGOs), the Working Group met in January 2004 and drafted a text for negotiation. The Committee devoted its third to eight sessions to negotiations. Following these negotiations, the text of the Convention was finalized on August 26, 2006. A drafting group tasked with ensuring uniformity of terminology throughout the text of the draft convention and harmonizing the versions in the official languages of the United Nations, reviewed the text from September to November 2006, following which, on December 13, 2006, the UN General Assembly adopted the text of the CRPD and its Optional Protocol. Ibid.

12. See "Ratification Status for Nigeria," UN Treaty Body Database, Office of the UN High Commissioner for Human Rights, https://tbinternet.ohchr.org/_layouts/15/TreatyBodyExternal/Treaty.aspx?CountryID=127&Lang=EN.

13. Under the law of treaties, minor yet important differences exist between signature, ratification, and accession. When a treaty is *signed*, a state party or entity qualified as such (such as a regional integration organization), signals its intention in good faith to take steps to be bound by the treaty at a later date. *Signing* also creates an obligation, in the period between signature and ratification, for a state party to refrain from acts that would defeat the object and purpose of the treaty. *Ratification* is the next step in becoming a party to a treaty. It is a concrete action taken by a would-be state party which signals its intention to assume the legal rights and obligations contained in the treaty. In the case of the CRPD and its Optional Protocol, regional integration organizations express their consent to be bound through "formal confirmation," an act with the same effect as ratification. Like ratification, *accession* conveys the consent of a state or regional integration organization to be bound by a treaty in whose negotiations it did not feature. Accession has the same legal effect as ratification, the difference being that, unlike ratification, which, under the law of treaty, is preceded by signature to create binding legal obligations under international law, accession requires only one step, namely, depositing the instrument of accession. "What is the Difference between Signing, Ratification[,] and Accession of UN treaties?" Dag Hammarskjöld Library, https://ask.un.org/faq/14594.

14. See "Ratification Status for Nigeria," note 12.

15. See Erwin Chemerinsky and Michael Stokes Paulsen, "Common Interpretation: The Preamble," Interactive Constitution, https://constitutioncenter.org/interactive-constitution/interpretation/preamble-ic/interps/37 (commenting on the U.S. Constitution); and Makane Moïse Mbengue, "Preamble," *Max Planck Encyclopedias of International Law* (New York and Oxford: Oxford University Press, 2006), https://opil.ouplaw.com/view/10.1093/law:epil/9780199231690/law-9780199231690-e1456.

16. CRPD, note 2, art. 1 ("Purpose").

17. See Book's Introduction, note 60, and accompanying text.

18. CRPD, note 2, art. 2 (defining "Reasonable accommodation").

19. CRPD, note 2, art. 2 (defining "Universal design").

20. Ibid.

21. See Book's Introduction, note 60, and accompanying text.

22. CRPD, note 2, art. 3(a)-(h).

23. Ibid., art. 5(3).

24. Ibid., art. 5(4).
25. CRPD, note 2, art. 6(1).
26. Ibid., art. 7(1).
27. Ibid., art. 7(2).
28. Ibid., art. 7(3).
29. Ibid., art. 8(1)(a)-(c).
30. Ibid., art. 9(1).
31. Ibid.
32. "Frequently Asked Questions regarding the CRPD," note 11 ("How is the Convention Monitored").
33. "Frequently Asked Questions regarding the CRPD," note 11 ("What is the Committee on the Rights of Persons with Disabilities?").
34. Ibid.
35. "Committee on the Rights of Persons with Disabilities," Office of the UN High Commissioner for Human Rights, https://www.ohchr.org/en/hrbodies/crpd/pages/crpdindex.aspx.
36. "Frequently Asked Questions regarding the CRPD," note 11 ("What is Periodic Reporting?").
37. Ibid.
38. CRPD, note 2, art. 36(4)
39. Ibid., art. 39. Founded in 1945, the UN General Assembly is "the chief deliberative, policymaking and representative organ of the United Nations [and] comprise[s] [. . .] all 193 Members of the United Nations." "About the General Assembly," UN General Assembly, https://www.un.org/en/ga/about/background.shtml#:~:text=The%20Assembly%20is%20empowered%20to,of%20people%20throughout%20the%20world. Under the UN Charter, the Economic and Social Council (ECOSOC) is responsible for promoting higher standards of living, full employment, and economic and social progress; identifying solutions to international economic, social and health problems; facilitating international cultural and educational cooperation; and encouraging universal respect for human rights and fundamental freedoms. The Council coordinates the work of the 14 UN specialized agencies, ten functional commissions and five regional commissions, receives reports from nine UN funds and program and issues policy recommendations to the UN system and to Member States. "What Does ECOSOC Do?" https://www.un.org/en/ecosoc/meetings/2005/hl2005/ECOSOCinfo%20rev%20et.pdf.
40. The CRPD leaves open the exact nature of the role of the Conference of States Parties. The much that is known is that its responsibilities include electing the members of the Committee on the Rights of Persons with Disabilities and debating and adopting proposed amendments to the Convention. "Frequently Asked Questions regarding the CRPD," note 11 ("What is the Conference of State Parties").
41. See OPCRPD, note 3, art. 3(1)-(5).
42. See *From Exclusion to Equality: Realizing the Rights of Persons with Disabilities,* Handbook for Parliamentarians No. 14 (New York: Office of the UN High Commissioner for Human Rights, 2007), 35 (comparing and contrasting the two procedures).

43. OPCRPD, note 3, art. 12.1.

44. See CRPD, note 2, preamble, items (d), (f), and (u).

45. Compare *From Exclusion to Equality,* note 42, pp. 10–11 with *Monitoring the Convention on the Rights of Persons with Disabilities: Guidance for Human Rights Monitors*, Professional Training Series No. 17 (New York and Geneva: Office of the UN High Commissioner for Human Rights, 2010), 14. For example, From *Exclusion to Equality* includes the Declaration on the Rights of Mentally Retarded Persons (1971), and Tallinn Guidelines for Action on Human Resources Development in the Field of Disability (1990), p. 10, not included in *Monitoring the Convention*, which source our table tracks.

46. Declaration on the Rights of Disabled Persons, UN General Assembly No. A/RES/3447 (XXX) (December 9, 1975), https://www.refworld.org/docid/3b00f1c18.html.

47. Ibid., item 3.

48. Ibid., preamble.

49. World Program of Action concerning Disabled Persons, UN General Assembly Resolution No. A/RES/37/52 (December 3, 1982), https://www.equalrightstrust.org/sites/default/files/ertdocs//world%20program%20of%20action%20on%20disabled%20persons.pdf. The instrument comprises three parts: an analysis of principles, concepts and definitions relating to disabilities; survey of the world situation regarding persons with disabilities; and recommendations for action at the national, regional and international levels. Ibid.

50. Ibid.

51. Principles for the Protection of Persons with Mental Illness and the Improvement of Mental Health Care, UN General Assembly Resolution No. 46/119 (December 17, 1991), Office of the UN High Commissioner for Human Rights, https://www.who.int/mental_health/policy/en/UN_Resolution_on_protection_of_persons_with_mental_illness.pdf.

52. Ibid., Principle 4(1).

53. Ibid., Principle 4(2)-(5).

54. Ibid., Principle 5.

55. Ibid., Principle 3.

56. Ibid., Principle 7.

57. Ibid., Principle 8 (“Standard of Care”).

58. Ibid., Principle 11.

59. Ibid., Principle 9(4).

60. Ibid., Principle 1(6).

61. Ibid., Principle 1(7).

62. See T.W. Harding, “Human Rights Law in the Field of Mental Health: A Critical Review,” *Acta Psychiatr. Scand. Suppl.*, 399 (2000) (abstract), DOI: 10.1111/j.0902-4441.2000.007s020[dash]6.x.

63. “Frequently Asked Questions regarding the CRPD,” note 11 (“What Other International Instruments Recognize the Rights of Persons with Disabilities?”).

64. Standard Rules on the Equalization of Opportunities for Persons with Disabilities, UN General Assembly Resolution No. A/RES/48/96 (December 20, 1993], https://www.refworld.org/docid/3b00f2e80.html [hereinafter Standard Rules].

65. Declaration on the Rights of Disabled Persons, note 46, preamble. The UN General Assembly defines "equalization of opportunity" to mean "the process through which the various systems of society and the environment, such as services, activities, information and documentation, are made available to all[,]" able or disabled. Ibid., 24. For the UN, equal opportunity is a principle that signifies "that the needs of each and every individual are of equal importance, that those needs must be made the basis for the planning of societies and that all resources must be employed in such a way as to ensure that every individual has equal opportunity for participation." Ibid., 25.

66. Ibid., 26.

67. Ibid., 27.

68. Ibid.

69. See Standard Rules, note 64.

70. Ibid., Rules 1–4, pp. 11–14.

71. Ibid., Rules 5–12, pp. 14–20.

72. International Convention on the Elimination of All Forms of Racial Discrimination, UN General Assembly, United Nations, Treaty Series, Vol. 660 (December 21, 1965), 195, https://www.refworld.org/docid/3ae6b3940.html.

73. See *The United Nations Human Rights Treaty System: An introduction to the Core Human Rights Treaties and the Treaty Bodies*, Fact Sheet No. 30/Rev. 1 (August 2012),Office of the UN High Commissioner for Human Rights, https://www.refworld.org/docid/5289d3e84.html, p. 10 (highlighting definition of "torture" in the CAT); and p. 16 (highlighting "enforced disappearance").

74. See Universal Declaration of Human Rights, UN General Assembly, 217 A (III) (December 10, 1948), https://www.refworld.org/docid/3ae6b3712c.html.

75. See "ILO Welcomes New UN Convention on Rights of People with Disabilities," International Labor Organization, Press Release (December 14, 2006), https://www.ilo.org/global/about-the-ilo/newsroom/news/WCMS_080627/lang--en/index.htm (referencing ILO Convention on Vocational Rehabilitation and Employment of Disabled Persons (No. 159) of 1983, ILO Human Resources Development Recommendation (No. 195) of 2004, and the *ILO Code of Practice on Managing Disability in the Workplace* of 2001).

76. *Monitoring the Convention on the Rights of Persons with Disabilities,* note 45, p. 13.

77. See generally Gerard Quinn and Theresia Degener, *Human Rights and Disability: The Current Use and Future Potential of United Nations Human Rights Instruments in the Context of Disability* (New York and Geneva, United Nations, 2002).

78. Margaret Chan [Director-General, WHO] and Robert B Zoellick [President, World Bank Group], "Preface," in *World Report on Disability* (Geneva Switzerland and Washington, DC: World Health Organization and the World Bank, 2011), xi, https://www.who.int/disabilities/world_report/2011/report.pdf.

79. "Frequently Asked Questions regarding the CRPD," note 11 ("Why is the Convention Unique?").

80. Ibid.

81. Navanethem Pillay [United Nations High Commissioner for Human Rights], "Foreword," in *The Convention on the Rights of Persons with Disabilities,* Training Guide, Professional Training Series No. 19 (New York and Geneva: United Nations, 2014) [hereinafter Training Guide No. 19], https://www.ohchr.org/Documents/Publications/CRPD_TrainingGuide_PTS19_EN%20Accessible.pdf.

82. Ibid.

83. Navanethem Pillay, United Nations High Commissioner for Human Rights, "Foreword," in *Monitoring the Convention on the Rights of Persons with Disabilities,* note 45.

84. Ibid.

85. Pillay, "Foreword," Training Guide No. 19, note 81.

86. "Convention on the Rights of Persons with Disabilities (CRPD)," UN Department of Economic & Social Affairs, https://www.un.org/development/desa/disabilities/convention-on-the-rights-of-persons-with-disabilities.html.

87. CRPD, note 2, preamble, k.

88. See "Frequently Asked Questions regarding the CRPD," note 11 ("Why is it Necessary to Have a Convention on the Rights of Persons with Disabilities?")

89. Training Guide No. 19, note 81, p. 24.

90. "[Tenth] Anniversary of the Adoption of Convention on the Rights of Persons with Disabilities (CRPD)," UN Department of Economic & Social Affairs, https://www.un.org/development/desa/disabilities/convention-on-the-rights-of-persons-with-disabilities/the-10th-anniversary-of-the-adoption-of-convention-on-the-rights-of-persons-with-disabilities-crpd-crpd-10.html.

91. CRPD, note 2.

92. "Frequently Asked Questions regarding the CRPD," note 11 (Commenting on the role of the UN Secretariat with respect to the CRPD).

93. Ibid.

94. Ibid.

95. Protocol to the African Charter on Human and Peoples' Rights on the Rights of Persons with Disabilities in Africa (hereinafter PACRD), https://au.int/sites/default/files/treaties/36440-treaty-protocol_to_the_achpr_on_the_rights_of_persons_with_disabilities_in_africa_e.pdf.

96. Ibid., 7th item or paragraph.

97. See note 22 and accompanying text.

98. See note 27 and accompanying text.

99. PACRD, note 95, art. 4(b).

100. Ibid., art. 4(i).

101. Ibid., art. 4(j).

102. Ibid., art. 4(f).

103. Ibid., art. 4(d).

104. Ibid., art. 31(1).

105. Ibid., art. 31(2).

106. Ibid., art. 32.

107. Ibid., art. 33(a).

108. Ibid., art. 34(1).
109. Ibid., art. 35.
110. Ibid., art. 36(1).
111. For the meanings and distinctions among these terms under the law of treaty, see note 13.
112. See Book's Introduction, note 101, and accompanying text.
113. See Grace Antwi-Atsu, "The African Disability Protocol: A Call to Leave No One Behind," *Sightsavers* (August 2021), https://www.sightsavers.org/blogs/2021/08/the-importance-of-the-african-disability-protocol.
114. See note 104 and accompanying text.
115. "International Norms and Standards Relating to Disability," United Nations Enable, https://www.un.org/esa/socdev/enable/comp303.htm#:~:text=Groups%20with%20Disabilities-,3.1%20African%20Human%20Rights%20Instruments,its%20recognition%20of%20collective%20rights.&text=The%20other%20distinctive%20feature%20is%20the%20recognition%20of%20the%20right%20to%20development.
116. Organization of African Unity (OAU), African Charter on Human and Peoples' Rights ("Banjul Charter") (June 27, 1981), CAB/LEG/67/3 rev. 5, 21 I.L.M. 58 (1982), art. 18 (4), https://www.refworld.org/docid/3ae6b3630.html.
117. Ibid., art. 16 (1).
118. African Charter on the Rights and Welfare of the Child, Organization of African Unity (OAU), CAB/LEG/24.9/49 (July11, 1990), art. 13, https://www.refworld.org/docid/3ae6b38c18.html.
119. See "Human Rights Instruments for Children with Disabilities," *Global Disability Rights Now!* (October 17, 2016), https://www.globaldisabilityrightsnow.org/es/tools/human-rights-instruments-children-disabilities.
120. African Decade of Disabled Persons (2000–2009), UN Department of Economic & Social Affairs, https://www.un.org/esa/socdev/enable/disafricadecade.htm.
121. Ibid.
122. Ibid.
123. Ibid.
124. Ibid.
125. *Purohit and Moore v. The Gambia*, Communication No. 241/2001 (2003), https://africanlii.org/afu/judgment/african-commission-human-and-peoples-rights/2003/49.
126. Ibid., 44, 59.
127. See "African Commission on Human and Peoples' Rights," Open Society Justice Initiative, https://www.justiceinitiative.org/publications/african-commission-human-and-peoples-rights. The Commission comprises 11 members elected for a six-year term, renewable once. It has been in operation since October 21, 1986. Ibid. The legal tribunal distinguished from this Commission is the African Court on Human and Peoples' Rights (African Court). Established on June 9, 1998, the African Court is the judicial arm of the African Union tasked with protection and promotion of human and peoples' rights in Africa principally through delivery of judgments. The Court has

its headquarters in Arusha, Tanzania. "African Court on Human and Peoples' Rights," https://www.african-court.org/wpafc/basic-information/.

128. Royal Victoria Hospital is a 540-bed medical facility, the largest hospital in the country, founded in 1853 by British colonial authorities. In 2013, the name of the hospital was changed to Edward Francis Small Teaching Hospital. "Edward Francis Small Teaching Hospital (The Royal Victory Hospital)," https://www.electives.net/hospital/3661/preview; "Royal Victoria Teaching Hospital, Banjul," http://www.accessgambia.com/information/rvh.html.

129. See *Purohit and Moore v. The Gambia*, note 125, 3–4.

130. Ibid., 5–6.

131. Ibid., 7–8

132. See ibid., 9. Article 6 on the right to personal integrity is not listed among the provisions, but the African Commission decision includes it. See ibid., ¶ 62.

133. Ibid., 24.

134. Ibid., 28.

135. Ibid., 28, 50.

136. Ibid., 29, 51.

137. Ibid., 54.

138. Ibid.

139. Ibid., 56.

140. Ibid., 59.

141. Ibid., 61.

142. See ibid., 57.

143. Ibid., 68.

144. Ibid.

145. Ibid.

146. Ibid.

147. Ibid.

148. Ibid., 71.

149. Ibid.

150. Ibid.

151. Ibid., 36, 53.

152. Ibid., 76.

153. Ibid.

154. Ibid., 77–85.

155. Ibid., 80.

156. Ibid., 81.

157. Ibid., 83.

158. Ibid., 84.

159. International Covenant on Economic, Social and Cultural Rights (December 16, 1966), UN General Assembly, United Nations, Treaty Series (Vol. 993), 3, https://www.refworld.org/docid/3ae6b36c0.html. Art. 2 (1) of the treaty provides that "Each State Party to the present Covenant undertakes to take steps, individually and through international assistance and cooperation, especially economic and technical, to the maximum of its available resources, with a view to achieving progressively

the full realization of the rights recognized in the present Covenant by all appropriate means, including particularly the adoption of legislative measures." The same clause is found in the Convention on the Rights of the Child (art. 4), and in the CRPD, art. 4(2). The reference to "available resources" reflects a recognition that realizing these rights can be hampered by a lack of resources, thereby permitting achievement over a reasonable period of time. In other words, the compliance of a state party with its obligation to take appropriate measures is assessed in the light of the financial and other resources that it has. "Frequently Asked Questions on Economic, Social[,] and Cultural Rights," Office of the UN High Commissioner for Human Rights (December 2008), 13, https://www.ohchr.org/documents/publications/factsheet33en.pdf.

160. Gambia ratified the ICESCR on December 29, 1978; Nigeria on July 29, 1993. See "Ratification Status for CESCR—International Covenant on Economic, Social and Cultural Rights," UN Treaty Body Database, https://tbinternet.ohchr.org/_layouts/15/TreatyBodyExternal/Treaty.aspx?Treaty=CESCR&Lang=en. Both countries did so by accession, meaning simply that they joined a treaty other state parties earlier negotiated. For explanation of the term, see note 13.

161. Reading a matter into something creates a different interpretation to what is presented. See "Read into (Something)," *Free Dictionary*, https://idioms.thefreedictionary.com/read+into (idiom means "[t]o find, infer, or attribute some additional meaning or different interpretation based on what is presented").

162. *Purohit and Moore v. The Gambia*, note 125, 84.

163. Ibid., 85(a).

164. Ibid., 42.

165. Ibid.

166. *Purohit and Moore v. The Gambia*, note 125 ("Decision").

167. See "The Gambia: Disability Bill is Key Step toward Greater Inclusion in Society," *Article 19* (September 10, 2021), https://www.article19.org/resources/the-gambia-disability-bill-is-a-key-step-towards-greater-inclusion-in-society/.

168. Ibid.

169. "African Commission Adopts Draft Protocol on Persons with Disabilities' Rights," International Justice Resource Center (April 20, 2016), https://ijrcenter.org/2016/04/20/african-commission-adopts-draft-protocol-on-persons-with-disabilities-rights/.

170. Ibid.

171. Ibid.

172. Ibid.

173. See ibid. See also Kathryn Jagoe, "The Disability Rights Movement: Its Development in South Africa," Independent Living Institute, https://www.independentliving.org/toolsforpower/tools6.html (observing that "for centuries," PLWDs "were either cast out of families or hidden behind closed curtains and doors for fear they would bring shame upon and ostraciz[e] the entire family").

174. See note 112 and accompanying text.

Chapter 3

Record of the Nigerian National Government since 1999

Regarding Implementation of Its Disability Obligations

INTRODUCTION

President Muhammed Buhari, Nigeria's current leader under the Fourth Republic as we write, once posited that integrating PLWDs into the mainstream of Nigeria's society is key to poverty alleviation in particular and economic development in general.[1] Buhari made the statement on January 7, 2021, when he received members of the newly-established Governing Council of the National Commission for Persons with Disability who paid him a courtesy visit at State House, Abuja.[2] President Buhari disclosed that he relied on them to realize the goal of his government to lift 100 million citizens out of poverty.[3] He enjoined them "to realize that [their] work forms a critical aspect in achieving the objective of [his] administration to removing 100 million Nigerians out of poverty[,]" and that, with their help, he "look[s] forward to commissioning projects and programs of high impact to the disabled community in line with this vision."[4] He urged them to help his administration ensure that it "touch[ed] the lives of our fellow citizens with special needs[.]"[5] The president pledged that his administration would give effect to treaties that give inclusion to PLWDs.[6] He complimented state governors who had enacted laws on disability in their own states and enjoined those yet to do so to "take necessary action to enable [the] Federal Government efforts have the desired impact at the subnational levels."[7]

This chapter critically assesses the record of the Nigerian national government under the Fourth Republic, the longest period of civilian rule in the country since independence, regarding performance of its international obligations related to PLWDs in Nigeria. For, as the African Commission on Human and Peoples' Rights observed in *Purohit and Moore v. The Gambia*, when countries become state parties of treaties, using the African Charter on Human and Peoples' Rights as case in point, they do so voluntarily, awake to their responsibilities to implement the provisions of such instruments.[8] Such is the wisdom that informs this chapter. The performance this chapter gauges is the implementation of the global and regional treaties related to PLWDs, unveiled in Chapter 2, that Nigeria ratified, especially the CRPD and its Optional Protocol. This chapter comprises three interrelated parts: overview of the Discrimination Against Persons with Disabilities (Prohibition) Act of 2018, abbreviatedly referred to in this book as the Nigerian Disabilities Act, ten sectors of inaccessibility for PLWDs in Nigeria under the Fourth Republic, and a statement on the negative legacy of prolonged military rule in Nigeria on the welfare of PLWDs.

THE DISCRIMINATION AGAINST PERSONS WITH DISABILITIES (PROHIBITION) ACT OF 2018

The Nigerian Disabilities Act made the CRPD, a landmark treaty on disability that, as indicated in Chapter 2, upgraded antecedent global measures and pronouncements related to this topic dating back to the formation of the United Nations after World War II, part of Nigerian laws. The incorporation into Nigerian domestic law followed the country's adoption of the CRPD and its Optional Protocol in September 2010. The Nigerian Disabilities Act is also, for this reason, the major legislation pertaining to PLWDs that the Fourth Republic is linked with. As can be seen from its very title, the Act prohibits discrimination based on disability, "by any person or institution in any manner or circumstance,"[9] under pain of monetary fines and time in prison,[10] with a view to promoting the full integration of PLWDs in the Nigerian society.[11] The law permits a PLWD discriminated against to bring a civil action against his or her discriminator,[12] and empowers the Commission tasked with enforcing the act, of which more below, to receive complaints of PLWDs regarding violation of their rights under the Act; and, if it comes to that, to support the right of a PLWD to seek redress in court regarding that violation.[13] Going further, under pain of monetary penalty or imprisonment or both, the law forbids anybody from using PLWDs in soliciting for alms in every form:[14] employing, using or involving a PLWD in begging, parading a PLWD in public with the intent to solicit for alms, or using the condition of disability as a guise for begging in public.[15] On its face, this could be read as banning PLWDs from begging for alms in Nigeria. But there are disability activists who maintain that this amounts to putting the cart before the horse in the sense that outlawing begging on Nigerian streets will not be effective, unless it is accompanied by action by the government to provide employment and rehabilitation for PLWDs.[16] To make matters worse, some parents of disabled children perpetrate discrimination against their own children, when they take them to the street to beg for alms, rather than take them to school.[17]

The law defines "disability" to "include long[-]term physical, mental, intellectual[,] or sensory impairment which[,] in interaction with various barriers[,] may hinder full and effective participation in society on equal basis with others."[18] In other words, the law adopts the definition of the CRPD,[19] enshrined in human rights. Building on the definition of "disability," the law defines a "person living with disability" as someone with the features of disability above who, additionally, possesses a certificate to that effect, showing substantial limitations to the functional ability of the individual, but not limited to, activities of daily living, such as seeing, hearing, thinking, ambulating, climbing, descending, lifting, grasping, and rising.[20] Instructively, this definition recites verbatim the definition in the Nigerian with Disability Decree of 1993, enumerated in Chapter 1.[21]

The Nigerian Disabilities Act stipulates a five-year transitory period during which timeframe owners and operators of facilities, whether physical structures, road transport, or non-road transport (such as railways, airports, and seaports) must make them accessible and usable for PLWDs.[22] One of its highlights is the creation of an agency, the National Commission for Persons with Disabilities (hereinafter the NCPD or National Disabilities Commission), tasked with responsibility for the wellbeing of PLWDs in Nigeria, beginning with their healthcare and education. The Nigerian Disabilities Act has ten complementary parts. Part I prohibits discrimination based on disability, stipulates penalties in money and prison time for individuals and groups who perpetrate such discrimination, and empowers the Federal Ministry of Information to make provisions for awareness programs to promote respect for the rights and dignity of PLWDs and their contributions to society.

Part II deals with accessibility of PLWDs to public physical structures, such as road side-walks, pedestrian crossings, and public buildings, embodied on a list of sixteen special facilities in the First Schedule to the law that includes ramps, handrails, elevators, windows, entrance doors, water fountains, toilets, and parking spaces. Highlights of this Part are the right to these physical structures that it creates for PLWDs,[23] and the stipulation of a five-year transitional period for modifying these public structures to render them accessible to and usable by PLWDs.[24] There are some who will consider the five-year transitory period long. Moreover, there are unanswered questions like when does the five years start: From the passage of the law in 2018? Or with the inauguration of the Commission which, as indicated later in this discussion, did not take place until December 2020? These questions are especially on point, given the contention by perceptive disability activists that there has been no regulation issued "to inform companies, [and owners of] buildings and other structural environments what is expected of them."[25]

Part III focuses on access to road transportation for PLWDs. Among other things, it requires providers of transport services to equip their vehicles with lifts, ramps, and related fixtures, and in good conditions, to make these vehicles accessible to and usable by PLWDs, including persons on wheelchairs.[26] A key highlight of this Part is the provision for reserved spaces in parking lots for PLWDs, under pain of monetary penalty for noncompliance.[27] Part IV deals with accessibility of railways, seaports, and airports to PLWDs. It stipulates the same five-year transitional period in § 6 for other modes of transportation, and mandates that any general information providers of these transportation services give to nondisabled persons be translated into an accessible format appropriate for PLWDs.[28]

Part V focuses on the right to education, health, and related benefits. In addition to forbidding the use of PLWDs to solicit for alms, as indicated before,[29] this Part guarantees PLWDs "unfettered right to education," free of discrimination on ground of disability or segregation,[30] "delivered in the most appropriate language, mode, and means of communication for the individual, and in environments which maximize [their] academic and social development."[31] Similarly, Part V guarantees PLWDs "unfettered access to adequate health care," free of discrimination based on disability,[32] with most of the provisions focused on mental impairment.[33] Highlights of this Part are the requirements that, in situations of humanitarian emergencies, such as violence, and natural disaster, the government must take "steps to ensure the safety and protection of [PLWDs], taking cognizance of their peculiar vulnerability,"[34] and that, in receiving services, PLWDs will get "first consideration," outside any queue.[35] What makes this provision meaningful is that long queues for medical attention are common in Nigerian hospitals and medical centers, given the scarcity of medical facilities in the country, including limited access to physicians and other healthcare professionals.[36]

The prohibition related to using the PLWDs to solicit alms calls for more comments here. The proscription brings to mind the practice of Almajiri, a system of Islamic education practiced in northern Nigeria.[37] Almajiri children "are used as an object of begging for alms on the street in order to bring income for" their Koranic teachers known as Malams.[38] However, oftentimes, these teachers fail to provide these children with adequate shelter or food, with the result that many of the children became effectively homeless.[39] At a highpoint of the COVID-19 pandemic in 2020, governors of 19 northern states reached a decision to ban Almajiri schools and send the children back to their parents.[40] But it did not take long before these children returned to the streets begging for alms.[41] In northern states which apply Sharia law, it is "difficult to prosecute people who violate" this and other rights of children, given that Sharia law fails to forbid the practice of begging for alms.[42]

Part VI focuses on employment opportunities for PLWDs and on their participation in politics and public life. It guarantees PLWDs a right to work, free of discrimination based on disability, including the "opportunity to gain a living by work freely chosen and accepted in a labor and [open] work environment."[43] A key highlight of this Part is a mandate for public agencies to "have persons [living] with disabilities constitut[e] at least 5 [percent] of their" labor force.[44] While on the surface this might read as an impermissible quota or reverse discrimination against nondisabled persons, the CRPD permits the use of measured, nonpermanent, preferential programs to rectify past discrimination against PLWDs.[45] Next to participation in politics, Part VI stipulates that PLWDs "shall be encouraged to fully participate in politics and public life[,]"[46] in a conducive environment that the government "actively promote[s]."[47]

Part VII deals with the National Disability Commission, placed under the Office of the President, rather than designed to operate as a freestanding entity.[48] The law stipulates that the finances of the Commission must be audited by the Auditor-General of the Federation, an agency of the Nigerian national government conferred with a measure of independence in conformity with its constitutional mandate.[49] However, this ameliorates, but does not rectify the appearance of dependence indicated by placement under the presidency. The Commission has a Governing Council of 19 members, headed by a part-time chairman, charged with the conduct of its affairs.[50] The members are appointed for a four-year term, subject to reappointment for another four-year term.[51] The several duties of the Governing Council include receiving complaints from PLWDs regarding violation of their rights with a view to helping them redress such violations,[52] "ensur[ing] research, development[,] and education on disability issues" and PLWDs,[53] and "procur[ing] assistive devices,"[54] among other responsibilities. In December 2020, the Minister of Humanitarian Affairs, Disaster Management, and Social Development, Hajiya Sadiya Umar Farouq, inaugurated the Governing Council.[55] To the extent that they remain uncovered, Parts VIII to X are immaterial to this discussion. Part VIII deals with the appointment and duties of the Executive Secretary and other staff of the National Disability Council, Part IX with miscellaneous matters, and Part X with interpretations.

Although 25 long years separate the Nigerians with Disability Decree of 1993 and the Nigerian Disabilities Act of 2018, their provisions ring eerily similar for the new dispensation, tracking the CRPD, that the latter law signifies—although concededly the name is our own abbreviation from the awkwardly long name of the Act. The names of the two Commissions under each act is similar, except for the term *People* in the 1993 Decree, vis-à-vis the term *Persons* in the Nigerian Disabilities Act. The sizes of their memberships are also intriguingly similar, 14 for the Nigerians with Disability Decree vis-a-vis 19 for the Nigerian Disabilities Act, especially considering the growth of the country's population within the two and half decades between the two laws.

TEN SECTORS OF INACCESSIBILITY FOR PERSONS LIVING WITH DISABILITY IN NIGERIA UNDER THE FOURTH REPUBLIC

Accessibility is necessary "[t]o enable [disabled persons] to live independently and participate fully in all aspects of life."[56] It is present when a PLWD "is afforded the opportunity to acquire the same information, engage in the same interactions, and enjoy the same services as a person without a disability in an equally effective and equally integrated manner, with substantially equivalent ease of use."[57] Many people at some point in their lives will encounter barriers, defined by the WHO as "[f]actors in a person's environment that, through their absence or presence, limit functioning and create disability."[58] Examples of these factors, according to the WHO, are "services, systems[,] and policies that are either nonexistent or that hinder the involvement of all people with a health condition in all areas of life."[59] Because of their vulnerability, these barriers are more frequent, and more negatively impactful for PLWDs.[60] For PLWDs, therefore, barriers can be more than just physical obstacles.[61] Worse still, oftentimes, multiple barriers are present that can make it extremely difficult for PLWDs to function.[62]

Ten sectors of inaccessibility for PLWDs in Nigeria under the Fourth Republic since 1999 include health, education, employment, physical structure, road transportation, non-road transportation (such as railways, airports, and seaports), information and communications technology (ICT), social protection, technological and digital resources (TDR), and political participation. On a note of caveat, several observations preface the discussion in this section. First, the sectors are illustrative; they do not begin to exhaust the amenity inaccessibility load of Nigeria since 1999 for nondisabled persons, much more for the PLWDs that form the object of this book. Accordingly, the term "include" that begins the enumeration of the ten sectors is used deliberately and advisedly.[63] For example, although not listed here as a sector, negative attitudes toward PLWDs, discussed in Chapter 1, is a major factor because of its impact on each of the sectors analyzed here. Negative attitudes mean that some nondisabled persons see only the impairment, rather the person with a disability. The inaccessibility comes from the fact that believing in the stigma attached to a disability can result in a range of negative responses that includes bullying, isolation, or straight out violence.[64] In fact, this barrier may be seen as the mother of all sectors of inaccessibility because it underlines all the other barriers.[65] It is a foundational barrier that "contribute[s] to other barriers."[66] Second, as the following discussion shows, the ten sectors of inaccessibility reinforce, rather than cross-cut, themselves.[67] For example, the materials on ICT and TDR substantially overlap. Third, the sectors are equal in the negative impact they distinctively interject into the lives of PLWDs. Therefore, the differences in the length of analysis assigned to each sector should not be read to mean that some are more important than the others, since each sector is important in its own right and a necessary part of a seamless whole. Table 3.1 summarizes the record of the Nigerian national government under the Fourth Republic.

Health

Health is the first of the ten sectors of inaccessibility PLWDs face in Nigeria since 1999 and before. The CRPD stipulates that state parties must guarantee for PLWDs the right to enjoy the highest standard of health, free of any discrimination based on disability, that is also gender-sensitive and includes health-related rehabilitation.[68] It enjoined state parties to provide PLWDs "with the same range, quality and standard of free or affordable health care and programs as provided to other persons";[69] and to require health professionals to provide care of the same quality to persons [living] with disabilities as to others[.]"[70] The treaty also enjoined state parties to "protect the privacy of personal, health and rehabilitation information of persons [living] with disabilities on an equal basis with others."[71] Similarly, the PACRD stipulates that "every [PLWD] has right to the highest attainable standard of health."[72] It enjoined state parties to ensure that PLWDs "have, on an equal basis with others, access to health services," including "providing to [PLWDs] [. . .] the same range, quality, and standard" of care afforded to nondisabled persons.[73]

Under the Nigerian Disabilities Act, the Nigerian government guaranteed PLWDs "unfettered access to adequate health care," free of discrimination based on disability.[74] The guarantee includes "free [. . .] health service[s] in all public institutions[,]"[75] provision for special communication in any public hospital that gives treatment to a person with communicational disabilities,[76] "first consideration" in queues for PLWDs,[77] under pain of fines or term of imprisonment for violation,[78] Finally, in situations of humanitarian emergencies, such as risk, violence, and natural disaster, the government is obligated

Table 3.1. Recap on the disability implementation record of the Nigerian national government under the Fourth Republic

Item No.	*Sector*	*CRPD*	*PACRD*	*Nigerian Disabilities Act (2018)*	*Heuristic assessment*
1.	Health	PLWDs have the right to enjoy the highest standard of health, free of discrimination based on disability	"Every [PLWD] "has the right to the highest attainable standard of health," free of discrimination based on disability	PLWDs have "unfettered access to adequate health care," free of discrimination based on disability	Suboptimal; more negative than positive
2.	Education	PLWDs have the right to an inclusive education and life-long learning	"Every [PLWD] has the right to education, that state parties must provide "on an equal basis with others"	PLWDs have "unfettered right to education," free of discrimination or segregation, based on disability	Suboptimal; more negative than positive
3.	Employment	State parties must guarantee for PLWDs "right to work on an equal basis with others"	"Every [PLWD] has the right to decent work" and related benefits, whose enjoyment state parties must facilitate "on an equal basis with others"	PLWDs have the "right to work on an equal basis with others"	Suboptimal; more negative than positive
4.	Physical structures	State parties must ensure for PLWDs "on an equal basis with others," access to physical structures, in rural and urban areas	"Every [PLWD] has the right to barrier-free access to" physical structures, without discrimination based on disability	PLWDs have "the right to access the physical environment and building on an equal basis with others"	Suboptimal; more negative than positive
5.	Road transportation	State parties must ensure for PLWDs, "on an equal basis with others," access to transportation, in rural and urban areas	"Every [PLWD] has the right to barrier-free access to" transportation, that state parties must provide, without discrimination based on disability	Motor vehicles, parks, and bus stops will be outfitted with accessibility devices like lifts, and ramps; parking lots must have reserved spots for PLWDs	Suboptimal; more negative than positive

6.	Railways, seaports and airports	Right not specified in the text of the instrument	"Every [PLWD] has the right to barrier-free access to" [non-road] transportation that state parties must provide, without discrimination based on disability	Facilities in these modes of transportation shall be made accessible to PLWDs	Suboptimal; more negative than positive or hardly applicable with respect to seaports and airports
7.	Information and communications technology (ICT)	State parties must ensure for PLWDs "on an equal basis with others," access to ICT, in rural and urban areas	"Every [PLWD] has the right to barrier-free access to" ICT that state parties must provide, free of discrimination based on disability	Right not specified in the text of the instrument	Suboptimal; more negative than positive
8.	Social protection	State parties must work to realize for PLWDs the right "to an adequate standard of living for themselves and their families"	PLWDs "have a right to an adequate standard of living for themselves and their families" that state parties must help them realize, without discrimination based on disability.	Right not specified in the text of the instrument	Suboptimal; more negative than positive
9.	Technological and digital resources (TDR)	Right not specified in the text of the instrument	Right not specified in the text of the instrument	Right not specified in the text of the instrument	Suboptimal; more negative than positive
10.	Political participation	State parties must work to realize for PLWDs "political rights and the opportunity to enjoy them on an equal basis with others"	"Every [PLWD] has the right to participate in political and public life" that state parties must help them realize, free of discrimination based on disability	The government will encourage PLWDs "to fully participate in politics and public life"	Probably more positive than negative

Source: Created by the authors

to take "necessary steps to ensure the safety and protection of [PLWDs], taking cognizance of their peculiar vulnerability."[79]

Here is why the record with respect to health is more negative than positive, rendering the achievement of the Nigerian government under the Fourth Republic suboptimal, as highlighted in Table 3.1. In April 2001, Nigeria and other African countries made a commitment, known as the Abuja Declaration, after the Nigerian capital where the Declaration was hammered out, to devote at least 15 percent of their national budget to healthcare.[80] The reservation of that percentage was motivated by a need to improve healthcare across the continent, given the underinvestment in this sector that dates back to the early days of independence in many countries—despite the burdensome challenges of infectious and non-infectious diseases in the region that include HIV/AIDS, tuberculosis, malaria, and mental illnesses.[81] A recent report published by the Partnership for Advocacy in Child and Family Health at Scale (PACFAH@Scale), a nonprofit based in Abuja and Kano, found that the Nigerian government failed woefully to keep the pledge.[82] Instead, oftentimes its budgetary allocation to healthcare barely reached a third of the pledged benchmark.[83] The finding was based on an analysis of the budgets of the Federal Ministry of Health in the 21 years between 2001 to 2021. According to the report, over the 21-year period from 2001 to 2021, budgetary allocation to healthcare averaged about 4.7 percent.[84]

In a nutshell, Nigeria has a healthcare system, in many respects dysfunctional, that PLWDs have enormous difficulty in accessing at many points of contact.[85] When they manage to get access at all, oftentimes PLWD confront the negative attitude of some health workers.[86] Some healthcare workers are not adequately trained to address some of the health issues that PLWDs face. These are among the "programmatic barriers," revolved around "[p]rovider's attitudes, knowledge, and understanding of people with disabilities[,]" which invariably "limit the effective delivery of a public health or healthcare program for people [living] with different types of impairments."[87] None of the 65 sections of the National Health Act of 2014, divided into 7 distinct parts, made provision, for instance, for mental health.[88] So much for a law avowedly aimed "to provide a framework for the regulation, development, and management of a national health system and set standards for rendering health services in the" country.[89]

Education

Education is another sector of inaccessibility, second only to health(care), that foregrounds the Fourth Republic. Just like health, education ranks among barriers, factors within the environment whose absence, in this case, can serve to limit functioning for PLWDs.[90] Arguably, this falls under issues that, in the literature of disability studies, may be classified as "social barriers," or "social determinants of health," obstacles "related to the conditions in which people are born, grow, live, learn, work and age, [. . .] that can contribute to decreased functioning among people with disabilities."[91] To use the US as example, persons 18 years and above living with disabilities "are less likely to have completed high school compared to their peers without disabilities (22.3 [percent] compared to 10.1 [percent])."[92]

For PLWDs, there are multiple marks of significance attached to education. First, a foremost picture of access to PLWD is educational opportunity.[93] It is the key to the acquisition of knowledge and skills that PLWDs need to develop their potentials and live productive lives.[94] With this tool, a PLWD can earn a living and "be able to have a family," with likely diminution of the harsh effects of disability.[95] When provided with good education, women living with disabilities "are able to lead better, respectful lives and possibly marry men of good education and understanding."[96] Little wonder that, in opinion surveys, PLWD respondents expressed the hopeful belief that, regardless of the specific disabilities that afflict them, with quality education they could live productive lives as members of their own communities.[97] Second, education can serve as a handy tool for challenging inaccurate stereotypes related to PLWDs by providing factual information, provided that programs designed to reduce stigma are "carefully matched to the unique culture, community, and mind-set of the population to which it is applied."[98]

The CRPD mandates state parties to provide for PLWDs an inclusive education and life-long learning, designed to develop their human potentials, creativity, and effective participation in a free society.[99] It mandates states parties to provide reasonable accommodation of the individualized requirements of PLWDs, including in tertiary and related education;[100] provide required support—within the general education system—to facilitate effective education for PLWDs;[101] facilitate the learning of communicational and mobility skills, such as Braille, alternative script, and augmentative and alternative modes;[102] facilitate the learning of sign language and the promotion of the linguistic identity of the deaf community;[103] ensure that the education of the blind, deaf, and deaf-blind, particularly children, is delivered in the most appropriate languages, means of communication, and conducive academic environments;[104] and employ teachers, including teachers with disabilities, qualified in sign language and/or Braille.[105] Some of these suggestions dovetail with the ones under information and communications technology (ICT).

The PACRD stipulates that every PLWD has the right to education, that state parties must provide "on an equal basis with others."[106] It enjoined these state parties to ensure "inclusive quality education and skills training" for PLWDs, free of any discrimination based on disability.[107] For the Protocol, education of PLWDs shall be aimed at fully developing their human potentials and self-worth; improving their "personality, talents, skills, professionalism and creativity" to the fullest extent possible; promoting their participation and inclusion in society; and strengthening "positive African values."[108]

The Nigerian Disabilities Act promised PLWDs "an unfettered right to education," free of "discrimination or segregation in any form."[109] The guarantee includes "free education to [the] secondary school level."[110] It also includes education accessible to PLWDs that is inclusive at all levels (primary, secondary, and tertiary), complete with "educational assistive devices," qualified teaching personnel, some of whose training will be subsidized by the government, and special facilities necessary for effective education of PLWDs, including Braille and sign language.[111] Going further, the Commission tasked with responsibility for enforcing the law is empowered to facilitate scholarship awards for PLWDs up to university level;[112] and for promoting inclusive schools, including vocational and rehabilitation centers for the development and edification of PLWDs.[113] Last but not least, the Nigerian Disabilities Act promised PLWDs "first consideration" in issues related to housing in educational and other settings.[114] The law solidified the National Policy on Education of 2013, "a statement of intentions [and] expectations [. . .] for quality education delivery," meant to facilitate the implementation of education at levels of government in the country.[115] Section 7 of the policy focuses on special education, defined as "a customized educational program, designed to meet the unique needs of persons with special needs that the general education program cannot cater for[,]"[116] including beneficiaries of this program, its aims, the role of the Federal Ministry of Education and related stakeholders, equipment, and training of special education teachers.[117]

Like health services, in Nigeria, numerous limitations impede access to education for PLWDs. First, special education for children living with disabilities is expensive to the point of unaffordability. It costs "more than four times" to educate a child living with disabilities than it does educating a nondisabled child.[118] Given that, like health, education for PLWDs is inadequately funded, parents and wards of children must bear much of the cost.[119] Second, education for PLWDs in the country is segregated. This is an institutionalization that is innocuously dubbed boarding schools.[120] Other impediments for parents and wards of disabled children include poor access to learning facilities, long distance to school and lack of transportation, as well as low expectation of returns for educational opportunities afforded to disabled children.[121] Small wonder that the vast majority of PLWDs in the country have little education.[122]

For PLWDs who beat the odds to the point of readiness for higher education, the obstacles are daunting.[123] First, admission is not guaranteed for certain disabled persons, such as those living with blindness.[124] Those who manage to get in are confronted with all manner of accessibility challenges in all the amenities that for both able and disabled students are necessary for a good educational experience—dormitories, cafeteria, restrooms, bathroom, transit buses, among other facilities—given that, in many institutions, operators of these facilities tailor these services to nondisabled students, with little regard for the needs of students living with disabilities. Some institutions have dormitories with no ramps, which render them inaccessible to disabled students on wheelchair. Others have classrooms on non-ground-level floors in story buildings not fitted with elevators, making it impossible for wheelchair users to access those classrooms. Yet others operate transit buses not wheelchair accessible, making it necessary for students living with disability to be helped manually into these vehicles, to certain discomfort and an affront to their dignity. There are also institutions where school administrators designate some buildings to students with disabilities, rather than take the trouble to make all dormitories accessible. Whatever the justification for such decision, some PLWDs and organizations who advocate for them read ulterior motives into those actions, such as the desire to render PLWDs invisible. Yet other institutions have acute shortage of basic learning aids, such as Braille and audio materials.[125] This and other realities give a hollow ring to the promise of "an unfettered right to education," free of "discrimination or segregation in any form," made to PLWDs in the Nigerian Disabilities Act.

Employment

Employment centrally ranks among the sectors of inaccessibility that impede the lives of PLWDs in Nigeria. Like education, employment falls within the category of social barriers, "conditions in which people are born, grow, live, learn, work and age," that impede the effective functioning of PLWDs.[126] To use the US as example, in 2017, 35.5 percent of PLWD, aged 18 to 64 years, were employed, compared to 76.5% of nondisabled people employed—about double that of people living with disabilities.[127] One's job is his friend, as one saying goes. Therefore, employment takes its significance in the fact that it is a dependable source of regular income, more so in developing societies like Nigeria where there is little social protection for many people, including PLWDs and even nondisabled poor people.

The CRPD enjoins state parties, as a matter of human right, to afford PLWDs the opportunity "to work, on an equal basis with others," including the freedom "to gain a living by work freely chosen or accepted in a labor market" and in an open, inclusive, and accessible work environment.[128] Among other means, they should promote for PLWDs "opportunities for self-employment, [including] entrepreneurship, the development of cooperatives[,] and starting [their] own business[es]";[129] promote the employment of PLWDs in the private sector through appropriate policies and measures, like preferential programs that take into account past discriminations perpetrated against the group;[130] provide them reasonable accommodation in the workplace;[131] and protect them, "on an equal basis with others, from forced or compulsory labor."[132]

Similarly, the PACRD provides that "[e]very [PLWD] has the right to decent work, and to just and favorable conditions of work," among related benefits, such as protection from compulsory labor, whose enjoyment state parties must facilitate "on an equal basis with others."[133] To achieve this goal, state parties should adopt a range of measures, anchored on a recognition of "the social and cultural value of" PLWD work, including: promoting opportunities for PLWDs "to initiate self-employment, entrepreneurship[,] and to access financial services"; reasonable accommodation of PLWDs in the workplace; the use of set-aside programs to benefit PLWDs in the public sector; and ensuring that employees with disabilities or those who become disabled on the job do not lose their jobs on ground of disability.[134]

The Nigerian Disabilities Act is not left out in the scheme of things regarding employment. The law provides that PLWDs have the "right to work on an equal basis with others," including the freedom "to gain a living by work freely chosen" and in an open work environment.[135] This guarantee includes monetary penalties for employers who violate the provision, including damages to any disabled person discriminated against,[136] and the mandate that employers of public agencies do their best to "constitute at least 5 [percent] of their" labor force with PLWDs.[137] The National Commission tasked with responsibility for enforcing the Act is also empowered to reserve "not less than 5 [percent] of the work force [for] qualified" PLWDs.[138] Except for the set aside of 5 percent of the labor force to PLWDs, the provision is similar, down to language, to the CRPD.[139]

Unemployment is exceedingly high for nondisabled persons in Nigeria, much more so for PLWDs. In the country, even PLWDs with university education have difficulty finding a job. This is why, by their self-description in opinion surveys and other forums, unemployment ranks among two of the most intractable challenges PLWDs say they face, the other being mobility.[140] And for those lucky to find a job, some report mixed treatment in the workplace because of the attitudes of nondisabled colleagues. Some disability activists take the position that the intent of the government to outlaw begging on the street will be ineffective if its leaders in Abuja did not act to improve the employment situation of persons living with disability.[141]

Physical Structures

The CRPD mandates state parties to ensure for PLWDs "access, on an equal basis with others," to physical structures, both in rural and urban areas.[142] The PACRD provides similarly, with its stipulation to the effect that "[e]very [PLWD] has the right to barrier-free access to" physical structures,[143] including "modification of all inaccessible infrastructure and the universal design of all new infrastructure."[144] Not to be outdone, the Nigerian Disabilities Act follows suit with its own stipulation which guarantees PLWDs the right of access to physical structures, free of discrimination based on disability, which structures it defines to include public buildings, road sidewalks, pedestrian crossings, elevators, ramps, entrance doors, windows, handrails, drinking-water fountains, and toilets, among other facilities,[145] and within the five-year transitory framework allowed for modification, where necessary, under this law.[146] The same law also empowered the National Commission tasked with responsibility for enforcing the rights of PLWDs to ensure that facilities across the country are "bult or modified, where and when feasible, to accommodate the special needs of" PLWDs.[147] The Commission also has responsibility for procuring assistive devices for all types of disabilities.[148]

But now with what result? Despite this wealth of impressive provisions, access to public buildings are not "disability-friendly."[149] Instead, "[p]laces of business, healthcare, education, employment, transport, recreation, sport and leisure, and the justice system have major structural barriers, which prevented people with disabilities from accessing programs and services provided by these entities."[150] More elaborately, the barriers include: relatively few wheel chair access for street crossings; unsuitability of housing facilities, such as the presence of ramps too steep that PLWDs trying to use these facilities will require assistance to get into the building; toilets inaccessible with wheel chairs; pedestrian bridges with no access for persons on wheel-chairs; steps or stairs with no ramps; rough, unpaved, and uneven floor surfaces; uncovered drainages or other openings in premises; high-rise buildings with no elevators (one study of Ibadan in 2005 found that only one out of twelve story buildings had an elevator connecting the different levels); absence of side walk; and curbs, hilly and undulating terrain PLWDs are not able to navigate.[151]

Physical structures are a sector that overlaps with several other sectors like health(care) and education, analyzed above. In healthcare, medical personnel examine patients with disabilities on examination tables that cannot be lowered or easily manipulated for transfer of wheelchair users during medical checkups. This lack leads to scenarios where, time and again, caregivers physically transfer the wheelchair user to the examination table, in encounters the PLWDs themselves assess as uncomfortable and dehumanizing.[152] For education, the same mark of inaccessibility occurs when PLWDs attempt to use educational resources, such as public libraries.[153]

Road Transportation

The CRPD enjoins state parties to ensure for PLWDs "access, on an equal basis with others," to transportation in both rural and urban areas.[154] The PACRD contains a similar guarantee with its stipulation to the effect that "[e]very [PLWD] has the right to barrier-free access to" transportation that state parties must fill.[155] Last but not least, the Nigerian Disabilities Act mandates the equipment of motor vehicles, parks, and bus stops with elevators, ramps, and related devices of accessibility, along with the provision of reserved spots for PLWDs in parking lots.[156]

Here, as in some of the other sectors under review, the reality on the ground is different. Nigeria has a history of underinvestment in road transportation, among numerous other items of infrastructure.[157] For this reason, the transportation problems nondisabled persons confront in the country are daunting,[158] more so for people living with disabilities, including those on wheelchair. In the graphic description of one scholar, PLWDs

> face difficulties in boarding available public transport, most especially the uncomfortable yellow painted buses or the large "geriatric clumsy buses" in Lagos called "molues" and the siblings of the molues known as "damfos." The attitude and driving behavior of most drivers as well as the overcrowding of available modes of travel, prolong[ed] waiting time, poor travel information and unaffordable travel cost are major travel difficulties to the disabled persons. Drivers of most public transport in Nigerian cities do not give disabled people enough time to board and alight in comfort and safety. Those using wheelchairs and other mobility aid, like walking stick, are unable to use public transport in most Nigerian cities.[159]

In some portions of the country, the modes of transportation available to paraplegics are such that they expose them "to numerous traffic dangers."[160] Three years after passage of the Nigerian Disabilities Act of 2018, in the assessment of one newspaper reporter, the reality is still "anguish" for PLWDs in some parts of the country with respect to access to public transportation.[161] Small wonder that, along with unemployment, described above, mobility embedded in transportation, ranks among the great challenges PLWD respondents in opinion surveys indicate they face in Nigeria.[162]

Non-Road Transportation

Facilities like railways, airports, and seaports are an extension of transportation as a broad category. It is obviously for this reason that the CRPD and the PACRD do not make separate provisions for them besides the guarantee for transportation generally. Instructively, the Nigerian Disabilities Act, which translated the CRPD into Nigerian law, did. The law stipulates that facilities, such as railways, airports, and seaports, must be made accessible to and usable by PLWDs, and within the transitory period of 5 years for these changes.[163] Going forward, it mandates operators of these facilities to translate any general information into the accessible format as appropriate to the PLWD they are providing service.[164]

Inexplicably, much of the provision was devoted to airports. Operators of these airports must provide "presentable and functional wheelchairs" for conveying PLWDs using their services to and from their aircraft,[165] ensure that they "are assisted to get on and off board in safety and reasonable comfort,"[166] and ensure that they "are accorded priority while boarding and disembarking from the aircraft."[167] Vis-à-vis seaports and airports, in Nigeria, the facility many PLWDs are familiar with are railways, partly because of its tie to road transportation. For that reason, the discussion on road transportation applies here and is, therefore, incorporated to this conversation by reference.

Information and Communications Technology (ICT)

In its most basic sense, information and communications technology (ICT) refers to "an electronic medium for creating, storing, manipulating, receiving and sending information from one place to another."[168] The field deals extensively with communication technology, including its impacts on other fields of human endeavor.[169] This source of inaccessibility exists when information and communications for the general public is effectively denied to PLWDs because it is not accessible. This means that, due to their disabilities, oftentimes, PLWDs are the last to receive information. This sector of inaccessibility signifies barriers suffered by persons "who have disabilities that affect hearing, speaking, reading, writing, and or understanding, and who use different ways to communicate than people who do not have these disabilities."[170] Scenarios which exemplify these barriers include:

Use of small print or no large-print versions of material,

No Braille or versions for people who use screen readers.

Auditory health messages inaccessible to people with hearing impairments, such as videos with no captioning, and oral communications unaccompanied with manual interpretation like sign language, and

the use of technical language, long sentences, and words with many syllables which impedes understanding for people with cognitive impairments.[171]

What these scenarios have in common is that they are supposed information materials with impairments that prevent disabled persons, whether visually or hearing impaired, from receiving the message in question.[172]

The CRPD enjoins state parties to ensure for PLWDs, "access, on an equal basis with others," "to information and communications, [. . .] both in urban and rural areas."[173] More elaborately, the CRPD mandates state parties to "[p]rovide information intended for the general public," to PLWDs in "accessible formats and technologies appropriate to different kinds of disabilities in a timely manner and without additional cost";[174] facilitate "the use of sign language, Braille, augmentative and alternative communication" to PLWDs in official interactions;[175] urge private entities that provide communicational services to the general public, such as the Internet, to provide information and services in accessible and usable formats for PLWDs;[176] encourage the mass media and providers of information through the Internet to do the same;[177] and recognize and promote the use of sign languages.[178] The treaty defines "Communication" broadly to "include languages, display of text, Braille, tactile communication, large print, accessible multimedia as well as written, audio, plain-language, human-reader and augmentative and alternative modes, means and formats of communication, including accessible information and communication technology."[179] Similarly, with respect to personal mobility, it enjoined state parties to "[f]acilitat[e] access by [PLWDs] to quality mobility aids, devices, assistive technologies and forms of live assistance and intermediaries, including by making them available at affordable cost,"[180] and to "[e]ncourag[e] entities that produce" these goods "to take into account all aspects of mobility for persons [living] with disabilities."[181]

The PACRD stipulates that "[e]very [PLWD] has the right to barrier-free access to" information and communication that state parties must help them realize, free of discrimination based on disability, in rural and urban settings alike.[182] In the same vein, "[e]very [PLWD] has the right to freedom of expression and opinion," that includes "the freedom to seek, receive[,] and impart information and ideas through all forms of communication of their choice," that state parties are obligated to help them realize "on an equal basis with others."[183] Finally, "[e]very [PLWD] has the right to access information," that state parties must help them realize, free of discrimination, based on disability.[184] To this effect, state parties need to provide information meant for the general public to PLWDs "in accessible formats and technologies appropriate to different kinds of disabilities in a timely manner, and without additional cost to" PLWDs; require private entities who provide services to the general public to do the same; ensure that persons with visual impairment or related disability have effective access to published works; and recognize and promote the use of sign language and deaf culture.[185] The treaty defined "deaf culture" to mean "the way deaf people interact," including the set of social beliefs and institutions influenced by deafness, which use sign languages as means of communication.[186]

Nigeria has not ratified the PACRD and Nigeria remains far off from the requirement of "access, on an equal basis with others," "to information and communications, [. . .] both in urban and rural areas" laid down by the treaty. This begins to explain but does not justify why, as some perceptive analysts point out, major television stations do not hire the services of sign language interpreters, and programs with video captions for the deaf are practically non-existent.[187]

Social Protection

Social protection refers to "public and private initiatives that provide income or consumption transfers to the poor, protect the vulnerable against livelihood risks[,] and enhance the social status and rights of the marginalized," in an attempt to reduce the economic and social fragility of these groups,[188] and minimize "the lifelong consequences of poverty and exclusion."[189] It is "a set of nationally owned policies and instruments that provide income support and facilitate access to goods and services by all households and individuals at least at minimally accepted levels, to protect them from deprivation and social exclusion, particularly during periods of insufficient income, incapacity or inability to work."[190] Examples of social protection programs include cash transfers, child grants, school meals, food subsidies, housing allowances, as well as job training and skills development.[191] In addition to PLWDs, beneficiaries of these programs include children, women, older people, displaced people, the unemployed, and the sick.[192]

The CRPD provides that PLWDs have the right "to an adequate standard of living for themselves and their families, including adequate food, clothing and housing, and to the continuous improvement of living conditions," and mandates state parties to work to realize this right for PLWDs, free of discrimination based on disability.[193] Similarly, word to word, the PACRD stipulates that PLWDs "have a right to an adequate standard of living for themselves and their families" that state parties must help them realize, free of discrimination based on disability.[194] The right subsumes access to basic needs and social amenities like adequate food, clothing, safe drinking water, housing, sanitation, and "continuous improvement of living conditions," as well as to social security protections.[195] The Nigerian Disabilities Act provides that the National Commission tasked with responsibility for enforcing the law shall prepare schemes designed to promote the social welfare of PLWDs, including the cost of implementing such proposals.[196]

Under Decree No. 73 of 1993, during the period of the second generation of military rule in Nigeria, the national government introduced the Nigeria Social Insurance Trust Fund (NSITF).[197] The Fund is a "defined benefit" program which enables contributors "to enjoy pension and grants far beyond their contributions."[198] In 2002, the program was amended to encompass disability benefits.[199]

Like with other programs, the reality on the ground is negatively different. Instead, based on studies of key poor states in Northern Nigeria, PLWDs benefit the least from social protetion program.[200] Because PLWDs face disadvantages in the labor market, disability benefits should not be limited to contributory schemes or PLWDs will be left out in the scheme of economic protection.[201] The trick though for decision makers is how to "strike a delicate balance between providing income security and adequate support services, on the one hand, and promoting participation in the labor force as much as possible, on the other."[202] In addition to disability-specific social protection, PLWDs should have access to other program, such as child and family allowances, and unemployment compensation, so long as they meet the criteria for such allowances, rather than excluded out of hand on ground of disability.[203] For, due to high rates of poverty and exclusion from the labor market, oftentimes PLWDs are eligible for mainstream social protection programs that, however, policy designers and implementers often keep beyond their reach.[204] Sometimes, application for these programs contain conditions that PLWDs have difficulty meeting.[205]

Technological and Digital Resources (TDR)

Inaccessibility to technological and digital resources (TDR) is a sector related to ICT, covered above, that should be read as complementary to that conversation and material.[206] Yet, given its importance, the topic is sufficiently distinct to form its own separate material. For optimal result, the two presentations should be read side by side in conjunction with each other.

TDR consists of "electronic code that can be rendered audibly, visually, or tactilely."[207] These resources derive their distinctive significance from the fact that they "break traditional barriers to communication, interaction, and access to information for persons [living] with disabilities."[208] As Mary Pat Radabaugh, then Director of IBM National Support Center for Persons with Disabilities, poignantly stated in 1988

> For most people, technology makes things easier. For people with disabilities, technology makes things possible. In some cases, especially in the workplace, technology becomes the great equalizer and provides the person with a disability a level playing field on which to compete.[209]

In other words, technology has many benefits for people with disability. Thanks to technology, in many parts of the world in this age of COVID-19, PLWDs can communicate with friends and family, build new connections and cement existing ones, access education, and work remotely.

On the other hand, "[w]hen traditional written or verbal communications are the only forms of communication available, they can be completely inaccessible to persons depending on type of disability."[210] This is where web-accessibility comes into play. Accessibility techniques are designed specifically to improve access for people with disability. For example, transcripts and captions on videos assist those with hearing impairments, using plain English helps those with cognitive or learning disabilities, and the use of calm colors is most effective when communicating with people with mental health conditions.[211] Web Content Accessibility Guidelines, often known as WCAG, is an internationally-recognized benchmark for measuring the accessibility of websites.[212]

Following the issuance in 1998 by the World Wide Web Consortium of the first guidelines for ensuring that websites are accessible to all persons with disabilities, in 2000, the U.S. Access Board established the standards for the accessibility of government websites.[213] The many fruits of ICT, including the growth of mainstreams that ICT makes possible, have changed and continue to change "the paradigm of technology-enabled development for" PLWDs. The key is to ensure that benefits enabled by ICT development remain accessible to PLWD, rather than create new divides.[214] Information providers should ensure that their website is accessible to all users, nondisabled persons and disabled alike. For technology to benefit people living with disability, web accessibility tools need to be utilized by everyone. There lies the key to minimizing major accessibility barriers that come with technology.[215]

How does Nigeria fit into this picture? A conceivable way to approach this question is to take a quick look at the Digital Rights and Freedom Bill in the National Assembly since 2016. The bill aims to protect Internet users from infringement of their basic rights.[216] More elaborately, the bill was designed to promote freedom of expression, assembly, and association online; protect the data privacy rights of citizens and set the boundaries for the legal framework pertaining to surveillance; secure the digital liberty of Nigerians; and equip the judiciary with the legal framework necessary for the protection of human rights online.[217] The legislation was passed by the House of Representatives in December 2017 and by the Senate in March 2018, after which it was sent to the president for assent.[218] In March 2019, President Muhammadu Buhari refused to sign the Digital Rights and Freedom Bill into law, on the ground that the bill covered many technical subjects, none of which, according to the President, it addressed extensively.[219] Many, including non-lawmakers within the media who need the protection of digital rights the bill seeks to guarantee, disagree with his position.[220]

Political Participation

The CRPD mandates state parties to guarantee for PLWDs "political rights and the opportunity to enjoy them on an equal basis with others," including ensuring that PLWDs "can effectively and fully participate in political and public life on an equal basis with others, directly or through freely chosen representatives," all the way down to the opportunity to vote and run for office.[221] The PACRD provides that "[e]very [PLWD] has the right to participate in political and public life" that state parties must help them realize, free of discrimination based on disability.[222] Measures state parties can adopt to help them realize this right for PLWDs include: robust "civic education" to promote full participation of PLWDs in democracy and development processes, as members of political parties, electors, or public office holders; and by changing laws that restrict the rights of PLWDs "to vote, stand for or remain in public office."[223] The Nigerian Disabilities Act mandates that PLWDs be "encouraged to fully participate in politics and public life."[224] To this effect, the national government must promote the environment for an effective participation, free of discrimination based on disability,[225] whether, for example, in the conduct of public affairs,[226] in nongovernmental organizations dealing with the political and public life of the country,[227] or in the work of political parties.[228]

Disability activists and non-governmental organizations advocating for disabled persons regrettably note that PLWDs "are noticeably absent in politics and public offices in Nigeria," and they posit that "Nothing About Us Without Us," the mantra of the disability right movement in Nigeria, amounts to little "if there are no [PLWDs] occupying key positions in the decision[-]making process" of the land.[229] In 2018, the Independent Electoral Commission (INEC), the national agency that oversees the conduct of elections in Nigeria, introduced a Braille ballot guide that allowed voters who are blind or low vision to cast their ballots independently and confidentially for the first time in the country's history.[230] Subsequently, for the February 2019 election, INEC promoted awareness on the political participation of PLWDs via publication of an electoral framework to defend their rights.[231] These activities were climax to a broader advocacy campaign, "Access Nigeria: Disability Votes Matter," spearheaded by Inclusive Friends Association.[232]

These distinctive marks of progress count among the reasons we have rated the performance of the Nigerian national government on this sector as more positive than negative. In *Purohit and Moore v. The Gambia*, described in Chapter 2, decided before the advent of the CRPD and its Optional Protocol, the African Commission on Human and Peoples' Rights found no violation by the Gambian government of the right of mental patients in the country to participate freely in the government under Article 13 of the African Charter on Human and Peoples' Rights.[233] The Commission reasoned that it found no indication that the Gambian government meant to impede the political participation of mental patients in the country.[234] In the light of the positive developments recounted above, the same logic appears to hold, justifying our assessment of the record of the Nigerian government as probably more positive than negative with stress on the word "probably."

Negative Legacy of Prolonged Military Rule in Nigeria on the Welfare of People Living with Disabilities

There is an Igbo saying to the effect that an individual drenched by rain will not dry from his wetness unless the individual is able to pinpoint where the rain started beating the person. That wisdom informs the ensuing discussion. For nearly thirty years from 1966 until 1998 with a brief pause under the Second Republic from 1979 to 1983, Nigerians lived under more or less repressive military dictatorships. Many of the country's major policies, such as the division of the country into 36 states, the move to a new national capital, and the controversial Land Use Decree, among numerous other policy initiatives, took place during military rule.[235]

Repressive military rule in Nigeria cast a negative shadow over many aspects of the country's national life whose effects, onto the present period, are still keenly felt. These include the welfare of PLWDs. One of the few visible progressive monuments of long military rule in the country, which appeared toward the end of that era, was the Nigerians with Disability Decree of 1993, discussed at some length in Chapter 1. As we indicated therein, the law used a rights-privilege dichotomy that falls below the standard of human rights of the kind that drives this book, and it purported to "guarantee" rights like access to voting that, by its repressive nature, a military regime was in no position to secure for PLWDs.[236]

Testament to the lingering effects from the military era is the domination of the Fourth Republic by former military generals who packaged themselves as "converted democrat[s],"[237] but still govern more or less as dictators in a civilian dispensation.[238] Two of them—Olusegun Obasanjo, 1999–2007 and Muhammadu Buhari, 2015–2023—won two terms in office, accounting for 16 of the 24 years of the Fourth Republic by May 2023 when Buhari completes his second term in office. The 16 years represent two-thirds of the Fourth Republic. To seal the domination by former military rulers, Obasanjo handpicked the two civilian leaders, Umaru Musa Yar'Adua (2007–10), and Goodluck Jonathan (2010–15), sandwiched between these two retired generals.[239] Little wonder that the Nobel laureate Wole Soyinka denominates much of Nigeria's leadership structure since 1999 as "militarized democratic experiment."[240] We will return to this theme of quality in the Fourth Republic in Chapter 4 which unveils a package of ten targeted proposals for advancing disability laws under the Fourth Republic.

A substandard healthcare system ranks among the negative bequeaths and legacies of long military rule in Nigeria. The dysfunctionality extends to PLWDs and their welfare, beginning with healthcare. First, military rule laid the notorious foundation for the alignment of national priorities in favor of guns (defense) over butter (social programs),[241] that explain, but does not justify, the low funding for healthcare that has marked the Fourth Republic. Secondly, many of the ills that currently bedevil healthcare delivery in Nigeria, including repeated strikes among health workers, ill-equipped laboratories, ill-stocked pharmacies, dilapidated hospital buildings, unsanitary hospital environments, and poor remuneration of health workers, are carryovers from the era of military rule.[242] These effects extend to the welfare of PLWDs.

Military dictatorship and proper management of any economy are two oxymoronic phenomena that do not go together.[243] In its compositeness, development is "a big cultural moment, a complex process [. . .] entail[ing] changes in people's minds as well[,]"[244] that rarely occurs under military rule. Broadly speaking, this supports the seminal position of the political scientist Claude Ake who portrayed authoritarian political conditions in Nigeria and other Africa countries as the greatest impediment to development in these countries, an occurrence that he traced back to colonial rule in these lands.[245] An antidote to military rule, as we argue in Chapter 4, is not just the nominal maintenance of civilian rule, but one with power enough to implement Nigeria's international obligations related to the welfare of PLWDs, including their healthcare and education.

CONCLUSION

This chapter addressed three main issues necessary for critically appraising the performance of the Nigerian national government since 1999 under the Fourth Republic regarding its responsibilities toward PLWDs: the Nigerian Disabilities Act, signature accomplishment of the Fourth Republic; ten sectors of inaccessibility for PLWDs; and a statement on the negative legacy of military rule on the welfare of PLWDs. In July 2019, the Nigerian national government confessed multiple unresolved challenges in fulfilling its treaty obligations related to the welfare of PLWDs in the country. The setting for this confession was a response to a request on inputs (questionnaire) from the Human Rights Council, embodied in its Resolution 3722, regarding the rights of PLWDs, specifically Article 8 of the CRPD on raising awareness about PLWDs. The challenges are weak enforcement of the law relating to protecting the rights of PLWDs; inadequate budgetary allocation, including insufficient funding to conduct campaigns and organize seminars; negative attitudes; lack of data and information; inadequate policies and standards, indicated by policy designs that take little consideration of PLWD needs; and lack of political will to ensure full implementation of PLWD rights. The admitted challenges track the ten sources of inaccessibility for PLWDs that we identified and discussed in this chapter. Even though we refer to the PACRD in this presentation, it should be borne in mind that Nigeria is not a state party to this instrument, integral to the African human rights system. We return to this matter in the conclusion of this book.

There is no suggestion that the Nigerian national government is a complete failure when it comes to its duties toward PLWDs embodied in the implementation of the global and regional regimes pertaining to these duties. It is just that it is a horrible example, both for itself and its neighbors within and outside the West Africa subregion. Failure is seldom absolute, given that "[n]o man is ever a complete failure—he can always serve as a horrible example."[246] On this issue, Nigeria is a horrible example. This is despite the vastness of its human and material resources, including home to the largest economy in Africa, which potentials many analysts accord giant status.[247] Such is the record of the Nigerian national government under the Fourth Republic since 1999 on issues relating to its international obligations related to PLWD that observers familiar with this topic have made appeal for the formation of an independent body to monitor accessibility in all sectors pertaining to the welfare of PLWDs.[248] This is a recommendation that deserves to be borne in mind along with the other steps set forth in Chapter 4.

NOTES

1. "Buhari Urges Commission to Assist in Lifting 100 m[illion] Nigerians Out of Poverty," *Guardian* (Lagos) (January 7, 2021), https://guardian.ng/news/buhari-urges-commission-to-assist-in-lifting-100m-nigerians-out-of-poverty/.
2. Ibid.
3. Ibid.
4. Ibid.
5. Ibid.

6. Ibid.
7. Ibid.
8. *Purohit and Moore v. The Gambia*, Communication No. 241/2001 (2003), 41, https://africanlii.org/afu/judgment/african-commission-human-and-peoples-rights/2003/49
9. Discrimination Against Persons with Disabilities (Prohibition) Act (2018), §1(1), *Nigeria Health Watch*, https://nigeriahealthwatch.com/wp-content/uploads/bsk-pdf-manager/2019/02/1244-Discrimination-Against-Persons-with-Disabilities-Prohibition-ACT-2018.pdf [hereinafter DPDP or Nigerian Disabilities Act].
10. Ibid., § 1(2).
11. Ibid. ("Explanatory Memorandum").
12. Ibid., § 1(3).
13. Ibid., § 38(n)-(o).
14. Ibid., § 16(1)-(2).
15. Ibid., § 1(a)-(c).
16. "Government and Disability Activism in Nigeria," *Poor Magazine* (posted July 1, 2016), https://www.poormagazine.org/node/5549 (interview of Julius Shemang, a deaf journalist and disability activist).
17. *Nigeria: Children and Young People with Disabilities* (London: Asylos and ARC Foundation, October 2021), 22 (quoting Timothy Ali Yohanna, a disability researcher and advocate).
18. Nigerian Disabilities Act, note 9, Part X, § 57 ("Interpretation").
19. See Chapter 2, notes 85–87, and accompanying texts.
20. Nigerian Disabilities Act, note 9, Part X, § 57 ("Interpretation").
21. See Chapter 1, note 112, and accompanying text.
22. Nigerian Disabilities Act, note 9, § 6, 10(2) (road transportation), and § 13(3).
23. Nigerian Disabilities Act, note 9, § 3.
24. Ibid., § 6.
25. *Nigeria: Children and Young People with Disabilities,* note 17, p. 271 (written correspondence with Danlami Umaru Basharu, Director of Anglo-Nigerian Welfare Association for the Blind, August 14, 2021).
26. Nigerian Disabilities Act, note 9, § 11(1)-(5).
27. Ibid., § 12(1)-(5).
28. Ibid., § 15.
29. Ibid., § 16(1)-(2); see also note 14 and accompanying text.
30. Nigerian Disabilities Act, note 9, § 17(1).
31. Ibid., § 20.
32. Ibid., § 21(1).
33. See ibid., § 21(2), § 22(1)-(4), and § 23.
34. Ibid., § 25.
35. Ibid., § 26.
36. See Joseph A. Balogun and Philip C. Aka, "Strategic Reforms to Resuscitate the Nigerian Healthcare System," in E. Ike Udogu, ed., *Nigeria in the Fourth Republic: Confronting the Contemporary Political, Economic, and Social Dilemmas* (Lanham, Boulder, New York, and London: Lexington Books, 2022), 79–111.

37. Akali Omeni, "The Almajiri in Northern Nigeria: Militancy, Perceptions, Challenges, and State Policies," *African Conflict and Peacebuilding Review,* 5 (2) (2015), 128–142, doi:10.2979/africonfpeacrevi.5.2.128.

38. *Nigeria: Children and Young People with Disabilities,* note 17, p. 248 (interview with an anonymous source).

39. Ibid., citing "Nigeria," in U.S. Department of State, *2020 Country Reports on Human Rights Practices* (March 30, 2021), § 6.

40. Ibid.

41. Ibid.

42. *Nigeria: Children and Young People with Disabilities,* note 17, p. 271 (interview with an anonymous source).

43. Nigerian Disabilities Act, note 9, § 28(1).

44. Ibid., § 29.

45. See Chapter 2, note 24, and accompanying text.

46. Nigerian Disabilities Act, note 9, § 30(1).

47. Ibid., § 30(2).

48. See ibid., § 31(1); and § 39(3) ("The Commission shall not be subject to a direction, control[,] or suspension by any other authority or person in the performance of its functions under this Act[,] except the President").

49. See Office of the Auditor-General for the Federation, https://www.oaugf.ng/about-us/about-oaugf (stating that the Auditor-General "is a separate and independent entity," who, in the exercise of his duties under the Nigerian Constitution, is not "subject to the direction or control of any [. . .] authority or person").

50. Nigerian Disabilities Act, note 9, § 31(2).

51. Ibid., § 34.

52. Ibid., § 37(n)-(o).

53. Ibid., § 37(p).

54. Ibid., § 37(r).

55. Joseph Erunke, "Farouq Inaugurates Governing Council of National Commission for Persons with Disabilities," *Vanguard* (Lagos) (December 22, 2020), https://www.vanguardngr.com/2020/12/farouq-inaugurates-governing-council-of-natl-commission-for-persons-with-disabilities/.

56.Convention on the Rights of Persons with Disabilities, UN General Assembly Resolution No. A/RES/61/106, Annex I (December 13, 2006), art. 9(1), https://www.refworld.org/docid/4680cd212.html [hereinafter CRPD].

57. "What is Accessibility?" Case Western Reserve University, https://case.edu/accessibility/what-accessibility (quoting the Office for Civil Rights in the U.S. Department of Education).

58. World Health Organization, *International Classification of Functioning, Disability[,] and Health* (Geneva, Switzerland: World Health Organization, 2001), 214.

59. Ibid.

60. "Common Barriers to Participation Experienced by People with Disabilities," CDC: Centers for Disease Control and Prevention (USA), https://www.cdc.gov/ncbddd/disabilityandhealth/disability-barriers.html.

61. Ibid.

62. Ibid.

63. For example, see *Disability Inclusion in Nigeria: A Rapid Assessment* (Washington, DC: World Bank, 2020), ix-xiv (including table) (counting features, such as community-based (services) rehabilitation, as well as assistive device and technology among the items of inaccessibility in the country).

64. "The Biggest Barrier for People with Disability is How Society Disables Them," *Epic* (July 22, 2021), https://epicassist.org/the-biggest-barrier-for-people-with-disability/.

65. Ibid.

66. "Common Barriers to Participation Experienced by People with Disabilities," note 60.

67. An imagery that comes to mind here is the possible harm arising from reinforcing ethnic cleavages in Nigeria and many other African countries. Cleavages are lines of division in society capable of producing conflict or disagreement. The chances for conflict heighten when cleavages are reinforcing or cumulative, meaning they overlap each other, but such chances diminish when cleavages cross-cut, meaning they cut across each other. See "Reinforcing and Cross-Cutting Cleavages," *Desart*, http://desart.us/courses/3180/cleavages.html.

68. CRPD, note 56, art. 25.

69. Ibid., art. 25(a).

70. Ibid., art. 25(d).

71. Ibid., art. 22(2).

72. Protocol to the African Charter on Human and Peoples' Rights on the Rights of Persons with Disabilities in Africa (January 29, 2018), art. 17(1), https://au.int/sites/default/files/treaties/36440-treaty-protocol_to_the_achpr_on_the_rights_of_persons_with_disabilities_in_africa_e.pdf [hereinafter Protocol of the African Charter Related to Disabilities or PACRD].

73. Ibid., art.17(2)-17(2)(b).

74. Nigerian Disabilities Act, note 9, § 12(1).

75. Ibid., § 21(2).

76. Ibid., § 24.

77. Ibid., § 26(1).

78. Ibid., § 26(2).

79. Ibid., § 25.

80. See Balogun and Aka, note 36.

81. See ibid.; and *[Fifteen Percent] Benchmark to Health Sector in Nigeria—The Journey So Far* (Abuja: Partnership for Advocacy in Child and Family Health at Scale (PACFaH@Scale), April 2021), https://drpcngr.org/15-benchmark-to-health-sector-in-nigeria-the-journey-so-far/.

82. *[Fifteen Percent] Benchmark to Health Sector in Nigeria*, note 81.

83. See ibid., pp. 3–4 (including Table 2).

84. Ibid., p. 4 (Table 2).

85. See, for example, Akeem Olalekan Ayub and Anifowose Jimoh Rasaki, "Barriers in Accessing Healthcare Services by Patients with Disabilities in Nigerian

Hospitals," *Gusau International Journal of Management and Social Sciences, Federal University, Gusau*, 4(1) (2021), 280–296.

86. See ibid. (abstract) ("[S]ystemic barriers and attitudes of the healthcare providers affect the access and quality of healthcare services received by" PLWDs); Mohammed Awaisu Haruna, "The Problem of Living with Disability in Nigeria," *Journal of Law, Policy[,] and Globalization*, 65 (2017), 103, 108, https://www.iiste.org/Journals/index.php/JLPG/article/viewFile/39027/40128.

87. "Common Barriers to Participation Experienced by People with Disabilities," note 60.

88. National Health Act, 2014, Federal Republic of Nigeria Official Gazette, 101(145) (October 27, 2014), https://nigeriahealthwatch.com/wp-content/uploads/bsk-pdf-manager/2018/07/01_-Official-Gazette-of-the-National-Health-Act-FGN.pdf.

89. Ibid.

90. World Health Organization, note 58.

91. "Common Barriers to Participation Experienced by People with Disabilities," note 60.

92. Ibid.

93. Felix Silwimba, "Possibilities of Independent Living of Persons with Disabilities in Africa," Independent Living Institute, https://www.independentliving.org/toolsforpower/tools5.html.

94. C. Jonah Eleweke and Jannine Ebenso, "Barriers to Accessing Services by People with Disabilities in Nigeria: Insights from a Qualitative Study," *Journal of Educational & Social Research*, 6(2) (2016), 113, 119, doi:10.5901/jesr.2016.v6n2p113.

95. Ibid.

96. Ibid.

97. Ibid.

98. "Disability Stigma in Developing Countries," p. 18, https://assets.publishing.service.gov.uk/media/5b18fe3240f0b634aec30791/Disability_stigma_in_developing_countries.pdf. For this source, simply educating people about the true medical causes of impairments to reduce stigma without taking into account the local social and normative nuances would not do. The trick is how to overcome false belief and counter stereotypes and not create new ones. Therefore, celebratory events like the International Day of Persons with Disabilities, the International Day of the African Child, and the Day for International Albinism Awareness should not be used to invoke pity or purely to inspire nondisabled persons. Ibid., p. 19.

99. CRPD, note 56, art. 24(1)(a)-(c).

100. Ibid., art. 24(2)(c) and 24(5).

101. Ibid., art. 24(2)(d).

102. Ibid., art. 24(3)(a).

103. Ibid., art. 24(3)(b).

104. Ibid., art. 24(3)(c).

105. Ibid., art. 24(4).

106. Ibid., art. 16(1)-16(2).

107. Ibid., art. 16(3).

108. Ibid., art. 16(4)(a)-(d).

109. Nigerian Disabilities Act, note 9, § 17(1).
110. Ibid., § 17(2).
111. Ibid., §§ 17(3), 18(1)-(2), and 19.
112. Ibid., § 38(i).
113. Ibid., § 38(j).
114. Ibid., § 27.
115. Federal Republic of Nigeria, *National Policy on Education, 6th ed.* (Lagos: Nigerian Educational Research and Development Council (NERDC), 2013), https://educatetolead.files.wordpress.com/2016/02/national-education-policy-2013.pdf.
116. Ibid., p. 35.
117. Ibid., pp. 35–37.
118.See Odirin Omiegbe, "Poverty and Persons Living with Disabilities in Nigeria," in *Africa's Radicalisms and Conservatisms, Volume 1: Politics, Poverty, Marginalization, and Education* (Leiden, The Netherlands: Brill Publishing, January 11, 2021), 164, 170–171.
119. Ibid.
120. See, for example, "Institutionalizing Inclusive Education in Nigeria: A Way to End Poverty," Human Development Initiatives (HDI) Blog (December 3, 2019), https://hdinigeria.org/blog/2019/12/03/institutionalizing-inclusive-education-in-nigeria-a-way-to-end-poverty/.
121. Haruna, note 86, p. 108.
122. Eleweke and Ebenso, note 94, p. 119.
123. Except where indicated otherwise, this paragraph draws on ibid., pp. 119–120 (enumerating the barriers to accessing education students face in Nigeria, as the students themselves recounted them in a survey).
124. See Unini Chioma, "ABU Zaria Denied Me Admission to Study Law Because of My Disability, Blind Young Man, Deshi Godwin Justin Laments," *Nigeria Lawyer* (October 10, 2020), https://thenigerialawyer.com/abu-zaria-denied-me-admission-to-study-law-because-of-my-disability-blind-young-man-deshi-godwin-justin-laments/.
125. Eleweke and Ebenso, note 94, pp. 119–121.
126. Ibid.
127. Ibid.
128. CRPD, note 56, art. 27(1).
129. Ibid., art. 27(1)(f).
130. Ibid., art. 27(1)(h).
131. Ibid., art. 27(1)(i).
132. Ibid., art. 27(2).
133. PACRD, note 72, art, 19(2).
134. Ibid., art. 19(4), and art. 19(2)(c), (d), (f), (g).
135. Nigerian Disabilities Act, note 9, § 28(1).
136. Ibid., § 28(2)-(3).
137. Ibid., § 29.
138. Ibid., § 38(d).
139. CRPD, note 56, art. 27.

140. "Government and Disability Activism in Nigeria," *Poor Magazine* (posted July 1, 2016), https://www.poormagazine.org/node/5549 (interview of Julius Shemang, a deaf journalist and disability activist).

141. Ibid. In a statement that calls to mind the negative attitude toward disability analyzed in Chapter 1, Shemang observed that Nigerians "are very religious, they love to give beggars so they can pray for them. These [. . .] government officials want Nigerian cities to be clean like New York and London without providing necessary infrastructure first and they are banning beggars. You know what? The same elites will be looking for beggars to donate to when they are facing storms of life like business collapse, health problems etc. In other words, they are just being hypocrites!" Ibid.

142. CRPD, note 56, art. 9(1).

143. Nigerian Disabilities Act, note 9, § 15(1)-(15(2)(b).

144. Ibid., § 15(2) (f).

145. Nigerian Disabilities Act, note 9, §§ 3–5.

146. Ibid., § 6.

147. Ibid., § 38(g).

148. Ibid., § 38(r).

149. Eleweke and Ebenso, note 94, p. 116.

150. Ibid. See also "Nigeria Situational Analysis Version II–June 2020," *Inclusive Futures: Promoting Disability Inclusion* (Brighton, UK: Institute of Development Studies, July 2020), 8, https://opendocs.ids.ac.uk/opendocs/bitstream/handle/20.500.12413/15561/DID%20SITAN%20Nigeria%20V2%20July%202020.pdf?sequence=1&isAllowed=y (stating that many public buildings in Nigeria are inaccessible to PLWDs).

151. Haruna, note 86, p. 109.

152. Eleweke and Ebenso, note 94, p. 117.

153. Ibid.

154. CRPD, note 56, art. 9(1).

155. Nigerian Disabilities Act, note 9, §§ 15(1)-15(2(b).

156. Nigerian Disabilities Act, note 9, § 10.

157. See Philip C. Aka and Joseph A. Balogun, *Healthcare and Economic Restructuring: Nigeria in Comparative Perspective* (Gateway East, Singapore: Palgrave Macmillan, 2022), 119–146.

158. See Chapter 1, notes 94–95, and accompanying texts (portraying many roads in Nigeria as "death traps for commuters" and commenting that Nigeria ranks among the countries with the worst roads in Africa).

159. Haruna, note 86, p. 109.

160. Ibid.

161. Tessy Igomu, "Disabled by Fate, Denied Rights to Mobility: Nigerians Living with Disabilities Tell Tales of Anguish Accessing Public Transportation," *Punch* (Lagos) (September 12, 2021), https://punchng.com/disabled-by-fate-denied-rights-to-mobility-nigerians-living-with-disabilities-tell-tales-of-anguish-accessing-public-transportation/ (reporter toured the Lagos Bus Rapid Transit terminals and routes,

reports how discriminatory attitudes and lack of assistive facilities deprive Persons Living With Disabilities access to public transportation).

162. "Government and Disability Activism in Nigeria," note 140 (interview of Julius Shemang, journalist and disability activist).

163. Nigerian Disabilities Act, note 9, § 13(1)-(3).

164. Ibid., § 15.

165. Ibid., § 14(1)(b).

166. Ibid., § 14(1)(c).

167. Ibid., § 14(1)(d).

168. "Information and Communication Technology (ICT): Meaning, Importan[ce]," Yo University TV, https://www.youniversitytv.com/college-tips/information-and-communication-technology-ict-meaningimportan/.

169. Ibid.

170. "Common Barriers to Participation Experienced by People with Disabilities," note 60. See also "The Biggest Barrier for People with Disability is How Society Disables Them," note 64.

171. See "Common Barriers to Participation Experienced by People with Disabilities," note 60.

172. See ibid.

173. CRPD, note 56, art. 9(1).

174. Ibid., art. 21(a).

175. Ibid., art. 21(b).

176. Ibid., art. 21(c).

177. Ibid., art. 21(d).

178. Ibid., art. 21(e).

179. CRPD, note 56, art. 2 ("Definition").

180. Ibid., art. 20(b).

181. Ibid., art. 20(d).

182. PACRD, note 72, art. 15(1)-(2)(a).

183. Ibid., art. 23(1)-(2).

184. Ibid., art. 24(1)-(2).

185. PACRD, note 72, art. 24(2)(a)-(d).

186. Ibid., art. 1 ("Definitions").

187. Eleweke and Ebenso, note 94, p. 121.

188. Stephen Devereux and Rachel Sabates-Wheeler, *Transformative Social Protection*, IDS Working Paper 232 (Brighton, Sussex: Institute of Development Studies, October 2004), https://www.ids.ac.uk/download.php?file=files/dmfile/Wp232.pdf ("Summary").

189. "Social Protection," UNICEF, https://www.unicef.org/social-policy/social-protection.

190. *Leaving No One Behind: A Social Protection* (New York, NY: United Nations Development Program, October 6, 2016).

191. See, for example, "Types of Social Protection," GSDRC, https://gsdrc.org/topic-guides/social-protection/types-of-social-protection/; and "Social Protection and

Labor Overview," World Bank (last updated April 20, 2020), https://www.worldbank.org/en/topic/socialprotection/overview#1.

192. See, for example, "Other Benefits," Social Protection and Human Rights, https://socialprotection-humanrights.org/key-issues/social-protection-systems/other-benefits/.

193. CRPD, note 56, art. 28.

194. PACRD, note 72, art. 20(1)-(2).

195. Ibid., art. 20(1)-(2), and art. 20(2)(b).

196. Nigerian Disabilities Act, note 9, § 38(b).

197. Nigeria Social Insurance Trust Fund Decree 1993 (No. 73 of 1993) (August 23, 1993), published in *Federal Republic of Nigeria Official Gazette*, 80(24) (September 1, 1993), A811-A27. Reprinted in Laws Africa: Legislation Commons, https://commons.laws.africa/akn/ng/act/1993/73/eng@2002-12-31.pdf.

198. "About Us," Nigeria Social Insurance Trust Fund, https://www.nsitfweb.com.ng/html/AboutUs.cfm ("2:0. Contributory Pension Scheme (1993)").

199. Ibid., §16 ("Categories of Benefits"). See also "Nigeria Situational Analysis Version II–June 2020," note 150, p. 19.

200. Ebuka Onyeji, "PWDs Not Benefitting Enough from Social Protection Programs in Four Nigerian States—Survey," *Premium Times* (Abuja) (May 14, 2021), https://www.premiumtimesng.com/news/more-news/461527-pwds-not-benefitting-enough-from-social-protection-programmes-in-four-nigerian-states-survey.html. The four states in question were Jigawa, Kaduna, Kano, and Zamfara.

201. *The Report on the World Social Situation 2018* (New York: United Nations, September 2018), 73, https://doi.org/10.18356/c107798c-en.

202. Ibid.

203. Ibid.

204. Ibid.

205. Ibid.

206. See "Understanding Barriers to Accessibility," Council of Ontario Universities, https://www.uottawa.ca/respect/sites/www.uottawa.ca.respect/files/accessibility-cou-understanding-barriers-2013-06.pdf (stating that, sometimes, technological barriers are related to information and communication barriers).

207. Daniel Goldstein and Gregory Care, "Disability Rights and Access to the Digital World: An Advocate's Analysis of an Emerging Field," *Federalist Lawyer* (December 2012), https://lawreview.law.miami.edu/wp-content/uploads/2013/02/Goldstein-Care-Disability-Rights-and-Access-to-the-Digital-World.pdf.

208. Deepti Samant Raja, *Digital Dividends: Bridging the Disability Divide through Digital Technologies*, Background Paper, World Development Report 2016 (Washington, DC: World Bank, 2016), https://thedocs.worldbank.org/en/doc/123481461249337484-0050022016/original/WDR16BPBridgingtheDisabilityDividethroughDigitalTechnologyRAJA.pdf (abstract).

209. "Assistive Technology," *Disability Insider*, https://disabilityinsider.com/technology/.

210. Raja, note 208, p. 9. See also ibid., Table 1, pp. 8–9 (highlighting barriers to participation by disability type and relevant ICT solutions).

211. "Digital Accessibility Benefits Everyone," *Epic* (May 10, 2021), https://epicassist.org/digital-accessibility-benefits-everyone/.

212. Ibid.

213. Ibid.

214. Goldstein and Care, note 207.

215. See "The Biggest Barrier for People with Disability is How Society Disables Them," note 64.

216. Abisola Olasupo, "Why Nigeria Needs to Sign Digital Right and Freedom Bill into Law as the World Goes Digital," *Guardian* (Lagos) (July 2, 2020), https://guardian.ng/features/why-nigeria-needs-to-sign-digital-right-and-freedom-bill-into-law-as-the-world-goes-digital/.

217. Ibid.

218. Ibid.

219. Ibid.

220. See ibid.

221. CRPD, note 56, art. 29(a).

222. PACRD note 72, art. 21(1)-(2).

223. Ibid., art. 21(2)(a), (b), and (e).

224. Nigerian Disabilities Act, note 9, § 30(1).

225. Ibid., § 30(2).

226. Ibid., § 30(2)(a).

227. Ibid., § 30(2)(b).

228. Ibid., § 30(2)(c).

229. "People with Disabilities and Politics in Nigeria," *World Pulse* (September 23, 2013), https://www.worldpulse.com/community/users/vweta/posts/28511.

230. See "How NDI Supports the Political Inclusion of Persons with Disabilities," *National Democratic Institute* (USA) (November 27, 2019), https://www.ndi.org/our-stories/how-ndi-supports-political-inclusion-persons-disabilities; and "Nigerians with Visual Impairments Vote Independently for the First Time," *National Democratic Institute* (USA) (April 23, 2019), https://www.ndi.org/our-stories/nigerians-visual-impairments-vote-independently-first-time.

231. "Human Rights Council Resolution 37/22 Concerning the Rights of Persons with Disabilities—Inputs by National Human Rights Commission, Nigeria" (July 22, 2019).

232. Lauren Moses, "Nigerian Disability Advocates Conduct First-Ever Election Accessibility Audits," *Democracy Works*, https://www.demworks.org/nigerian-disability-advocates-conduct-first-ever-election-accessibility-audits. Inclusive Friends Association is a disability advocacy nonprofit, led by women, that "employs data to address inclusion and participation challenges of [PLWDs] in Nigeria through advocacy, training, and research[,]" focusing on gender, democracy, good governance. "About Us, Inclusive Friends Association (IFA)," http://inclusivefriends.org/about-us/.

233. Chapter 2, note 152, and accompanying text.

234. Chapter 2, note 153, and accompanying text.

235. See Philip C. Aka, *Human Rights in Nigeria's External Relations: Building the Record of a Moral Superpower* (Lanham, MD: Lexington Books, 2017), 126.

236. See Chapter 1, notes 119–120, and accompanying texts.

237. See Alexis Akwagyiram, "Muhammadu Buhari: Nigeria's Converted Democrat Comes Back from the Brink," *Reuters* (February 26, 2019), https://www.reuters.com/article/us-nigeria-election-buhari-newsmaker/muhammadu-buhari-nigerias-converted-democrat-comes-back-from-the-brink-idUSKCN1QF2SN.

238. See John Campbell and Matthew T. Page, *Nigeria: What Everyone Needs to Know* (New York: Oxford University Press, 2018), 1 (pointing out that even though Obasanjo's presidency was ostensibly civilian, "his [governance] style was that of a military ruler"). For example, Obasanjo did not enforce court judgments that he did not like. Ibid., pp. 1–2. See also Wole Soyinka, "Lessons from Nigeria's Militarized Democratic Experiment," *New York Times*, Op-Ed. (October 19, 2019), https://www.nytimes.com/2019/10/09/opinion/nigeria-militarized-democratic-experiment.html; and Etim O. Frank and Wilfred I. Ukpere, "The Impact of Military Rule on Democracy in Nigeria," *Journal of Social Sciences*, 33(3) (2012), 285–292, https://www.researchgate.net/publication/261672856_The_Impact_of_Military_Rule_on_Democracy_in_Nigeria.

239. See Aka, *Human Rights in Nigeria's External Relations*, note 235, p. 82; and Michelle Gavin, "The Post-Presidential Legacy of Nigeria's Goodluck Jonathan," Council on Foreign Relations (July 16, 2019), https://www.cfr.org/blog/post-presidential-legacy-nigerias-goodluck-jonathan.

240. Soyinka, note 238.

241. For an elaboration of the guns-over-butter dichotomy, see Alan Farley, "What Does 'Guns and Butter' Refer To?" *Investopedia* (updated February 11, 2020), https://www.investopedia.com/ask/answers/08/guns-butter.asp.

242. See, for example, Dennis A. Ityavyar, "The State, Class[,] and Health Services in Nigeria," *Africa Spectrum*, 22(3) (1987), 285–314, https://www.jstor.org/stable/40174297.

243. See Annalisa Merelli, "No Benevolent Dictators: 150 Years of Data Proves It: Strongmen are Bad for the Economy," *Quartz* (August 19, 2019), https://qz.com/1688397/data-proves-it-authoritarian-leaders-are-bad-for-the-economy/

244. See Philip C. Aka, "The Senegambia Confederation in Historical Perspective," *in African Intellectuals and the State of the Continent: Essays in Honor of Professor Sulayman S. Nyang*, eds. Olayiwola Abegunrin and Sabella Abidde (Newcastle upon Tyne, UK: Cambridge Scholars Publishing, 2018), 37, 50. As this piece elaborated, political culture consists of basic attitudes about political life that are widely shared within a particular community. These shared values are divisible into the three clusters of: attitudes toward authority, attitudes toward society, and attitudes toward politics, especially the state. Ibid., p. 51.

245. See generally Claude Ake, *Democracy and Development in Africa* (Washington, DC: Brookings Institution Press, 1996).

246. Opoku Agyeman, *The Failure of Grassroots Pan-Africanism: The Case of the All-African Trade Union Federation* (Lanham, Boulder, New York, and Oxford, Lexington Books), 345, note 96, citing T.M. Frank, ed., *Why Federations Fail* (New York: New York University Press, 1968), 169.

247. See Aka and Balogun, note 157, pp. 25–47 ("Primer on Nigeria, 'Giant of Africa'").

248. Ngozi C. Umeh and Ramola Adeola, "Nigeria," in *African Disability Rights Yearbook* (2013), 277, 290.

Chapter 4

Improving Disability Laws under Nigeria's Fourth Republic

Ten Steps into the Future

INTRODUCTION

This chapter sets forth proposals for improving the capability of the Nigerian national government, under the Fourth Republic, to design and implement disability laws aimed at improving the welfare of PLWDs in the country. The proposals consist of a package of ten measures, underlain by improved civilian rule as predicate. With Chapter 3, this material ranks as the centerpiece of the book. While Chapter 3 chronicles, arguably negatively, the failures of the national government relating to the welfare of PLWDs, this chapter looks, arguably positively, on what can be done to remediate or minimize the effect of those failures on the lives of PLWDs. The discussion has two interconnected parts: a set of ten targeted measures for improving disability laws under the Fourth Republic; and a statement on the predicate of improved civilian rule that underlies the ten steps.

IMPROVING DISABILITY LAWS UNDER NIGERIA'S FOURTH REPUBLIC:

A Parade of Ten Measured Steps

Consistent with the thoughts of Karl Marx (1818–1883), philosophical analysis must be complemented by solutions designed to change the condition an investigator and his or her society complain about.[1] The wisdom about analysis as a springboard to action in an attempt to address a problem animates this chapter. There are ten steps this chapter identifies and discusses: Better funding of disability initiatives and services; taking data collection on disabilities more seriously; more investment on infrastructure, especially disability-sensitive facilities; taking treaty reporting on disabilities more seriously; and more participation of PLWDs in policymaking related to disabilities. Others are: Minimizing the impact of political violence as a source and driver of disability; minimizing the impact of religion as a source and driver of disability; increased governmental and policymaking attention to issues related to women and girls living with disabilities; more work on raising awareness related to disabilities; and the imperative of a national strategy and action plan on disabilities.

These steps are flipsides of sort to the disabling barriers, pieced together in the preceding chapter as sectors of inaccessibility, which individually and collectively impede the lives of PLWDs. First, the list is more illustrative than exhaustive, and draws from the extensive literature on the subject, including studies published by the WHO,[2] and the World Bank.[3] Second, as the following discussion makes clear, these steps are not mutually exclusive but instead more or less overlap, at some points inextricably. Third, for the best result, these steps must be synchronized, rather than implemented sequentially. Like the sectors of inaccessibility enumerated in Chapter 3, some of the steps generate more discussion than others. However, that, by itself, does not make them more important than others, since, in its own right, irrespective of length, each step is important and part of a seamless whole. A variable underlying these steps as predicate is improved civilian rule under the Fourth Republic. This is consistent with James Madison's timeless notion of "auxiliary precautions," elaborated upon below. The list of proposals comports with the admonition in the *World Report on Disability* to the effect that countries "tailor their actions to their specific contexts."[4] Table 4.1 encapsulates the ten steps, along with conceivable means for realizing each step.

Better Funding of Disability Initiatives and Services

We indicated elsewhere that, because financial barriers impede access to healthcare delivery—including health services for persons living with mental illnesses and other impairments—the hallmark of a good healthcare system is good funding.[5] We reasoned that: Robust funding is the lifeblood of a good healthcare system, and that good healthcare delivery is not a value amenable to realization on a shoestring budget; that how much a nation is willing to devote to healthcare, along with the "opportunity cost," embedded in the level of material sacrifices it is ready to endure to get healthcare for the vast majority of its citizens, including PLWDs, speaks to its seriousness about

Table 4.1. Recap on the ten measured steps for improving disability laws in Nigeria

Item No.	*Step*	*Means*
1.	Better funding of disability initiatives and services	Restructure Nigeria's economy away from its current overdependence on oil to generate money that goes into PLWD welfare; More money from tax that goes into PLWD welfare
2.	Taking data collection on disabilities more seriously	Increased funding and related institutional support for the National Bureau of Statistics (NBS)
3.	More investment in infrastructure, especially disability-sensitive facilities	To reverse the pattern of underinvestment in infrastructure, allocate say 5 percent of the GDP to infrastructural development sensitive to the needs of PLWDs, including maintenance of existing infrastructure, such as mental care centers; Pursue access to basic physical infrastructure as a key element of future economic and human development strategies.
4.	Taking treaty reporting on disabilities more seriously	Revamp the agency charged with this task in a manner that increases salience on disability issues
5.	More participation of PLWDs in policy-making related to disabilities	Legal provision that mandates PLWD participation in policymaking at the pain of penalty for noncompliance
6.	Minimizing the impact of political violence as a driver of disabilities	Provide better funding for disability issues; Promote non-military solutions to conflicts
7.	Minimizing the impact of religion as a driver of disabilities	Maintain the status of Nigeria as a secular state by means that include return to the settlement of 1960 that made Sharia law, alongside with customary law in non-Islamic areas of the country, private law.
8.	Increased attention to women and girls living with disabilities	A government more sensitive to this factor, possible under an environment of improved civilian rule that we propose as predicate to this and other steps.
9.	More work on raising awareness on disability issues	Vigorous media campaign that, for lasting result, should be incorporated into the training of teachers, doctors, architects, lawyers, construction engineers, nurses and the like.
10	The imperative of a national strategy and action plan on disabilities	Fashioning a national strategy and action plan on disabilities, draped in clear lines of responsibility and mechanisms for coordination, monitoring, and reporting across sectors, that integrates all or some of the foregoing steps.

Source: Created by the authors

improving healthcare; and that because few countries in the world have all the resources that they need to meet their healthcare needs, delivery of robust healthcare services requires the use of creative steps in funding, including reducing waste and efficient management of available resources.

The same logic applies here with equal force.[6] We begin broadly with budgetary allocations on healthcare services. As we saw in Chapter 3, over a two-decade period from 2001 until 2021, Nigeria devoted only an average of 4.7 percent of its annual budget to healthcare.[7] This is over 10 percentage point below the Abuja Declaration of 15 percent of the budget—barely enough to scratch the surface of the huge burden of infectious and chronic diseases, mental illness included, that convulses the country.[8] In 2021, the Nigerian national government allocated a paltry 4.45 percent of the budget to health.[9] The niggardly allocation epitomizes a traditionally low budget for public services characteristic of the Fourth Republic. As one British commentator familiar with Nigerian affairs points out, at about $US 30 billion, the Nigerian national government's budget for all services in 2021 is "derisory for a population of more than 200 million people."[10] As the commentator pungently elaborated, "[o]utside oil, [the Nigerian] government raises a petty amount of revenue, proportionally much less than other African states."[11] Many Nigerians are unwilling to pay their taxes not just because they believe their tax proceeds will go down the drain in political corruption, but also because they receive poor services for amenities of every kind, beginning with electricity and water supply.[12]

Next to funding of disability initiatives and services, in Nigeria and many other developing countries, public services for PLWDs "are often inadequately funded," an occurrence which negatively "affect[s] the availability and quality of such services."[13] Consequently "[a]dequate and sustainable funding of publicly[-]provided services is needed to ensure that they reach all targeted beneficiaries and that good quality services are provided."[14] This would minimize the incidence of "excessive out-of-pocket" while making such services more affordable for persons living with disabilities.[15]

In September 2021, the Nigerian House of Representatives announced that it will establish a Disability Trust Fund (DTF) to provide more funding for issues related to disabilities in an attempt to end discrimination against PLWDs.[16] The Chairperson, House Committee on Disability, Ms. Miriam Onuoha, conveyed this information, after a two-day disability-inclusive retreat in Owerri.[17] She indicated that the purpose of the retreat was "to fashion out a robust inclusion of persons with disability in all facets of life[,] [w]hether in mobility or recruitment."[18] She elaborated that "rights and privileges" provided for PLWDs in the country under the Discrimination Against Persons with Disabilities Prohibition Act of 2018, abbreviatedly referred to in this book as the Nigerian Disabilities Act, "have not been properly implemented[,]" adding: "[t]he problem of implementing the law is where we are now."[19] She stated that the DTF idea was a way around "the lack of funds" necessary to facilitate the work of the Committee created in an attempt to facilitate implementation of the Act.[20] Many PLWDs in Nigeria receive rehabilitation from families, friends and, in rare cases, governmental agencies.[21] Many educational institutions in Nigeria lack assistive technologies for disabled students because of lack of money.[22] Also, due to inadequate funding, many PLWDs in the country, especially those resident in rural communities, lack access to disability services.[23]

Where will the money for better funding of disability services come from? As we suggested elsewhere, the Nigeria government can restructure its economy away from excessive dependence on export of crude oil to the world economy to raise money that then goes into funding of healthcare, including mental health services.[24] Secondly, in tandem, the Nigerian national government can generate more internal revenue by reducing corruption and providing more dependable services to citizens that include benefits to PLWDs. Political corruption takes place when an office holder uses his or her public office to pursue private ends and gains.[25] The vice is the bane of public service in Nigeria that, despite the Buhari administration's anticorruption agenda, still remains widespread; during an anticorruption summit in the UK in 2016, then British Prime Minister David Cameron grouped Nigeria among "fantastically corrupt" countries.[26]

Finally, the proposal for a trust fund by the House of Representatives would be a step in the right direction, if the lawmakers will match talk with concrete action. Given the known negative influence of corruption in Nigerian politics and society, such concrete action must necessarily include antigraft safeguards to ensure that any money set aside is used for the purpose and in uninflated contracts.[27] These points make self-evident the imperative of our advocacy for improved civilian rule as predicate to the steps laid out in this chapter for improving disability laws under the Fourth Republic.

Taking Data Collection on Disabilities More Seriously

In addition to improved funding, the Nigeria national government must take data collection on issues relating to disability more seriously. Regrettably, like many countries in Africa, Nigeria has a weak "data culture,"[28] one marked by a deficiency in "credible and robust statistics" that leaves "a big knowledge gap that needs to be bridged."[29] It is a deficiency that one analyst analogizes to "flying blindly,"[30] one which another analyst likens to not "having [one's] own army," an imagery signifying decision making in the absence of reliable data in an Information Age when economic wars are won or lost, based on availability of reliable information.[31] No less than other countries, there is need for Nigeria to build "[a] critical mass of trained researchers on disability," with research skills strengthened in multiple fields like "epidemiology, disability studies, health and rehabilitation, special education, economics, sociology, and public policy," complemented with learning and research opportunities in universities abroad.[32]

The CRPD obligate states parties "to collect appropriate information, including statistical and research data," for various practical purposes, including facilitating formulation and implementation of policies to effectuate the treaty;[33] facilitating Research and Development (R & D) of standards and guidelines for universally-designed goods, services, equipment, and facilities, and the availability of these materials;[34] as well as identifying and resolving the barriers PLWDs face in exercising their rights.[35] In gathering such data, state parties must comply with international ethical standards, including respect for the privacy and confidentiality of PLWDs.[36] In addition, these state parties have a responsibility for disseminating the statistics to their populace, including PLWDs.[37] In the same vein, to facilitate planning and treatment, the National Commission charged with responsibility for enforcing the Nigerian Disabilities Act, the law that made the CRPD part of Nigerian domestic legislation, is empowered to regularly collect data and records on the special education of PLWDs.[38]

The Protocol to the African Charter on Human and Peoples' Rights on the Rights of Persons with Disabilities in Africa (PACRD)[39] provides similarly. To facilitate the protection and promotion of the rights of PLWDs, the Protocol mandates state parties to "ensure the systematic collection, analysis, storage[,] and dissemination of national statistics and data" pertaining to disability.[40] The collection, analysis, storage, and dissemination of these data must meet acceptable ethical standards, including respect for the privacy and confidentiality of PLWDs;[41] dissemination must be in form "accessible to all persons, including" PLWDs;[42] and state parties must involve PLWDs in the design, collection, and dissemination of these statistics.[43] Nigeria has not ratified this instrument. Therefore, the starting point with respect to this proposal is to ratify the instrument and make it part of Nigerian national law, ready for enforcement.

On a broader note, data collection on issues relating to disability is necessary for multiple reasons that overlap the ones above from the CRPD, PACRD, and Nigerian law. For one thing, "[u]nderstanding the numbers of people with disabilities and their circumstances can improve country efforts to remove disabling barriers and provide appropriate services for people with disabilities."[44] More elaborately, it is "essential for increasing public understanding about disability issues, informing disability policy and programs, and efficiently allocating resources[,]"[45] as well as for "monitoring [. . .] progress [. . .]" on policy evaluation, including "diagnosis of disparities in outcomes between people with or without functional difficulties."[46]

To uncover information about PLWDs, such as patterns, and trends, any collected data should then be "disaggregated by population features, such as age, sex, race, and socioeconomic status."[47] Various areas for research on disability the *World Report on Disability* recommends, which we endorse, include: the impact of environmental factors, including policies on disability and measurement of such impact, as well as the quality of life and well-being of PLWDs.[48] Other areas are barriers to mainstream and specialized services, along with strategies for overcoming those barriers in different contexts; accessibility and universal design programs appropriate in low-income settings; influence of factors like health and poverty on disability and the interactions of those factors; as well as the cost and cost-effectiveness of public spending on disability programs.[49]

In 2007, the Nigerian national government established the Basic Registry and Information System in Nigeria (BRISIN), touted as "an integrated and all[-]encompassing system for collection, storage and distribution of data and information to support the management of the economy and socio-economic development."[50] In 2018, the Nigeria Demographic and Health Survey (NDHS) included for the first time a disability module that is based on the Washington Group on Disability Statistics questions, which are themselves based on the framework of the World Health Organization's International Classification of Functioning, Disability, and Health (ICF).[51] The questions address six core functional domains: seeing, hearing, communication, cognition, walking, and self-care.[52] More recently, on January 25, 2019, the Nigerian government issued a new regulation, the Nigeria Data Protection Regulation, many of which concepts mirrored the European Union's General Data Protection Regulation.

These are all steps in the right direction. But the Nigerian government must go beyond these measures.[53] It should also, for example, increase the institutional capacity of the National Bureau of Statistics (NBS), beginning with sufficient funding to do its work. The Bureau was created under the Statistics Act of 2007 as the "apex statistical agency" of the government.[54] There is also the political aspect. "Data helps uncover truth and, in Nigeria, it has been better for the people that run the country for data to not be available."[55] Herein lies the necessity for improved civilian government, underlining this and other steps, as a predicate.

More Investment in Infrastructure, Especially Disability-Sensitive Facilities

Besides providing more money for disability initiatives and services and taking data collection on disabilities more seriously, the Nigerian national government needs more investment in infrastructure to repair the deficit in this sector, the result of an unceasing underinvestment, in the face of a steadily growing population, stretching back to the early days of the country's independence in 1960. Infrastructure comprises physical and organizational facilities necessary for the effective operation of a society and its economy.[56] These facilities include hospitals, clinics, and related healthcare centers.[57] They are the touchstone of a properly developed economy, necessary for improved healthcare delivery,[58] including medical treatment for persons living with disabilities.

In 2016, Nigeria ranked 32 out of 54 countries in infrastructure development.[59] Reports published by the Nigerian national government self-admit the severe disinvestment in infrastructure that the country faces. One such report was an economic recovery plan the national government published in 2017.[60] The Plan identified "deplorable infrastructure" as a main factor undermining economic performance in Nigeria.[61] Another, more recently, is the National Integrated Infrastructure Master Plan (NIIMP), published in October 2020.[62] The Plan "provides an integrated view of infrastructure development in Nigeria, evaluates current stock of infrastructure, establishes sector targets and identifies the investments required to achieve the country's growth and development aspirations over the next 23 years [. . .] from 2020–2043."[63] It is designed as a "blue-print for boosting and modernizing the nation's stock of infrastructure, over the next 23 years" from 2020 until 2043.[64] The Plan is linked to seven key sectors of the country's economy, namely: transportation, energy, social infrastructure, information and communications technology (ICT), housing, agriculture and related resources (i.e. water and mining), as well as security and vital registration.[65] The Plan indicated that "[t]here is widespread consensus that inadequate infrastructure is one of the major constraints to sustained economic growth and development in Nigeria."[66] It observed that despite certain progress, "substantial infrastructural deficit remains across the country[,]" one indicated by various measurement tools, including the Africa Infrastructure Development Index (AIDI), published by the African Development Bank which, in 2020, "placed Nigeria [. . .] at the bottom of the pyramid behind 23 other African countries."[67]

In the light of these diagnoses, it is estimated that Nigeria needs about US$ 100 billion every year to address its deficit in infrastructure.[68] Nigeria's infrastructure problem is so deep-seated it encompasses practically every aspect of the country's national life, all the way town to prison-correctional services.[69]

Take bad roads commented upon in Chapter 1.[70] Numerous accidents every day on Nigeria's poorly-maintained roads lead to injuries that have the potential to result in disabilities like "stroke, paralysis, and [. . .] mental illness."[71] Conversely, fixing Nigeria's infrastructure problem will "catalyze progress across multiple other systems, in particular the economy, health and education."[72] Left to fester, the problem could get worse by 2040.[73] The Nigerian government continues to lament the infrastructure deficit while doing little in practical terms to rectify it.[74] In a nutshell, despite some progress over the past decades, levels of access to basic physical infrastructure, such as clean water and improved sanitation, electricity and (paved) roads in Nigeria are inadequate, given its income levels, faced with rapid population growth, compared to peer middle-income countries in Africa and globally, who, on average, boast "more extensive and better road networks, and better access to electricity, clean water[,] and improved sanitation."[75]

Given the right infrastructure, PLWDs can engage in "basic activities for daily living, such as performing home activities, going to work, to school and using public and private facilities."[76] Nigeria's national government recognizes the key role of infrastructure in the tool-box for improving the welfare of PLWDs. This is judging by comments in the NIIMP. The Plan observed, in these statements so poignant that we need to quote them in full, that:

> Nigeria's infrastructure needs to take into account the needs of people with disabilities.The solution to addressing these needs should not be to create parallel institutions and processes, but rather to adapt existing services to include people with disabilities. [. . .] Accessibility of public and private amenities such as water, transport, education, and healthcare for all citizens is crucial to preventing exclusion and tapping into the full social and economic potential of the populace. Accessibility requires that the entire infrastructural service chain be fully accessible. As an example, in the Transport sector this means that stations, bus stops, airports, etc., should be fully accessible to and usable by people with disabilities. As Nigeria builds new and rehabilitates existing infrastructure, design-for-all or universal design principles should be a key requirement in order to ensure the accessibility needs of people with disabilities (such as the hearing, seeing or physically impaired) are fully met.[77]

Nigeria must invest in infrastructural facilities that meet the needs of PLWDs.[78] To reverse the historical pattern of underinvestment in infrastructure, it does not hurt, if, like with the Abuja Declaration, the National Assembly sets for the country a target of say 5 percent of the GDP for infrastructural development, including the building of new mental health centers and the upgrade of existing ones. Going further, Nigeria needs to pursue "access to basic physical infrastructure as a fundamental component of future economic and human development strategies in [the country]."[79] Keying to improved civilian rule as predicate, the *World Report on Disability*, an influential publication referred to repeatedly in this book, advised that Nigeria "build strong and effective institutions, as well as governance issues and public financial management systems."[80] Only a government stronger than the ones that have held shop since 1999 is in a position to build those strong institutions, within the best tradition of good governance.

Taking Treaty Reporting on Disabilities More Seriously

In addition to implementing the three steps enumerated above, the Nigeria government based in Abuja must take treaty reporting on disabilities more seriously. In its provisions dealing with implementation and monitoring, the CRPD mandates state parties, following their "system of organization," to "designate one or more focal points within government for matters relating to the implementation of the [. . .] Convention," and to "give due consideration to the establishment or designation of a coordination mechanism within government to facilitate related action in different sectors and at different levels."[81] It also requires state parties to "maintain, strengthen, designate or establish within [their country], a framework, including one or more independent mechanisms, as appropriate, to promote, protect and monitor implementation of the [. . .] Convention," taking "into account the principles relating to the status and functioning of national institutions for protection and promotion of human rights."[82] The PACRD embodies more or less similar provisions pertaining to implementation. The Protocol requires state parties "to establish or designate national mechanisms, including independent national institutions, to monitor [its] implementation."[83]

In Nigeria, the national agency tasked with responsibility for submitting reports related to compliance with treaties on PLWDs is the Ministry of Women Affairs and Social Development (MWASD).[84] The agency was established by Decree No. 30 of 1989, under the military regime of General Ibrahim Babangida.[85] The mandate of the agency was to advise the government on gender and children's issues, as well as on issues relating to PLWDs and elderly Nigerians.[86]

As we showed in Chapter 2, Nigeria ratified the CRPD and accepted the competence of its Optional Protocol in 2010. These instruments require state parties to submit initial and periodic reports to the Committee on the Rights of Persons with Disabilities. However, since ratifying the CRPD and accepting the competence of its Optional Protocol, Nigeria has not submitted its initial report, much less any periodic report.[87] The explanation provided for the failure to meet its reporting obligation under the CRPD was bureaucratic incapacity "due to lengthy national processes," in more clear terms, the challenge of "[n]on-existence of administrative structures for effective implementation."[88] As indicated repeatedly in this book, Nigeria is not a state party to the PACRD.

In the light of the reporting failure sketched above, Nigeria may need to revamp the agency responsible for producing and submitting these reports. Two possibilities open up in that revamp, both of which the government should consider adopting. The first is to create a new agency charged with responsibility for the welfare of PLWDs, including production and timely submission of periodic reports under the CRPD. The second is to promote visibility for disability affairs under the current Ministry of Women Affairs and Social Development by adding Disabilities in the nomenclature of the agency, including separate responsibility for production of the periodic reports. South Africa offers an administrative or organizational example here. Here, Nigeria can borrow an administrative and organizational leaf from South Africa. The country has a Department of Women, Youth, and Persons with Disabilities (DWYPD), headed by a director-general.[89]

Proper messaging here is important. Judging from the structure and mandate of the MWASD indicated above, under the Fourth Republic, the bureaucracy related to disabilities remains steeped in the administrative format from the military era, with negative ramifications for the production and submission of periodic reports under its obligations related to the CRPD. This points up the need for improvement in the quality of civilian rule under the Fourth Republic, including improved opportunity for participation in decision making for organizations advocating for PLWDs.

More Participation of PLWDs in Policymaking Related to Disabilities

Along with the four steps enumerated above, the Nigerian national government must strive harder for more involvement of PLWDs in decision making related to disabilities. The CRPD mandates state parties to closely consult and actively involve PLWDs in decision-making affecting them, through organizations that represent them.[90] The PACRD provides similarly, stipulating that PLWDs have a right to self-representation "in all spheres of life" that state parties are obligated to help them realize through various means, including actively consulting and involving them in formulating and implementing "all legislation, policies, programs[,] and budgets that impact" their lives.[91]

Increased involvement of PLWDs and organizations which advocate for them comports with the tenor of democracy which, in its ordinary sense, means that individuals have a voice in matters that affect them more or less directly.[92] On this matter, one notion that comes to mind is the concept of disability-inclusive development. The phenomenon exists when PLWDs can access all stages of the developmental process, specifically, when all persons, able and disabled alike, are afforded equal access to benefits, necessary for their socioeconomic edification and wellbeing, such as education, healthcare services, work and employment, and social protection.[93] One conceivable way to achieve such increased involvement could be a legal provision, well-enforced, that mandates such participation in policymaking at the pain of penalty for noncompliance.[94] Consistent with the abstract and popular constructions of democracy and its tenor, the chances for such proper enforcement increases when more quality is put into civilian rule, a property which, as we indicate repeatedly in this chapter and book, the Fourth Republic lacks.

Minimizing the Impact of Political Violence as a Driver of Disabilities

Under the Fourth Republic since 1999, much like during the military era preceding it, Nigeria has gyrated from one conflict to the other, with negative ramifications for socioeconomic development,[95] including access to healthcare.[96] We denominate these conflicts political violence because they embed some degree of force to achieve a political end, such as the replacement of a current regime with a supposedly better government that will subjectively improve the lives of members of the group perpetrating the conflict.[97] These conflicts include Boko Haram, referenced in Chapter 1,[98] kidnappings and generalized violence in northwestern Nigeria that goes by the name of "armed banditry,"[99] as well as rashes of post-election violence in Northern Nigeria, such as the destructive one that convulsed the country in 2011.[100] Because of these conflicts, compounded by the effects of global warming like flooding, as of December 2020, the number of internally-displaced persons (IDPs) in IDP camps across the country stood at 2.7 million.[101] This number is one of the largest in Africa and hard-hit states include Adamawa, Bauchi, Benue, Borno, Gombe, Kaduna, Kano, Nasarawa, Plateau, Taraba, Yobe, and Zamfara.[102]

Living with violence or in fear of violence is a grievous public health issue.[103] Unsurprisingly, many of the IDPs in Nigeria experienced trauma, depression, and related mental health problems.[104] In 2018, there were about 3.3 million people living with disabilities in Nigeria, amounting to a disability prevalence rate of 2.3 percent,[105] many of them from the northeast of the country due to Boko Haram.[106] In the light of these inauspicious developments, along with the measured steps enumerated above, the Nigerian national government must work to minimize the impact of political violence as a driver of disabilities. It can do so in the short term by providing better funding for disability issues, as indicated in the first proposal above, and ultimately by more quality civilian governance that places more premium on non-military solutions to conflicts.

Minimizing the Impact of Religion as a Driver of Disabilities

Under the Fourth Republic, twelve northern states in Nigeria adopted Sharia law as criminal code, dispensing with the practice since independence that made this variety of law and other species of nonnational law, private law in northern Nigeria.[107] The twelve states, in alphabetical order, are Bauchi, Borno, Gombe, Jigawa, Kaduna, Kano, Katsina, Kebbi, Niger, Sokoto, Yobe, and Zamfara.[108] The implementation of Sharia law in the country kicked off with Zamfara State in January 2000.[109]

The effects of the adoption and implementation of Sharia law were magnified by the introduction of private Sharia instruments, known as Independent Sharia Panels (ISPs), in non-northern cities with sizable Muslim populations, such as Ijebu-Ode, Ibadan, and Lagos in Western Nigeria.[110] Under ISPs, private parties embark on a private arrangement, not supported by the government, to apply Islamic law to settle disputes, whose jurisdiction they consent to and judgment they agree to abide by.[111] Going further, Nigeria's Sharia states created hisbah organization, or Sharia police, charged with responsibility for prosecuting a range of offenses, including "social vices," such as prostitution, mixing of the sexes, and drinking in public places.[112] In the assessment of one scholar, taken together, these actions had the effect of restoring Sharia law in Northern Nigeria "to a state of completeness and a degree of autonomy" never seen before in the country "for over a century."[113] Enforcers of Sharia law in these states include judges known as Alkalis and police that goes by the name Hisbah.[114]

The introduction of Sharia law by the twelve states in Northern Nigeria upset an agreement on the eve of independence, which confined the application of such law, just like customary law in non-Islamic portions of the country, to issues of family and personal status law, such as marriage, divorce, child custody, and inheritance.[115] The introduction also ended the former practice under which the entire nation, including the North, was governed by one criminal code that provided punishments for criminal offenses throughout the nation.[116] As one of the authors indicated elsewhere, the adoption of Sharia law as criminal code in Nigeria's Sharia states is an issue replete with possible negative implication for judicial independence, including the layer of complexity that it adds to the judicial system in the country that pre-1999 "remained nearly secular."[117]

More to the purpose of this discussion and as indicated in Chapter 1, a most visible effect from the implementation of Sharia laws is the amputation of the limbs of offenders for even basic offenses.[118] In these Sharia states, amputation could occur for a crime as bland or pedestrian as stealing a goat or grocery in a marketplace.[119] A conceivable antidote to religion as a source and driver of disability is to minimize the influence of religion in Nigerian politics by maintaining the status of Nigeria as a secular state through means that include return to the settlement of 1960 that kept Sharia law, alongside customary law in non-Islamic areas of the country, as private law.

Increased Attention to Women and Girls Living with Disabilities

In addition to the seven tailored proposals discussed above, the Nigerian government under the Fourth Republic must pay increased attention to the needs of women and girls living with disabilities. Females living with disabilities "are doubly disadvantaged, due to the stigma associated with gender as well as disability."[120] Arguably, this may be matched against the observation that, in many African communities, including Nigeria, men living with disabilities "face high rates of dependency and divorce," and endure the taunts of portrayal as "liabilities to society due to depression caused by the notion that they cannot contribute to their community as" real men.[121]

Yet, overall, women and girls living with disabilities come out much worse, compared to men and boys living with disabilities. "Cultural beliefs around gender roles that favor males magnify the challenges of women and girls [living] with disabilities, who may not meet the norms in terms of beauty or of being a wife and mother, compounded by the myth that women with disabilities will give birth to children who also have disabilities."[122] There are also factors impeding employment opportunities for females, "due to the imperatives of Nigeria's patriarchal society, and prejudice opinions about image."[123] In short, as indicated in Table 2.5 of Chapter 2, which summarized the key clauses in the preamble of the PACRD, as a group, women and girls living with disabilities face multiple forms of discrimination, epitomized by an increased risk of violence, abuse, neglect, and exploitation, amidst high levels of poverty.

Due to the vulnerability to "multiple discrimination[s]" women and girls face, the CRPD mandates state parties to take measures to ensure that these females living with disabilities fully enjoy their human rights and basic freedoms.[124] The PACRD stipulates similarly, including requirements for the design of "[s]pecific measures [. . .] to facilitate the equal participation" of women and girls living with disabilities on an equal basis with others in fields, such as "sports, culture[,] and technology."[125] To build its fledgling credential on human rights while contributing to the African human rights system, Nigeria will have to ratify the PACRD and make it part of its domestic legislation. In the final analysis, however, a durable solution to the whammy of multiple discrimination against women and girls is a government more sensitive to this factor, more likely under an environment of improved civilian rule that we propose as predicate to this and the other measures enumerated in this chapter.

More Work on Raising Awareness

Attitude shapes altitude the same way that awareness and self-education create empathy.[126] However, in Nigeria, as in many other parts of the world, "there is still much misinformation and ignorance surrounding disability."[127] Raising awareness related to disability helps bring to the fore, misconceptions and stereotypes around disabilities,[128] necessary "to improve public understanding of disability, confront negative perceptions, and represent disability fairly," ultimately building the "[m]utual respect and understanding [which] contribute to an inclusive society."[129]

"Collecting information on knowledge, beliefs and attitudes about disability can help identify gaps in public understanding that can be bridged through education and public information."[130] This connects this step to the proposal related to data collection on disabilities analyzed above. Conceivable means within and outside the workplace for promoting such awareness include more education on disabilities, use of correct or appropriate language in conversations bearing on disabilities, increased appreciation of the possible negative impact that a prejudiced society can have on PLWDs, the power of personal example, media engagement that uplifts disabled voices, and direct action, such as support of charities advocating for PLWDs.[131]

Here, media power is so very critical. "Governments, voluntary organizations, and professional associations should consider running social marketing campaigns that change attitudes on stigmatized issues, such as HIV, mental illness, and leprosy. Involving the media is vital to the success of these campaigns and to ensuring the dissemination of positive stories about persons with disabilities and their families."[132] For best result, disability awareness should be incorporated into the training of teachers, doctors, architects, lawyers, construction engineers, nurses and the like.[133]

The Imperative of a National Strategy and Action Plan on Disabilities

Good results do not happen by accident. To the contrary, they must be preceded by careful planning. The welfare of PLWDs is no different. In the light of this logic and wisdom, Nigeria needs to adopt a national strategy on disabilities with a plan of action that establishes "clear lines of responsibility and mechanisms for coordination, monitoring and reporting across sectors."[134] Central to the strategy here is which government agency does the coordination, monitoring, and reporting. The organ that naturally comes to mind is the National Human Rights Commission (NHRC) set up in 1995,[135] paradoxically, during the military dictatorship of General Sani Abacha from 1993 until 1998.[136]

Back to the foundation of the United Nations human rights system, national human rights institutions have been a tool of choice for the pursuit and achievement of human right values.[137] In Nigeria, the NHRC monitors human rights throughout the country, assists victims of human right abuses, and helps the Nigerian national government to formulate policies on human rights.[138] In going about its statutory responsibilities, the Commission adopts a national action plan featuring various activities like a complaint mechanism, seminars, workshops, rallies and related activities.[139] Designed initially as an extra-judicial body empowered to safeguard the human rights of Nigerians, the Commission metamorphosed into a quasi-judicial organ with the power to summon persons, gather evidence, award compensation, and enforce its decisions.[140]

However, given the repression that marked the Abacha dictatorship, its establishment was suspect and probably designed to give Abacha a patina of legitimacy to mask the human rights abuses that marked his government. Under the Fourth Republic since 1999, the Commission appeared to lack sufficient institutional independence necessary for its effective operations. This is judging by an Amnesty International press release in 2012 that advised the Nigeria police to refrain from intimidating the Commission.[141] The context for the issuance of this advice was a summon to Chidi Odinkalu, head of the NHRC's governing board, to appear before the Criminal Investigation Department of the Police for alleged "damaging remarks" made against it by the NHRC chief the Police claimed it was investigating.[142] The putative offensive remarks revolved around a statement on March 5, 2012, credited to Odinkalu regarding acts of massive torture and extrajudicial executions the Nigeria Police carried out annually.[143]

Independent research by Amnesty International (AI) confirmed the impunity, in the light of which finding AI expressed the view that the "intimidation and harassment of the NHRC [was] deeply disturbing."[144]AI advised the Nigeria Police to "immediately stop undermining the Commission's mandate, which is in line with Nigeria's international human rights obligations and commitments."[145] Improved independence for this and other constitutional and statutory agencies stand a better chance of crystallization under conditions for improved civilian rule under the Fourth Republic elaborated in the next section.

THE PREDICTATE OF IMPROVED CIVILIAN RULE

For best results and as a thing of what James Madison long ago likened to "auxiliary precautions,"[146] improved civilian must underlie the steps discussed above as a predicate. Nigeria needs to create an enabling environment that minimizes the likelihood of discrimination against PLWDs. The conceivable way to achieve this goal is to improve civilian rule under the Fourth Republic. The preference of *improved civilian rule* over the term *democracy*, which Nigeria claims to practice since 1999, is deliberate. This is because "government of the people, by the people, for the people," as Abraham Lincoln colloquially defined the term, byword for people-centered governance, has yet to take root in Nigeria.[147] For, although important, procedures, such as elections, are not the only constituent features of a democracy; instead, quality is also a key ingredient in the definition of any democracy.[148] In theory, as well as in practice, democracy is a dynamic notion that entails progressive and widespread application of democratic principles that proceed apace until the phenomenon becomes "the only game in town," through routinization and internalization "in social, institutional, and even psychological life, as well as in political calculations for achieving success."[149] Despite the numerous elections Nigeria has held under the Fourth Republic, Nigeria's electoral system remains flawed with irregularities, election season after election season.[150]

As we pointed out in Chapter 3, under Nigeria's Fourth Republic, two former military dictators, General Olusegun Obasanjo, and General Muhammadu Buhari, have governed for a total of 16 years, out of the 24 years by May 2023 of that Republic. The occurrence leaves only 8 years of rule by civilian leaders: Umaru Musa Yar'Adua from 2007–2010, and Goodluck Jonathan from 2010–2015. Of the two former military-dictators-turned-democrats, Buhari takes the dubious prize for pathetically low-quality governance. Under his "somnolent watch," one UK commentator points out, "Nigeria has sleepwalked closer to disaster," elaborating: "Buhari has overseen two terms of economic slump, rising debt and a calamitous increase in kidnapping and banditry—the one thing you might have thought a former general could control."[151] Because it raises questions regarding the civilian content of a supposedly democratic regime, domination of the political system by former military generals negates civilian control of the military and the police, a key element of democracy.[152] Civilian control of the military is present when there is supremacy of elected officials of state over appointed officers at all levels, but is lacking where, instead, security forces control the civilian population.[153]

It is hard to "underestimate the depth of Nigeria's quagmire" under the Fourth Republic, one analyst stated.[154] "The problem is not so much who leads the government as the nature of [the] government itself."[155] This is because for decades, including the period since 1999 under the Fourth Republic, "the business of government [. . .] has been to control access to oil revenues and earn patronage by spreading petro-dollars to federal and state supplicants."[156] The net result is that "[a]lmost all the energy, drive and wealth creation in Nigeria happens outside [the] government. [. . .] Nigeria grows at night while the government sleeps."[157] Nigeria desperately needs but has still yet to get after more than two decades of experiment with civilian rule under the Fourth Republic, a government "whose energies go not into preserving its own privilege but into providing public goods—basic education and health, rule of law, security, power, roads and digital infrastructure."[158] Nigerian leaders must reform their corrupt, unworking system before what remaining faith citizens still have in the Nigerian system of government evaporates, failing which they will be courting "disaster."[159]

More to the welfare of PLWDs at issue in this book, Nigeria needs a national leadership structure that can perform its treaty obligations relating to PLWDs and motivate other stakeholders to do their part. By its policies and examples, the government sets the tone for behavior in society. These obligations toward PLWDs include, but are by no means limited to, reviewing and revising existing legislation and policies for consistency with the CRPD; reviewing mainstream and disability-specific policies, systems, and services with a view to identifying gaps and barriers and planning actions to overcome them; ratifying the PACRD and making it part of its national law; and crafting a national disability strategy and action plan, with clear lines of responsibility and mechanisms for coordination, monitoring and reporting across sectors.[160] Other obligations include: Allocating adequate resources to existing publicly-funded services and appropriately funding the implementation of the national disability strategy and plan of action; adopting national accessibility standards and ensuring compliance in new buildings, transportation, as well as in information and communication technology (ICT); sponsoring social protection programs to help insulate PLWDs from abject poverty; integrating disability into national data collection systems and providing disability-disaggregated data wherever possible; designing and implementing communication campaigns to increase public knowledge and understanding of disability; and establishing channels for aggrieved PLWDs and organizations that advocate for them to lodge complaints.[161]

Consistent with the stress on duties in the African Charter on Human and Peoples' Rights,[162] in tandem with the national government, the following illustrative stakeholders have a complementary role in the struggle for a better future for PLWDs: academic institutions, PLWDs and their families, organizations representing PLWDs, service providers, communities, and the private sector.[163]

Academic institutions can help by: removing barriers to the recruitment and participation of students and staff with disabilities; ensuring that professional training courses include adequate information about disability, anchored on human rights principles; and, in partnership with organizations representing PLWDs, conducting research on the lives of PLWDs, including minimization of disabling barriers that impede the welfare of these individuals. Arguably, this ties to data collection but also ranges beyond it.

PLWDs can contribute their part to their own well-being by: supporting other people living with disabilities through peer support, training, information, and advice; promoting the rights of PLWDs within their local communities, for example, by conducting access audits, and campaigning for human rights; participating in awareness-raising campaigns and in forums pertaining to the welfare of PLWDs, such as influencing public policy or shaping service delivery; as well as participating in research projects on disabilities.[164] This role harmonizes with the right of self-representation for PLWDs in the PACRD.[165] This doctrine mandates state parties "to recognize and facilitate the right of persons [living] with disabilities to represent themselves in all spheres of life," through various means, including effective advocacy for their rights and inclusion in society, and active consultation and involvement in all laws, policies, and programs that impact their lives.[166] Nigeria is not a state party to the PACRD but needs to ratify the treaty as first step if it must live up to expectation in its responsibilities toward PLWDs. We return to this theme in the Conclusion of this book.

Organizations representing PLWDs can do their part by: engaging in the activities described above for PLWDs and their families, as well as by supporting PLWDs to become more aware of their rights, for example, to live independently, and to develop their skills, as well as supporting children with disabilities and their families to ensure inclusion in education.[167] Service provides can do their part by: carrying out access audits, in partnership with local disability groups, to identify physical and information barriers that may exclude PLWDs; ensuring that their staff are adequately trained about disability; implementing training as required and including service users in developing and delivering training; and ensuring that PLWDs are informed of their rights and the mechanisms for complaints, among other techniques or means.[168]

Communities can help enthrone non-discrimination of PLWDs by challenging their own beliefs and attitudes related to PLWDs in an attempt to improve those beliefs and attitudes; helping to protect the rights of PLWDs; helping to promote PLWD inclusion and participation in their community; ensuring that community environments, such as schools, recreational facilities, and cultural centers, are accessible to PLWDs; and challenging perpetration of violence and bullying against PLWDs.[169] Last but not least, the private sector in Nigeria can complement the efforts of the national government and other stakeholders by promoting diversity and inclusiveness in working environments; facilitating employment opportunities for PLWDs by ensuring that recruitment is equitable, that reasonable accommodations are provided, and that employees who become disabled are supported to return to work; removing barriers of access to microfinance, so that PLWDs can develop their own businesses; ensuring that construction projects, such as public accommodations, offices and housing, include adequate access for PLWDs; ensuring that Information and Communications Technology (ICT) products, systems, and services are accessible to disabled persons, among other means.[170] Given the essentialist capitalist character of Nigeria,[171] the contribution of the private sector is critical.

In a nutshell, civilian rule will become more improved when governance in the country become more people-centered, consistent with the colloquial definition of democracy as government of the people, by the people, for the people. As one observer aptly points out, including PLWDs as productive members of African societies requires "a strong democratic government."[172] The scenario in Nigeria before and during the COVID-19 pandemic was one that Inclusive Futures analogized to shrinking civic space.[173] In the word of one representative of a Disabled People's Organization in the country, "[o]ur relationship with [the Nigerian national] government even before the pandemic had not been quite encouraging. [. . .] [W]hen we talk about partnership with the government, it's not a very encouraging partnership because it's more or less one sided from our part."[174]

We advisedly called the steps enumerated in this Chapter "measured." Our advocacy for improved civilian rule as predicate to any sets of steps designed to protect, promote, and fulfil the rights of PLWD calls to mind the insights of the social scientists Elgin F. Hunt and David C. Colander, elaborating the concept of educated common sense in social science.[175] In their explanation,

> [C]ompared with the capabilities of the human mind, even the most powerful computer counts by using its fingers and toes. The mind processes trillions of pieces of information in illinanoseconds (we don't know what they are either, but we do know they are very small). When the results of the models and the minds diverge, it seems reasonable to rely on the more power computer—the mind. [. . .] Common sense is not sufficient; we must use educated common sense.[176]

The analogy holds here. There are no guarantees with a heterogenous country like Nigeria, but in the sense we conceptualize it here, improved civilian rule could be the glue to the various steps we propose for uplifting the welfare of PLWDs under the Fourth Republic. Various scholars on disability have made recommendations on how to improve the welfare of persons living with disability under the Fourth Republic. Haruna recommended passage of the Nigerian Disabilities Act, now adopted, and implementing it; that the national government should engage in a wide and rigorous public enlightenment campaign against the discrimination of disabled people in the Nigerian society; and that it should introduce a fund, the Disability Tax Fund (DTF), to be used to provide social security protection for PLWDs.[177] Similarly, Eleweke and Ebenso urged the passage of the law (again now accomplished), to be fully implemented across all states in the land, along with the setup of a presidential commission that reports directly to the president, with more money provided.[178]

None of these will count for much without the predicate of improved civilian rule under the Fourth Republic that will form the basis for these obviously insightful recommendations. One disability activist with a hearing impairment once noted that the real problem with lax passage and implementation of disability laws in Nigeria is really lack of political will.[179] The problem parallels the low quality of civilian rule in the country since 1999 under the Fourth Republic.

CONCLUSION

This chapter sets forth workable measures for boosting the capability of the Nigerian government under the Fourth Republic to implement disability laws. Its import is designed to be remedial: driven by the admonition of Karl Marx for social scientists to seek to change the world rather than merely analyze it, the chapter complements and completes Chapter 3 which chronicles the failures of the national government relating to the welfare of PLWDs. The highlight of the chapter is the set of ten measured proposals, underlain by the predicate of improved civilian rule, that it proposes for advancing disability laws in Nigeria under the Fourth Republic. There is no silver bullet solution to the intractable problems Nigeria faces regarding the welfare for PLWDs, but a journey of a thousand miles begins with one fateful step. Such is the wisdom that drives the discussion in this chapter.

NOTES

1. Karl Marx, "Theses on Feuerback, Thesis 11 (1845)," in *Selected Works, Vol. 1, Marx Engels* (Moscow: Foreign Languages Publishing House, 1950), 13–15 ("the philosophers have only interpreted the world, in various ways; the point is to change it"). See also Karl Marx and Friedrich Engels, *The German Ideology, Including*

Theses on Feuerbach (Amherst, NY: Prometheus, 1998), chap. 3 ("One of the most difficult tasks confronting philosophers is to descend from the world of thought to the actual world. [. . .] Just as philosophers have given thought an independent existence, so they were bound to make language into an independent realm").

2. See *World Report on Disability* (Geneva Switzerland and Washington, DC: World Health Organization and the World Bank, 2011), 263–267, https://www.who.int/disabilities/world_report/2011/report.pdf (setting forth a list of nine cross-cutting, rather than specific, recommendations). The list of ten recommendations is: enable access to all mainstream policies, systems, and services; invest in specific programs and services with PLWDs; adopt a national disability strategy and plan of action that is informed by a situation analysis; and involve people with disabilities. Ibid., pp. 263–265. Other recommendations are: improving human resource capacity through effective education, training, and recruitment; providing adequate funding and improving affordability; increasing public awareness and understanding of disability; improving data collection on disability; as well as strengthening and supporting research on disability. Ibid., pp. 266–267. The recommendations were informed by a list of widespread evidence of disabling barriers against PLWDs that the report uncovered, among them: inadequate policies, negative attitudes, inadequate services, problems with service delivery, inadequate funding, lack of accessibility, lack of consultation and involvement of PLWDs even in matters that directly affect their lives, and lack of data and evidence. Ibid., p. 262. These disabling barriers, in turn, contribute to some of the disadvantages PLWDs experience, such as poor health outcomes, vis-à-vis the general populace; lower educational achievements; lower participation in the economic system, evidenced by increased unemployment and lower wages for employed PLWDs; higher rates of poverty; inability to live independently, and non-robust participation in community events. Ibid., p. 263.

3. "World Bank Group Announces New Commitments on Disability Inclusion," World Bank, Press Release No. 2018/012/SUR (July 24, 2018) [hereinafter World Bank Press Release], https://www.worldbank.org/en/news/press-release/2018/07/24/world-bank-group-announces-new-commitments-on-disability-inclusion. See also "World Bank Group Commitments on Disability-Inclusive Development," World Bank, Brief (July 24, 2018), https://www.worldbank.org/en/topic/socialsustainability/brief/world-bank-group-commitments-on-disability-inclusion-development. At a global disability summit in London on July 24, 2018, the World Bank announced a set of ten commitments designed to accelerate global action for disability-inclusive development in key areas, such as education, digital development, data collection, gender, post-disaster reconstruction, transport, private-sector investments, and social protection. The commitments were consistent with the 2030 Agenda for Sustainable Development, adopted by the UN in September 25, 2015. World Bank Press Release. The agenda "is a plan of action for people, planet and prosperity[,]" designed "to strengthen universal peace in larger freedom[,]" with the recognition "that eradicating poverty in all its forms and dimensions, including extreme poverty, is the greatest global challenge and an indispensable requirement for sustainable development." "Transforming Our World: The 2030 Agenda for Sustainable Development." UN General Assembly (September 25, 2015), preamble, https://www.un.org/ga/search/

view_doc.asp?symbol=A/RES/70/1&Lang=E. Consistent with the Bank's strategy to develop human capital around the world, the commitments were also designed to help developing countries invest more effectively in accessible services for PLWDs. World Bank Press Release. The summit was co-hosted by the UK Department for International Development, in partnership with the Kenyan Government, and the International Disability Alliance. The ten commitments were: (1) ensuring that all World Bank-financed education programs and projects are disability-inclusive by 2025; (2) ensuring that all World Bank-financed digital development projects are disability sensitive, including through the use of universal design and accessibility standards; (3) scaling up disability data collection and use, guided by global standards and best practices, such as using the Washington Group's Short Set of Questions on Disability; (4) introducing questions on disability into the Women, Business and the Law survey to better understand the economic empowerment of women with disabilities; and (5) ensuring that all projects financing public facilities in post-disaster reconstruction are disability-inclusive by 2020. World Bank Press Release. Others are: (6) ensuring that all World Bank-financed urban mobility and rail projects that support public transport services are disability-inclusive by 2025; (7) enhancing due diligence on private sector projects financed by the International Finance Corporation (IFC) regarding disability inclusion; (8) ensuring that 75 percent of World Bank-financed social protection projects are disability-inclusive by 2025; (9) increasing the number of staff with disabilities in the World Bank Group; and (10) promoting the Disability Inclusion and Accountability Framework among World Bank staff as a way to support the World Bank's new Environmental and Social Framework (ESF). Ibid.

4. *World Report on Disability*, note 2, p. 264.

5. This whole paragraph draws from Philip C. Aka et al., *The Political Economy of Universal Healthcare in Africa: Evidence from Ghana* (London and New York: Routledge, 2022), 26.

6. This logic calls to mind the Pidgin saying in Nigeria to the effect that "Better soup na money kill am," translatable into "more money, more value" or result. See Akas Baba, "Nigerian Proverbs in Pidgin Language," *Rex Chimex* Blog (October 15, 2016), http://www.rexchimex.com/2016/10/nigerian-proverbs-in-pidgin-language.html.

7. Chapter 3, notes 82–84, and accompanying texts.

8. See Philip C. Aka and Joseph Abiodun Balogun, *Healthcare and Economic Restructuring: Nigeria in Comparative Perspective* (Gateway East, Singapore: Palgrave Macmillan, 2022), 1–24 ("Introduction").

9. *[Fifteen Percent] Benchmark to Health Sector in Nigeria—The Journey So Far* (Abuja: Partnership for Advocacy in Child and Family Health at Scale (PACFaH@Scale), April 2021), pp. 3–4 (including tbl. 2), https://drpcngr.org/15-benchmark-to-health-sector-in-nigeria-the-journey-so-far/.

10. David Pilling, "What is Nigeria's Government for?" *Financial Times* (UK) (January 31, 2022), https://www.ft.com/content/c4025da8-7951-4ed1-bccd-5d546f86786c.

11. Ibid.

12. Ibid.

13. *World Report on Disability*, note 2, p. 266.

14. Ibid.

15. Ibid.

16. Chinonso Alozie, "Establishment of Disability Trust Fund to End Discrimination—Reps," *Vanguard* (Lagos) (September 15, 2021), https://www.vanguardngr.com/2021/09/establishment-of-disability-trust-fund-to-end-discrimination-reps/.

17. Ibid.

18. Ibid.

19. Ibid.

20. Ibid.

21. "Nigeria Situational Analysis Version II–June 2020," *Inclusive Futures: Promoting Disability Inclusion* (Brighton, UK: Institute of Development Studies, July 2020), 8, https://opendocs.ids.ac.uk/opendocs/bitstream/handle/20.500.12413/15561/DID%20SITAN%20Nigeria%20V2%20July%202020.pdf?sequence=1&isAllowed=y.

22. Ibid.

23. Ibid., p. 9.

24. See Aka and Balogun, note 8, 25–47 ("Primer on Nigeria, 'Giant of Africa'").

25. "What is Corruption?" Transparency International, https://www.transparency.org/en/what-is-corruption; Gabriella R. Montinola, "Political Corruption" *Encyclopedia.com*, https://www.encyclopedia.com/international/legal-and-political-magazines/political-corruption. On the scale of this problem in the country, see, for example, Ebenezer Obadare, "Nigeria's All Too Familiar Corruption Ranking Begs Broader Questions Around Normative Collapse," Council on Foreign Relations (Blog) (February 24, 2022), https://www.cfr.org/blog/nigerias-all-too-familiar-corruption-ranking-begs-broader-questions-around-normative-collapse (opining that endemic corruption in Nigeria poses an immense challenge to its stability, despite efforts by the government to tackle the problem). See also *Corruption in Nigeria: Patterns and Trends: Second Survey on Corruption as Experienced by the Population* (Vienna, Switzerland: United Nations Office on Drugs and Crime, December 2019), https://www.undoc.org/documents/data-and-analysis/statistics/corruption/nigeria/Corruption-in-Nigeria_2019_standard_res_11MB.pdf. For a statement on the rifeness of corruption and related graft in Nigerian popular life, see Daniel Jordan Smith, *A Culture of Corruption: Everyday Deception and Popular Discontent in Nigeria* (Princeton, NJ: Princeton University Press, 2007).

26. See, for example, Don Melvin, "David Cameron calls Afghanistan, Nigeria 'Fantastically Corrupt,'" *CNN* (May 11, 2016), https://www.cnn.com/2016/05/10/europe/cameron-corrupt-countries-nigeria-afghanistan-queen/index.html; Sewell Chan, "David Cameron Calls Nigeria Corrupt, and Its President Agrees," *New York Times* (May 11, 2016), https://www.nytimes.com/2016/05/12/world/europe/david-cameron-calls-nigeria-corrupt-and-its-president-agrees.html; and Guy Faulconbridge, "Cameron Says Leaders of 'Fantastically Corrupt' Countries to Attend UK Anti-Graft Summit," *Reuters* (May 10, 2016), https://www.reuters.com/article/us-global-taxavoidance-cameron/cameron-says-leaders-of-fantastically-corrupt-countries-to-attend-uk-anti-graft-summit-idUSKCN0Y11NW.

27. See "Nigeria's Loss of ₦557 bn to Contract Inflation," *Blueprint* (October 7, 2021), https://www.blueprint.ng/nigerias-loss-of-n557bn-to-contract-inflation/.

28. Yomi Kazeem, "Flying Blind: African Governments Need to Fix Their Problematic Relationship with Data on Their Own Countries," *Quartz Africa* (October 16, 2019; last updated October 18, 2019), https://qz.com/africa/1725537/africa-has-a-data-problem-says-mo-ibrahim-governance-report/.

29. N. Amusat, "Disability Care in Nigeria: The Need for Professional Advocacy," *AJPARS*, (1) (2009), 30, 31.

30. Ibid.

31. Kazeem, note 28 (citing Yannick Lefang, founder of Kasi Insight, a consumer data-focused research firm).

32. *World Report on Disability*, note 2, p. 268.

33. Convention on the Rights of Persons with Disabilities, UN General Assembly Resolution No. A/RES/61/106, Annex I (December 13, 2006), art. 31(1), https://www.refworld.org/docid/4680cd212.html [hereinafter CRPD].

34. CRPD, note 33, art. 4(1)(f).

35. Ibid., art. 31(2).

36. Ibid., art. 31(1)(a)-(b).

37. Ibid., art. 31(3).

38. Discrimination Against Persons with Disabilities (Prohibition) Act (2018), *Nigeria Health Watch*, https://nigeriahealthwatch.com/wp-content/uploads/bsk-pdf-manager/2019/02/1244-Discrimination-Against-Persons-with-Disabilities-Prohibition-ACT-2018.pdf., §38(f) [hereinafter DPDP or Nigerian Disabilities Act].

39. Protocol to the African Charter on Human and Peoples' Rights on the Rights of Persons with Disabilities in Africa (hereinafter PACRD), https://au.int/sites/default/files/treaties/36440-treaty-protocol_to_the_achpr_on_the_rights_of_persons_with_disabilities_in_africa_e.pdf.

40. Ibid., art. 32.

41. Ibid., art. 32(c).

42. Ibid., art. 32(b).

43. Ibid., art. 32(d).

44. *World Report on Disability,* note 2, p. 267.

45. *World Report on Disability*, note 2, p. 267.

46. *Disability Inclusion in Nigeria: A Rapid Assessment* (Washington, DC: World Bank, 2020), p. 9.

47. *World Report on Disability,* note 2, p. 267.

48. Ibid., pp. 267–268.

49. Ibid., pp. 267–268.

50. "Basic Registry and Information System in Nigeria," https://brisin.ng/.

51. See "International Classification of Functioning, Disability[,] and Health (ICF)," National Center for Health Statistics, US CDC (January 24, 2008), http://www.cdc.gov/NCHS/about/otheract/icd9/icfhome.htm; *Toward a Common Language for Functioning, Disability and Health ICF* (Geneva, Switzerland: World Health Organization, 2002), https://www.who.int/classifications/icf/icfbeginnersguide.pdf.

52. *Disability Inclusion in Nigeria*, note 46, p. 11.

53. "Nigeria Issues New Data Protection Regulation," Hunton Andrews Kurth (April 5, 2019), https://www.huntonprivacyblog.com/2019/04/05/nigeria-issues-new-data-protection-regulation/.

54. "National Bureau of Statistics (Nigeria)," https://www.devex.com/organizations/national-bureau-of-statistics-nigeria-143915.

55. Kazeem, note 28 (citing Michael Famoroti, partner at Stears Data, a research firm based in Lagos).

56. See "Infrastructure," *Merriam-Webster*, https://www.merriam-webster.com/dictionary/infrastructure (portraying infrastructure as the "underlying structure" of a country's economy and the "fixed installations" necessary for its effective function).

57. There is no universal element to these fixed installations but, broadly speaking, these facilities include streets, roads, highways, and railways; bridges; mass transit, airports, and airways, water supply and resources, waste management and waste water management, power generation and transmission, and information and communication technologies (ICT) or telecommunications, and healthcare centers. See Julia Bello-Schüemann and Alex Porter, *Building the Future: Infrastructure in Nigeria Until 2040*, West Africa Report No. 21 (Pretoria, South Africa: Institute for Security Studies, November 2017), 3 ("Methodology") (dividing the term into four main categories: transportation, energy, water and sanitation, and information and communication technologies); Vivien Foster, and Nataliya Pushak, *Nigeria's Infrastructure: A Continental Perspective* (Washington, DC: World Bank Group, June 2011), 5, tbl. 1, https://doi.org/10.1596/1813-9450-5686 (identifying eight categories: air transport, information and communications technology (ICT), ports, power, railways, roads, water resources, as well as water and sanitation).

58. See William Ascher and Corinne Krupp, "Distributional Implications of Alternative Financing of Physical Infrastructure Development," in *Physical Infrastructure Development: Balancing the Growth, Equity, and Environmental Imperatives*, eds. William Ascher and Corinne Krupp (New York: Springer, 2010), 35–68 (portraying physical infrastructure as "the backbone of any developed economy and a pillar of quality of life").

59. Bello-Schüemann and Porter note 57, p. 7.

60. Federal Republic of Nigeria, *Economic Recovery and Growth Plan* (Abuja, Nigeria: Ministry of Budget and Planning, February 2017), https://estateintel.com/wp-content/uploads/2017/03/Nigeria-Economic-Refom-Plan-2.pdf.

61. Ibid., p. 11.

62. See generally *The National Integrated Infrastructure Master Plan* (Abuja: Federal Ministry of Finance, Budget, and National Planning, 2020).

63. Ibid., p. xv ("Executive Summary").

64. Ibid., p. ii ("Preface").

65. Ibid., pp. i and xvi ("Foreword"; "Executive Summary").

66. Ibid., p. 1.

67. Ibid.

68. See "Nigeria Needs $100bn Annually to Address Infrastructural Deficit–Emefiele," *The Will* (September 25, 2021), https://thewillnigeria.com/news/nigeria-needs-100bn-annually-to-address-infrastructural-deficit-emefiele/ (quoting Godwin

Emefiele, the country's Central Bank governor). See also Foster and Pushak, note 57, p. 1 ("Synopsis") ("Addressing Nigeria's infrastructure challenges will require sustained expenditure of almost [US]$ 14.2 billion per year over [ten years] or about 12 percent of GDP," over and above the estimated US$ 5.9 billion [as of 2011] the country [. . .] spends"); and *The National Integrated Infrastructure Master Plan,* note 62, p. 2 (recounting, citing the Global Infrastructure Hub, an estimate that Nigeria's cumulative infrastructure spending need between 2016 and 2040 was about US$ 878 billion, translating to about US$35 billion per year).

69. See "Nigeria 2020 Human Rights Report," *U.S. Dept. of State* (March 30, 2021), 7, https://www.state.gov/wp-content/uploads/2021/03/NIGERIA-2020-HUMAN-RIGHTS-REPORT.pdf ("Prison and Detention Center Conditions") (pointing out that "[m]any of the 240 prisons [in the country] were 70 to 80 years old and lacked basic facilities," like "potable water, inadequate sewage facilities," and were so overcrowded that one cell in Ikoyi Prison in Lagos State "held approximately 140 inmates despite a maximum capacity of 35").

70. See Chapter 1, notes 94–98, and accompanying texts. See also Bello-Schüemann and Porter note 57, p. 7 (pointing out that, in 2016, "only 16 [percent] of Nigeria's roads [were] paved, compared on average to half the roads in the world's lower middle-income countries"). That same year, only about "3 [percent] of Nigeria's population had access to improved sanitation facilities compared to, on average, more than half of the population in the country's global income peers." Ibid. The situation for access to clean water and electricity is similar. Ibid. Nigeria's African income peers were Cameroon, Cape Verde, Republic of the Congo, Ivory Coast, Djibouti, Egypt, Ghana, Kenya, Lesotho, Mauritania, Morocco, São Tomé and Príncipe, Sudan, Swaziland, Tunisia and Zambia. Ibid., p. 4 (tbl. 1). Its global income peers were Armenia, Bangladesh, Bhutan, Bolivia, Cambodia, El Salvador, Guatemala, Honduras, India, Indonesia, Kosovo, Kyrgyz, Laos, Federal States of Micronesia, Moldova, Mongolia, Myanmar, Nicaragua, Pakistan, Palestine, Papua New Guinea, Philippines, Samoa, Solomon Islands, Sri Lanka, Syria, Tajikistan, Timor-Leste, Tonga, Ukraine, Uzbekistan, Vanuatu, Vietnam and Yemen. Ibid.

71. Mohammed Awaisu Haruna, "The Problems of Living with Disability in Nigeria," *Journal of Law, Policy, and Globalization*, 65 (2017), 103–113, https://www.iiste.org/Journals/index.php/JLPG/article/viewFile/39027/40128.

72. Bello-Schüemann and Porter note 57, p. 3. Emphasis added. See also Foster and Pushak, note 57, p. 1 ("Synopsis") (positing that "[r]aising [Nigeria's] infrastructure endowment to that of the region's middle-income countries could boost annual growth by around 4 percentage points").

73. Bello-Schüemann and Porter note 57, p. 7 (predicting that on the current developmental trajectory, by 2040 Nigeria is expected to rank second to last among its peers of global lower middle-income countries).

74. See Abdullahi Maikudi, "Nigeria Needs [US]$ 2.3trn To Bridge Infrastructural Deficit–Osinbajo," *The Will* (March 18, 2021), https://thewillnigeria.com/news/nigeria-needs-2-3trn-to-bridge-infrastructural-deficit-osinbajo/ (quoting Nigerian Vice President Yemi Osinbajo's statement to the effect that Nigeria requires the equivalent of US$ 2.3 trillion over the next 30 years to address its infrastructural deficit).

According to this news story, the government held out partnership between the public and private sectors as the only viable way to close the gap because the government cannot do it alone. Ibid.

75. Bello-Schüemann and Porter, note 57, p. 1.. For the identity of these peer countries in Africa and globally, see note 70.

76. *The National Integrated Infrastructure Master Plan,* note 62, p. 26.

77. Ibid., p. 27.

78. See "ActionAid Nigeria Calls on Governments to Invest More in Infrastructure and Public Services That Meet the Needs of PWDs," Press Release, ActionAid Nigeria (December 3, 2021), https://nigeria.actionaid.org/news/2021/international-day-persons-disability-actionaid-nigeria-calls-governments-invest-more.

79. Bello-Schüemann and Porter note 57, p. 3.

80. *World Report on Disability,* note 2, p. 10.

81. CRPD, note 33, art. 33(1).

82. Ibid., art. 33(2).

83. PACRD, note 39, art. 34(2). Going further, the Protocol referenced two legal tribunals, namely, the African Commission on Human and Peoples' Rights, and an African court, charged with hearing disputes arising from implementation of the instrument. Ibid., art. 34(4)-(5).

84. Federal Ministry of Women Affairs and Social Development [MWASD], https://socialprotection.org/connect/stakeholders/nigeria-federal-ministry-women-affairs-and-social-development.

85. For more on General Babangida and the dictatorship that he headed, see, for example, Ayodele Akinkuotu, "IBB, the General Who Lost His Last Battle," *Guardian* (Lagos) (August 18, 2021), https://guardian.ng/opinion/ibb-the-general-who-lost-his-last-battle/; and Adewunmi James Falode, "The Military and Nation-Building in Nigeria: The General Ibrahim Babangida Regime, 1985–1993," *International Letters of Social and Humanistic Sciences*, 85 (2009), 37–48.

86. MWASD, note 84.

87. Ngozi C. Umeh and Ramola Adeola, "Nigeria," in *African Disability Rights Yearbook* (2013), 277, 278. See also Jenny Birchall, *Legislation, Policies and Social Exclusion in Nigeria*, K4D Helpdesk Report (Brighton, UK: Institute of Development Studies, November 18, 2019), 8, https://opendocs.ids.ac.uk/opendocs/bitstream/handle/20.500.12413/14810/693_Legislation_policies_and_social_exclusion_in_Nigeria.pdf?sequence=1&isAllowed=y.

88. Umeh and Adeola, note 87, p. 286.

89. See Department of Women, Youth[,] and Persons with Disabilities (DWYPD), National Government of South Africa, https://nationalgovernment.co.za/units/management/31/department-of-women-youth-and-persons-with-disabilities-dwypd.

90. CRPD, note 33, art. 4(3).

91. PACRD, note 39, art. 22(f).

92. See "What Does Democracy Mean for You?" *Everyday Democracy* (June 12, 2015), https://www.everyday-democracy.org/news/what-does-democracy-mean-you.

93. *Toolkit on Disability for Africa: Disability-Inclusive Development*, Module 3, UN Department of Economic & Social Affairs.

94. See Umeh and Adeola, note 87, p. 290.

95. See Philip C. Aka, "Bridging the Gap Between Theory and Practice in Humanitarian Action: Eight Steps to Humanitarian Wellness in Nigeria," *Willamette Journal of Int'l Law & Dispute Resolution*, 24 (Fall 2016), 1–50; and Philip C. Aka, "Understanding the Paradox of Civil Rule and Human Rights Violations under President Olusegun Obasanjo," *San Diego International Law Journal*, 4(2003), 209–276.

96. See Aka and Balogun, note 8, 49–78 ("Features of Nigeria's Healthcare System").

97. See "Political Violence," *Your Dictionary*, https//www.yourdictionary.com/political-violence.

98. See Chapter 1, notes 91–93, and accompanying texts.

99. See "Nigeria," Global Center for the Responsibility to Protect (March 1, 2022), https://www.globalr2p.org/countries/nigeria/; James Barnet et al., "Northwestern Nigeria: A Jihadization of Banditry, or a 'Banditization' of Jihad"? *CTC Sentinel*, 15(1) (January 2022), 46–69, https://ctc.usma.edu/northwestern-nigeria-a-jihadization-of-banditry-or-a-banditization-of-jihad/; James Barnett and Murtala Rafai, "The Other Insurgency: Northwest Nigeria's Worsening Bandit Crisis," *War on the Rocks* (November 16, 2021), https://warontherocks.com/2021/11/the-other-insurgency-northwest-nigerias-worsening-bandit-crisis/; and Oluwole Ojewale, "Rising Insecurity in Northwest Nigeria: Terrorism Thinly Disguised as Banditry," Brookings (Blog) (February 18, 2021), https://www.brookings.edu/blog/africa-in-focus/2021/02/18/rising-insecurity-in-northwest-nigeria-terrorism-thinly-disguised-as-banditry/.

100. See, for example, Dorina Bekoe, "Nigeria's 2011 Elections: Best Run, But Most Violent," United States Institute of Peace (August 19, 2011), https://www.usip.org/publications/2011/08/nigerias-2011-elections-best-run-most-violent; "Nigeria: Post-Election Violence Killed 800," *Human Rights Watch* (May 16, 2011), https://www.hrw.org/news/2011/05/16/nigeria-post-election-violence-killed-800#; and Joe Brock, "Nigeria Post-Election Violence Killed 800: Rights Group," *Reuters* (May 16, 2011), https://www.reuters.com/article/us-nigeria-violence/nigeria-post-election-violence-killed-800-rights-group-idUSTRE74F71S20110516.

101. "Nigeria," IDMC: Internal Displacement Monitoring Center, https://www.internal-displacement.org/countries/nigeria. See also "Number of Internally Displaced Persons (IDP) in Nigeria from 2013 to 2020," *Statista*, https://www.statista.com/statistics/1237374/number-of-internally-displaced-persons-in-nigeria/.

102. "Nigeria IDP Figures Analysis," IDMC (September 13, 2016), http://www.internal-displacement.org/sub-saharan-africa/nigeria/figures.analysis.

103. See Frederick Rivara, "The Effects of Violence on Health," *Health Affairs* (Millwood), 38(10) (October 2019), 1622–1629, https://doi.org/10.1377/hlthaff.2019.00480. According to Rivara, the health consequences of violence include increased incidence of post-traumatic stress disorder, anxiety, depression, suicide, increased risk of cardiovascular diseases, and premature death. Ibid.

104. "Nigeria Situational Analysis Version II—June 2020," note 21, p. 9.

105. Ibid., p. 15.

106. Ibid.

107. See Jude Egbas, "[Four] Things You Should Know about Sharia Law in Nigeria," *Pulse* (August 12, 2020), https://www.pulse.ng/news/metro/sharia-in-nigeria-4-things-you-should-know-about-islamic-law/y29g15v; "Analysis: Nigeria's Sharia Split," *BBC News* (January 7, 2003), news.bbc.co.uk/2/hi/Africa/2632939.stm; "Nigerian Muslims Welcome Sharia Law," *BBC News* (January 27, 2000), news.bbc.co.uk/2/hi/Africa/620058.stm.

108. See Egbas, note 107; and "Nigeria's Sharia Split," note 107.

109. "Nigerian Muslims Welcome Sharia Law," note 107.

110. Philip Ostien and Albert Dekker, "Sharia and National Law in Nigeria," in *Sharia Incorporated: A Comparative Overview of the Legal Systems of Twelve Muslim Countries in Past and Present*, ed. Jan Michiel Otto (Zuid-Holland, Netherlands: Leiden University Press, 2010), p. 577.

111. Ibid.

112. See Philip Ostein, compiler and editor, *Sharia Implementation in Northern Nigeria 1999–2006: A Sourcebook* (Sharia in Africa.net, 2007), http://www.sharia-in-africa.net/media/publications/sharia-implementation-in-northern-nigeria-volume-six/Chapter%208%20Part%20II.pdf.

113. Ostien and Dekker, note 110, p. 576.

114. Egbas, note 107.

115. Ostien and Dekker, note 110, p. 567 (commenting on "the Settlement of 1960"). Supported by the departing British colonial authorities, the settlement was necessary to protect basic rights for all citizens and to promote economic relations in the new nation. Ibid., pp. 566–67.

116. See Ostien & Dekker, note 110, pp. 555–612

117. Philip C. Aka, "Judicial Independence under Nigeria's Fourth Republic: Problems and Prospects," *California Western International Law Journal,* 45(1) (Fall 2017), 1, 41–42.

118. See Chapter 1, notes 106–107, and accompanying text.

119. Ibid.

120. Brigitte Rohwerder, "Disability Stigma in Developing Countries," *K4D Helpdesk Report* (May 9, 2018), 2, https://opendocs.ids.ac.uk/opendocs/bitstream/handle/20.500.12413/13795/Disability_stigma_in_developing_countries.pdf?sequence=1. See also "Factsheet on Persons with Disabilities," UN Department of Economic & Social Affairs Disability, https://www.un.org/development/desa/disabilities/resources/factsheet-on-persons-with-disabilities.html ("Women with disabilities are recognized to be multiply disadvantaged, experiencing exclusion on account of their gender and their disability").

121. Sarah G. Brouillard, "Disability Inequality in Developing African Countries: A Comparison of Disability Legislation and Social Rights in Mali and Niger," *Story Maps* (December 8, 2020), https://storymaps.arcgis.com/stories/e8f5bbadc9594b0da39cbaa7fa1bfbbb.

122. *Disability Inclusion in Nigeria,* note 46, p. ix.

123. "Nigeria Situational Analysis Version II–June 2020," note 21, p. 6.

124. CRPD, note 33, art. 6(1).

125. PACRD, note 39, art. 27(i).

126. "Why It's Important to Raise Awareness Around Disabilities," Weaver Industries (Blog), https://www.weaverindustries.org/blog-details/why-its-important-to-raise-awareness-around-disabilities#:~:text=Creating%20acceptance%20is%20a%20vital,posts%20with%20friends%20and%20family.

127. "How to Promote Disability Awareness," Calvert Trust Exmoor, https://calvertexmoor.org.uk/news/how-promote-disability-awareness/?gclid=CjwKCAjwur-SBhB6EiwA5sKtjilp4wG4Pny5jldbbt2BHXkW4TGLrF1vi3EEz2gQ5D-7u79Js1UdgRoCFo4QAvD_BwE. Founded in 1978, Calvert Trust is a UK charity which works to "challeng[e] disability through outdoor" activities in the countryside. "About Us," Calvert Trust Exmoor, https://calvertexmoor.org.uk/about-us/; "History," Calvert Trust Exmoor, https://calvertexmoor.org.uk/history/. The mission of the organization "is to enable people with disabilities to achieve their potential through the challenge of adventurous activities, to improve the understanding of disability[,] and to encourage the integration of disabled and able-bodied across society." "About Us," Calvert Trust Exmoor.

128. "Why It's Important to Raise Awareness Around Disabilities," note 126.

129. *World Report on Disability*, note 2, p. 267.

130. Ibid.

131. "How to Promote Disability Awareness," note 127.

132. *World Report on Disability*, note 2, p 267.

133. Umeh and Adeola, note 87, p. 290.

134. *World Report on Disability*, note 2, p. 268.

135. See May Agbamuche-Mbu, "Nigeria and its Human Rights Commission," *This Day Live* (Lagos) (April 2, 2015), http://www.thisdaylive.com/articles/nigeria-and-its-human-rights-commission/191769/.

136. See, for example, "Sani Abacha: Nigerian Military Leader," *Encyclopedia Britannica* (Last Updated March 3, 2022), https://www.britannica.com/biography/Sani-Abacha; and "Sani Abacha," Religion and Public Life, Harvard Divinity School, https://rpl.hds.harvard.edu/faq/sani-abacha.

137. See *National Human Rights Institutions: History, Principles, Roles[,] and Responsibilities*, Professional Training Series No. 4 (New York: Office of the UN High Commissioner for Human Rights, 2010), 9, https://www.ohchr.org/sites/default/files/Documents/Publications/PTS-4Rev1-NHRI_en.pdf.

138. Agbamuche-Mbu, "Nigeria and Its Human Rights Commission," note 135.

139. See Nneka Amalu and Moyosore Adetu, "The Role of the National Human Rights Commission (NHRC) in Post Conflict Situations in Nigeria," *AFRREV IJAH: An International Journal of Arts and Humanities*, 8(1) (March 2019), 132, doi: 10.4314/ijah.v8i1.12.

140. See "National Human Rights Commission of Nigeria" (October 17, 2013), https://www.upr-info.org/sites/default/files/document/nigeria/session_17_-_october_2013/nhrc-nigeria_upr17_nga_e_main.pdf.

141. See "Nigeria: End Police Intimidation of National Human Rights Commission," Amnesty International (April 13, 2012), https://www.amnesty.org/en/latest/news/2012/04/nigeria-end-police-intimidation-national-human-rights-commission/.

142. Ibid.

143. Ibid.

144. Ibid.

145. Ibid.

146. A notion that comes to mind here is James Madison's insights related to "auxiliary precautions." See James Madison, Federalist Paper No. 51 (1788), *reprinted* in Bill of Rights Institute, https://billofrightsinstitute.org/primary-sources/federalist-no-51 (opining that while popular sovereignty embedded in dependence on the people remains "the primary control on the government," at the same time, "experience has taught mankind the necessity of auxiliary precautions").

147. Philip C. Aka, *Human Rights in Nigeria's External Relations: Building the Record of a Moral Superpower* (Lanham, Boulder, New York, and London: Lexington Books, 2017), p. 125.

148. Ibid.

149. Ibid.

150. See Emmanuel Remi Aiyede, "Nigeria's Electoral System is Still Broken," *Conversation* (May 9, 2021), https://theconversation.com/nigerias-electoral-system-is-still-broken-heres-a-list-of-whats-urgent-159693.

151. Piling, note 10.

152. Aka, note 147, pp. 127–128.

153. Ibid., p. 128.

154. Piling, note 10.

155. Ibid.

156. Ibid.

157. Ibid.

158. Ibid.

159. Ibid.

160. See *World Report on Disability*, note 2, p. 268.

161. See ibid.

162. See Organization of African Unity (OAU), African Charter on Human and Peoples' Rights ("Banjul Charter"), CAB/LEG/67/3 rev. 5 (June 27, 1981), 21 I.L.M. 58 (1982), art. 27–29, https://www.refworld.org/docid/3ae6b3630.html. Of particular import here are: art. 27(2) ("The rights and freedoms of each individual shall be exercised with due regard to the rights of others, collective security, morality and common interest"); art. 28 ("Every individual shall have the duty to respect and consider his fellow beings without discrimination, and to maintain relations aimed at promoting, safeguarding and reinforcing mutual respect and tolerance"); and art. 29(2) (Every individual has a duty "[t]o serve his national community by placing his physical and intellectual abilities at its service").

163. See *World Report on Disability*, note 2, pp. 269–270.

164. See ibid., p. 270.

165. PACRD, note 39, art. 22

166. Ibid., art. 22(d) and 22(f).

167. *World Report on Disability*, note 2, p. 269.

168. Ibid.

169. Ibid., p. 270.

170. Ibid., p. 269.

171. See Piling, note 10, pointing out that, under the Fourth Republic since 1999, much of the energy, drive and wealth creation in Nigeria takes place within the private sector. "New unregulated businesses in the booming tech sector, fashion, design[,] and the creative arts are flourishing. Every day, tens of millions of Nigerians somehow get by, despite the efforts of those supposedly looking out for them." Ibid. Because of its enormous natural and human resource potentials that for some earn it the moniker of the "giant of Africa," Nigeria remains a haven for investors despite the proverbial dysfunctionality of its politics. See, for example, Olayinka Sodiq, "[Ten] Best African Countries to Invest in 2022," *Business Insider Africa* (February 5, 2022), https://africa.businessinsider.com/local/markets/10-best-african-countries-to-invest-in-2022/whvt6nq.

172. Brouillard, note 121.

173. *Consequences of Exclusion: A Situation Report on Organizations of People with Disabilities and COVID-19 in Bangladesh, Nigeria, and Zimbabwe* (London, UK: Inclusive Futures. September 2021), 38, https://www.sddirect.org.uk/media/2268/english-situation-report-opds-covid-19-report-final.pdf.

174. Ibid.

175. Elgin F. Hunt and David C. Colander, *Social Science: An Introduction to the Study of Society,* 12th Edition (Boston, New York, and San Francisco: Pearson, 2005), 20.

176. Ibid.

177. Mohammed Awaisu Haruna, "The Problem of Living with Disability in Nigeria," *Journal of Law, Policy[,] and Globalization,* 65 (2017), 103, 111, https://www.iiste.org/Journals/index.php/JLPG/article/viewFile/39027/40128.

178. C. Jonah Eleweke and Jannine Ebenso, "Barriers to Accessing Services by People with Disabilities in Nigeria: Insights from a Qualitative Study," *Journal of Educational & Social Research*, 6(2) (2016), 113–122, doi:10.5901/jesr.2016.v6n2p113.

179. Julius Shemang, interview in "Government and Disability Activism in Nigeria," *Poor Magazine* (July 1, 2016), https://www.poormagazine.org/node/5549.

Conclusion and Prospects for the Future

IMPROVING DISABILITY LAWS UNDER THE FOURTH REPUBLIC

Nigeria's ratification of the CRPD and its acceptance of the individual-complaint and inquiry procedures of the CRPD's Optional Protocol, was climaxed by its enactment in 2018 of its legislation prohibiting discrimination against PLWDs, referred to in this book as Nigerian Disabilities Act, which made these instruments part of its domestic law. This composite of positive occurrences presents an opportune moment for a midrange examination of the country's implementation of its obligations related to the welfare of PLWDs that this book undertakes.

The book's argument revolves around the proposition that the Nigerian national government, as the face of the Nigerian state in its relations with other countries, has been lethargic at best toward its international obligation, indicated by treaties that it has ratified, pertaining to the welfare of PLWDs in the country. To correct the lackadaisicalness, we have proposed a set of ten targeted measures for advancing disability laws under the latest instalment of civilian rule, in the lexicon of Nigerian constitutional history, referred to as the Fourth Republic. Nigeria's Nobel laureate Wole Soyinka once labelled Nigeria's democracy under the Fourth Republic as "militarized democratic experiment."[1] In the light of that assessment, the proposals for improvement this book makes are underlain by the predicate of improved civilian rule.

To support the argument of this study anchored on better implementation of disability laws this book makes, we sketched the background history of disabilities in Nigeria from the precolonial to postcolonial eras, including the characteristic features, that mark each era (Chapter 1); set forth the global and regional regimes of disability laws pertaining to the obligation of the Nigerian government for its own sake and as a guide to assessment of performance (Chapter 2); found the performance of the government severely wanting, based on a benchmark of ten sectors of inaccessibility for PLWDs (Chapter 3); and proposed a set of targeted measures, underlain by better civilian rule, Chapter 4, as solution to the problem we highlighted in Chapter 3.

Three characteristics features this book unearthed in Chapter 1 are the sources of disabilities and prevalence, representative laws and policies, and societal attitudes toward PLWDs. Key takeaways included the growth in the number and proportions of sources or drivers of disability in the postcolonial period, all the way up to the Fourth Republic, matched against a troubling paucity of representative laws and policies, especially in the field of mental health, and a recentness in disability activism. The analysis in Chapter 2 focused on the global regime on disability anchored on the UN human rights system, and on the regional regime, based on the African human rights system. Instructively, the examination covered the Protocol to the African Charter on Protocol to the African Charter on Human and Peoples' Rights on the Rights of Persons with Disabilities in Africa (PACRD), adopted by the African Union in 2018, that Nigeria has not yet ratified. We return to this issue shortly in this conclusion.

Chapter 3 marshals and discusses ten sectors of inaccessibility that impede the lives of PLWDs in Nigeria, including health, education, employment, and social protection—and the extent of the gap in the performance of the Nigerian national government relating to its responsibilities toward PLWDs. Consistent with our belief about the ability of the past to shape current policies, the discussion includes a statement on the negative role of long military rule until 1999 on the welfare of PLWDs in the country. Chapter 4 makes proposals on the viable way forward, packaged in a set of ten measures, including better funding of disability matters, better data collection, repairing the infrastructure deficit of the country that dates back to the early years of independence, and attention to women and girls with disabilities. The discussion concludes with a statement on the need to improve the quality of democratic rule in the country, for obvious reasons, deliberately denominated civilian rule, without which implementation of any proposals, no matter how high-minded, stands little chance of success.

Nigeria's ratification of the CRPD, its acceptance of the individual-complaint and inquiry procedures of the CRPD's Optional Protocol, and its enactment of the Nigerian Disabilities Act, which made these instruments part of its domestic law, afford an opportune moment for a midrange examination this book undertakes of the country's implementation of its obligations related to the welfare of PLWDs. The notion of PLWDs as a set of individuals "whose bodies do not work," or who "look different[] or act differently" or lack capacity for "productive work"[2] is an anachronistic one fit for relegation to the dustbin of history. Instead, as indicated in this book's introduction and reiterated subsequently, PLWDs are vectors of immense untapped potentials capable of contributing to socioeconomic development that the Nigerian national government must work diligently to unlock and harness.[3] As Bill Clinton said, in his contribution to the affirmative action debate in the US, campaigning for president many years ago, "I don't think we've got a person to waste."[4] The same wisdom applies here with respect to the untapped potentials of the estimated 25–30 million PLWDs in Nigeria. No different from their fellow citizens, PLWDs are *also* Nigerians, to whom the national government owes an obligation, freely and voluntarily assumed, of freedom from discrimination based on disabilities.[5]

PROSPECTS FOR THE FUTURE

Prospects for the future will depend on the actions of the Nigerian leadership, joined with civil society, including organizations who advocate for PLWDs. There is no better time than now to heed the appeal by enlightened voices for Nigeria and other countries to "create enabling environments" that benefit both PLWDs and the larger community.[6] First, Nigeria needs to unambiguously prohibit discrimination based on disability. The way to do that is to write it into its highest law, the constitution. The 1999 Constitution, undergirding the Fourth Republic, contains provisions that arguably prohibit discrimination based on disability. These include the likes of: § 42(2) which prohibits discrimination based on the circumstances of a person's birth;[7] § 34, which guarantees "e]very individual" respect for the dignity of his or her person, including freedom from torture, involuntary servitude, and forced labor;[8] and § 35 which guarantees "[e]very person" personal liberty, free of deprivation, except in specified circumstances permitted by law.[9] However, these provisions are indirect. Nigeria needs a constitutional provision that prohibits discrimination in clear terms.

It could even go further. A provision of the same higher law "*enjoins* the State to carry out its social objectives towards ensuring that all citizens without discrimination on any group whatsoever have the opportunity for securing adequate means of livelihood as well as adequate opportunity to secure suitable employment."[10] With respect to economic objectives, the constitution provides that "[t]he State *shall* direct its policy toward ensuring—[. . .] that suitable and adequate shelter, suitable and adequate food, reasonable national minimum living wage, old age care and pensions, and unemployment, sick benefits and welfare for the disabled are provided for all citizens."[11] However, these commands have little meaning because the provisions under the Fundamental Objectives and Directive Principles of State Policy of the Constitution[12] are statements of aspirations that are nonjusticiable, meaning that aggrieved citizens cannot bring a lawsuit to enforce these provisions when they are violated, as is often the case in Nigeria. The way to go is to make these provisions justiciable.[13] For example, South Africa has a Bill of Rights that explicitly forbids the "state," standing for the government, from "unfairly discriminat[ing] directly or indirectly against anyone on one or more grounds," that includes "disability."[14] Nigerian constitutionalism lacks this key protective feature.

Second, Nigeria needs to ratify the PACRD, whose provisions we have referred to repeatedly in various parts of this book, including Chapter 4 assessing the Nigeria national government's performance of its obligations relating to persons living with disabilities. Because the Protocol is patterned after the CRPD,[15] its ratification will solidify Nigeria's ratification of the CRPD, while simultaneously strengthening its commitment to and participation in the African regional human rights system.

NOTES

1. Wole Soyinka, "Lessons from Nigeria's Militarized Democratic Experiment," *New York Times*, Op-Ed. (October 19, 2019), https://www.nytimes.com/2019/10/09/opinion/nigeria-militarized-democratic-experiment.html.

2. Tom Shakespeare, "Disability, Identity, and Difference," in *Exploring the Divide: Illness and Disability*, eds. Colin Barnes and Geof Mercer (Leeds, UK: The Disability Press, 1996), 95.

3. See Book's Introduction ("Organization of the Book").

4. Quoted in Philip C. Aka, "The Supreme Court and Affirmative Action in Public Education, with Special Reference to the Michigan Cases," *Brigham Young University Education and Law Journal*, 2006(1) (2006), 1, 5, n.19. Then as President, Clinton released a policy statement on affirmative action preceded by a long study. The statement came one month following the handing down of *Adarand Constructors, Inc. v. Pefia*, 515 U.S. 200 (1995), wherein the Supreme Court applied strict scrutiny, its highest standard of constitutional review, to all affirmative action programs. He said, "While our Nation has made enormous strides toward eliminating inequality and barriers to opportunity, the job is not complete." Ibid. Clinton said his administration will comply with the decision, guided by "four standards of fairness," namely: no quotas in theory or practice; no illegal discrimination of any kind, including reverse discrimination; no preference for people who are not qualified for any job or other opportunity; and as soon as a program has succeeded, it must be retired." Ibid. Clinton pled with Americans to mend, not end, preferential programs. Ibid.

5. See Augustine Edobor Arimoro, "Are They Not Nigerians? The Obligation of the State to End Discriminatory Practices against Persons with Disabilities,"

International Journal of Discrimination and the Law, 19(2) (2019), https://doi.org/10.1177/1358229119846764.

6. See Book's Introduction, note 82, and accompanying text.

7. See Constitution of the Federal Republic of Nigeria, 1999, reprinted in Constitute Project, § 42 (1)(a)-(b), https://www.constituteproject.org/constitution/Nigeria_1999.pdf (providing that "[a] citizen of Nigeria of a particular community, ethnic group, place of origin, sex, religion or political opinion shall not, by reason only that he is such a person—(a) be subjected either expressly by, or in the practical application of, any law in force in Nigeria or any executive or administrative action, of the government to disabilities or restrictions to which citizens of Nigeria of other communities, ethnic groups, places of origin, circumstance of birth, sex, religious or political opinions are not made subject; or (b) be accorded either expressly by, or in the practical application of, any law in force in Nigeria or any such executive or administrative action, any privilege or advantage that is not accorded to citizens of Nigeria of other communities, ethnic groups, places of origin, sex, religions or political opinions."); and § 41(2) (stipulating that "No citizen of Nigeria shall be subjected to any disability or deprivation merely by reason of the circumstances of his birth").

8. Constitution of the Federal Republic of Nigeria, note 7, § 34(1)(a)-(c).

9. Ibid., § 35(1)(a)-(e). Instructively, the exceptions include: *persons suffering from infectious or contagious disease, persons of unsound mind,* persons addicted to drugs or alcohol or vagrants, for the purpose of their care or treatment or the protection of the community." Ibid., § 35(1)(e). Emphasis added. Note, however, that the denial of freedom under these circumstances is to provide medical treatment to those individuals and/or to protect other citizens.

10. Constitution of the Federal Republic of Nigeria, note 7, § 17(3)(a). Emphasis added.

11. Ibid., § 16(2)(d). Emphasis added.

12. See ibid., Chapter II, §§ 13–24.

13. For an explanation of this concept, see "Justiciability," Legal Information Institute, Cornell Law School, https://www.law.cornell.edu/wex/justiciability.

14. "Constitution of the Republic of South Africa, 1996, Chapter 2, Bill of Rights," *South African Government,* https://www.gov.za/documents/constitution/chapter-2-bill-rights#:~:text=This%20Bill%20of%20Rights%20is,in%20the%20Bill%20of%20Rights.

15. See Book's Introduction, note 79, and accompanying text. See also Chapter 2, Table 2.5 ("Key clauses in the African Protocol preamble"), and Table 2.6 ("Human rights protected by the African Protocol on disabilities").

References

About Us. Nigeria Social Insurance Trust Fund. https://www.nsitfweb.com.ng/html/AboutUs.cfm.

About Us. Inclusive Friends Association (IFA). http://inclusivefriends.org/about-us/.

Achebe, Chinua. 2012. *There Was a Country: A Personal History of Biafra.* London, UK: Penguin.

ActionAid Nigeria. 2021. ActionAid Nigeria Calls on Governments to Invest More in Infrastructure and Public Services That Meet the Needs of PWDs. Press Release. December 3. https://nigeria.actionaid.org/news/2021/international-day-persons-disability-actionaid-nigeria-calls-governments-invest-more.

Adebayo, Bukola. 2018. Nigeria Overtakes India in Extreme Poverty Ranking. CNN. June 26.https://www.cnn.com/2018/06/26/africa/nigeria-overtakes-india-extreme-poverty-intl.

Adeniyi, Adeyinka Samson, and Michael Emeka Ofiwe. 2015. The Impact of Ethnicity on Nigeria's Political Development: An Assessment, 1999–2011. *International Journal of Research and Development Organization.* 2(12), 71–99. December.

Adetiba, Adedamola, and Enocent Msindo. 2022. Chiefs and Rural Health Services in South-Western Nigeria, c. 1920—c. 1950s. *Social History of Medicine.* https://doi.org/10.1093/shm/hkab116.

Adeworan, Adejumoke. 2019. *The Realities of Living with Disability in Ibadan, Nigeria: An Ethnographic Study.* MA thesis, Department of Disability Studies, University of Manitoba, Canada.

African Center for Strategic Progress. Subregions. https://acstrap.org/subregions/.

African Commission Adopts Draft Protocol on Persons with Disabilities' Rights. 2016.

African Court on Human and Peoples' Rights. https://www.african-court.org/wpafc/basic-information/.

Afzal, Madiha. 2020. From 'Western Education is Forbidden' to the World's Deadliest Terrorist Group: Education and Boko Haram in Nigeria. *Foreign Policy at Brookings.* April. https://www.brookings.edu/wp-content/uploads/2020/04/FP_20200507_nigeria_boko_haram_afzal.pdf

Agbamuche-Mbu, May. 2015. Nigeria and its Human Rights Commission. *This Day Live* (Lagos). April 2. http://www.thisdaylive.com/articles/nigeria-and-its-human-rights-commission/191769/.

Agyeman, Opoku. 2003. *The Failure of Grassroots Pan-Africanism: The Case of the All-African Trade Union Federation*. Lanham, Boulder, New York, and Oxford: Lexington Books.

Aiyede, Emmanuel Remi. 2021. Nigeria's Electoral System is Still Broken. *Conversation.* May 9. https://theconversation.com/nigerias-electoral-system-is-still-broken-heres-a-list-of-whats-urgent-159693.

Ajuwon, Paul M. 2018. Disabilities and Disability Services in Nigeria: Past, Present[,] and Future. In *The Routledge History of Disability,* eds. Roy Hanes, Ivan Brown, and Nancy E. Hansen, 133–150. London and New York: Routledge.

Aka, Philip C. 2018. The Senegambia Confederation in Historical Perspective. In *African Intellectuals and the State of the Continent: Essays in Honor of Professor Sulayman S. Nyang,* eds. Olayiwola Abegunrin and Sabella Abidde, 37–66. Newcastle upon Tyne, UK: Cambridge Scholars Publishing.

Aka, Philip C. 2017. *Human Rights in Nigeria's External Relations: Building the Record of a Moral Superpower.* Lanham, Boulder, New York, and London: Lexington Books.

Aka, Philip C. 2016. Bridging the Gap Between Theory and Practice in Humanitarian Action: Eight Steps to Humanitarian Wellness in Nigeria. *Willamette Journal of International Law & Dispute Resolution.* 24 (Fall), 1–50.

Aka, Philip C. 2014. Judicial Independence under Nigeria's Fourth Republic: Problems and Prospects. *California Western International Law Journal.* 45(1), 1–79.

Aka, Philip C. 2006. The Supreme Court and Affirmative Action in Public Education, with Special Reference to the Michigan Cases. *Brigham Young University Education and Law Journal.* 2006(1), 1–96.

Aka, Philip C. 2003. Understanding the Paradox of Civil Rule and Human Rights Violations under President Olusegun Obasanjo. *San Diego International Law Journal.* 4, 209–276.

Aka, Philip C. 2002. The "Dividend of Democracy": Analyzing U.S. Support for Nigerian Democratization. *Boston College Third World Law Journal.* 22(2), 225–279.

Aka, Philip C. 2002. The Military, Globalization, and Human Rights in Africa. *New York Law School Journal of Human Rights.* 18(3), 361–438. Summer. https://digitalcommons.nyls.edu/cgi/viewcontent.cgi?article=1493&context=journal_of_human_rights.

Aka, Philip C., and Joseph Abiodun Balogun. 2022. *Healthcare and Economic Restructuring: Nigeria in Comparative Perspective.* Gateway East, Singapore: Palgrave Macmillan.

Aka, Philip C., Hassan Wahab, and Yvette M. Alex-Assensoh. 2022. *The Political Economy of Universal Healthcare in Africa: Evidence from Ghana.* London and New York: Routledge.

Ake, Claude. 1996. *Democracy and Development in Africa.* Washington, DC: Brookings Institution Press.

Akinkuotu, Ayodele. 2021. IBB, the General Who Lost His Last Battle. *Guardian* (Lagos). August 18. https://guardian.ng/opinion/ibb-the-general-who-lost-his-last-battle/.

Akinyoade, Akinwale. 2021. Strength Beyond All Odds: Living with Albinism in Nigeria. *Guardian* (Lagos). June 13. https://guardian.ng/life/strength-beyond-all-odds-living-with-albinism-in-nigeria/.

Akwagyiram, Alexis. 2019. Muhammadu Buhari: Nigeria's Converted Democrat Comes Back from the Brink. *Reuters.* February 26. https://www.reuters.com/article/us-nigeria-election-buhari-newsmaker/muhammadu-buhari-nigerias-converted-democrat-comes-back-from-the-brink-idUSKCN1QF2SN

Alozie, Chinonso. 2021. Establishment of Disability Trust Fund to End Discrimination—Reps. *Vanguard* (Lagos). September 15. https://www.vanguardngr.com/2021/09/establishment-of-disability-trust-fund-to-end-discrimination-reps/

Aluko-Olokun, Ayo. 2019. President Buhari Signs Long[-]Awaited Disability Bill into Law. *Nigeria Democratic Report.* January 24. https://www.ndr.org.ng/president-buhari-signs-long-awaited-disability-bill-into-law/.

Amalu, Nneka, and Moyosore Adetu. 2019. The Role of the National Human Rights Commission (NHRC) in Post Conflict Situations in Nigeria. *AFRREV IJAH: An International Journal of Arts and Humanities.* 8(1) (March), 132. doi: 10.4314/ijah.v8i1.12.

American Psychiatric Association. What Is Mental Illness? https://www.psychiatry.org/patients-families/what-is-mental-illness.

Americans with Disabilities Act (ADA). 1990. P.L. 101–336, including changes made by ADA Amendments Act, P.L. 110–325 (2008).

Amnesty International. 2012. Nigeria: End Police Intimidation of National Human Rights Commission. April 13. https://www.amnesty.org/en/latest/news/2012/04/nigeria-end-police-intimidation-national-human-rights-commission/.

Amusat, N. Disability Care in Nigeria: The Need for Professional Advocacy. 2009. *AJPARS* 1(1), 30–6.

Analysis: Nigeria's Sharia Split. 2003. *BBC News.* January 7. news.bbc.co.uk/2/hi/Africa/2632939.stm.

Antwi-Atsu, Grace. 2021. The African Disability Protocol: A Call to Leave No One Behind. *Sightsavers.* August. https://www.sightsavers.org/blogs/2021/08/the-importance-of-the-african-disability-protocol.

Arimoro, Augustine Edobor. 2019. Are They Not Nigerians? The Obligation of the State to End Discriminatory Practices against Persons with Disabilities. *International Journal of Discrimination and the Law.* 19(2). https://doi.org/10.1177/1358229119846764.

Ascher, William, and Corinne Krupp. 2010. Distributional Implications of Alternative Financing of Physical Infrastructure Development. In *Physical Infrastructure Development: Balancing the Growth, Equity, and Environmental Imperatives*, eds. William Ascher and Corinne Krupp, 35–68. New York: Springer.

Assistive Technology. *Disability Insider.* https://disabilityinsider.com/technology/.

Audiovisual Library of International Law. https://legal.un.org/avl/ha/crpd/crpd.html.

Ayub, Akeem Olalekan, and Anifowose Jimoh Rasaki. 2021. Barriers in Accessing Healthcare Services by Patients with Disabilities in Nigerian Hospitals. *Gusau International Journal of Management and Social Sciences, Federal University, Gusau.* 4(1), 280–296.

The Babangida Government. 1991. In *Nigeria: A Country Study*, Helen Chapin Metz, *ed.* Washington, DC: GPO for the Library of Congress. http://countrystudies.us/nigeria/73.htm.

Baba, Akas. 2016. Nigerian Proverbs in Pidgin Language. *Rex Chimex* Blog. October 15. http://www.rexchimex.com/2016/10/nigerian-proverbs-in-pidgin-language.html.

Balogun, Joseph A., and Philip C. Aka. 2022. Strategic Reforms to Resuscitate the Nigerian Healthcare System. In *Nigeria in the Fourth Republic: Confronting the Contemporary Political, Economic, and Social Dilemmas,* ed. E. Ike Udogu, 79–111. Lanham, Boulder, New York, and London: Lexington Books.

Barnet, James, Murtala Ahmed Rufa'i, and Abdulaziz Abdulaziz. 2022. Northwestern Nigeria: A Jihadization of Banditry, or a "Banditization" of Jihad? *CTC Sentinel.* 15(1) (January), 46–69. https://ctc.usma.edu/northwestern-nigeria-a-jihadization-of-banditry-or-a-banditization-of-jihad/.

Barnett, James, and Murtala Rafai. 2021. The Other Insurgency: Northwest Nigeria's Worsening Bandit Crisis. *War on the Rocks.* November 16. https://warontherocks.com/2021/11/the-other-insurgency-northwest-nigerias-worsening-bandit-crisis/.

Barrio, Brenda L., Darcy Miller, Caroline Ojeme, and Deborah Tamakloe. 2018. Teachers' and Parents' Knowledge about Disabilities and Inclusion in Nigeria. *Journal of International Special Needs Education.* 22(1), 14–24.

Basic Registry and Information System in Nigeria. https://brisin.ng/.

Beals, Monique. 2021. Surgeon General Warns of Mental Health Challenges Confronting Youth. *The Hill.* December 7. https://thehill.com/policy/healthcare/mental-health/584656-surgeon-general-warns-of-mental-health-challenges-confronting.

Bekoe, Dorina. 2011. Nigeria's 2011 Elections: Best Run, But Most Violent. United States Institute of Peace. August 19. https://www.usip.org/publications/2011/08/nigerias-2011-elections-best-run-most-violent.

Bello-Schüemann, Julia, and Alex Porter. 2017. *Building the Future: Infrastructure in Nigeria Until 2040.* West Africa Report No. 21. Pretoria, South Africa: Institute for Security Studies. November.

Belluck, Pam. 2022. Covid Patients May Have Increased Risk of Developing Mental Health Problems. *New York Times.* February 16. https://www.nytimes.com/2022/02/16/health/covid-depression-anxiety.html.

The Biggest Barrier for People with Disability is How Society Disables Them. 2021. *Epic.* July 22. https://epicassist.org/the-biggest-barrier-for-people-with-disability/.

Birchall, Jenny. 2019. *Legislation, Policies and Social Exclusion in Nigeria.* K4D Helpdesk Report. Brighton, UK: Institute of Development Studies. November 18. https://opendocs.ids.ac.uk/opendocs/bitstream/handle/20.500.12413/14810

/693_Legislation_policies_and_social_exclusion_in_Nigeria.pdf?sequence=1&isAllowed=y.

Boko Haram in Nigeria. 2022. Global Conflict Tracker, Council on Foreign Relations. Last updated February 24. https://www.cfr.org/global-conflict-tracker/conflict/boko-haram-nigeria.

Brants, Luc, Paul van Trigt, and Alice Schippers. 2018. A Short History of Approaches to Disability in the Netherlands. In *The Routledge History of Disability,* eds. Roy Hanes, Ivan Brown, and Nancy E. Hansen, 151–162. London and New York: Routledge.

Bratton, Michael, and Nicolas van de Walle. 1997. *Democratic Experiments in Africa: Regime Transitions in Comparative Perspective.* New York: Cambridge University Press.

A Brief History of the Disability Rights Movement. ADL. https://www.adl.org/education/resources/backgrounders/disability-rights-movement.

Brief Notes on Nigeria. *Online Nigeria.* http://www.onlinenigeria.com/history.asp.

Brock, Joe. 2011. Nigeria Post-Election Violence Killed 800: Rights Group. *Reuters.* May 16. https://www.reuters.com/article/us-nigeria-violence/nigeria-post-election-violence-killed-800-rights-group-idUSTRE74F71S20110516.

Brown, Ivan. 2018. When is Life Unworthy of Living? Lessons from the Systematic Killing of Children with Disabilities in Nazi Germany. In *The Routledge History of Disability,* eds. Roy Hanes, Ivan Brown, and Nancy E. Hansen, 421–433. London and New York: Routledge.

Brouillard, Sarah G. 2020. Disability Inequality in Developing African Countries: A Comparison of Disability Legislation and Social Rights in Mali and Niger. *Story Maps.* December 8. https://storymaps.arcgis.com/stories/e8f5bbadc9594b0da39cbaa7fa1bfbbb.

Buhari Urges Commission to Assist in Lifting 100 [M][illion] Nigerians Out of Poverty. 2021. *Guardian* (Lagos). January 7. https://guardian.ng/news/buhari-urges-commission-to-assist-in-lifting-100m-nigerians-out-of-poverty/.

Calvert Trust Exmoor. About Us. https://calvertexmoor.org.uk/about-us/.

Calvert Trust Exmoor. History. https://calvertexmoor.org.uk/history/.

Calvert Trust Exmoor. How to Promote Disability Awareness. https://calvertexmoor.org.uk/news/how-promote-disability-awareness/?gclid=CjwKCAjwur-SBhB6EiwA5sKtjilp4wG4Pny5jldbbt2BHXkW4TGLrF1vi3EEz2gQ5D-7u79Js1UdgRoCFo4QAvD_BwE.

Cameron, Debra L., Stephanie Nixon, Penny Parnes, and Mia Pidsadny. 2005. Children with Disabilities in Low-Income Countries. *Pediatric Child Health.* 10(5), 269–272. May-June. doi: 10.1093/pch/10.5.269

Campbell, John. 2020. Sharia Punishments Embarrass Nigeria. Council on Foreign Relations. September 30. https://www.cfr.org/blog/sharia-punishments-embarrass-nigeria.

Campbell, John, and Nolan Smith. 2021. What's Happening to Democracy in Africa. Council on Foreign Relations. May 26. https://www.cfr.org/article/whats-happening-democracy-africa.

Campbell, John, and Matthew T. Page. 2018. *Nigeria: What Everyone Needs to Know.* New York: Oxford University Press.

Cavendish, Richard. 1998. The Treaty of Westphalia. *History Today.* 48(1). October. https://www.historytoday.com/archive/months-past/treaty-westphalia.

Carter, Rosaylnn, Susan K. Golant, and Kathryn E. Cade. 2010. *Within Our Reach: Ending the Mental Health Crisis.* Emmaus, PA: Rodale.

CDC: Centers for Disease Control and Prevention (USA). Common Barriers to Participation Experienced by People with Disabilities. https://www.cdc.gov/ncbddd/disabilityandhealth/disability-barriers.html.

CDC: Centers for Disease Control and Prevention (USA). Disability and Health Overview. https://www.cdc.gov/ncbddd/disabilityandhealth/disability.html.

Chan, Margaret, and Robert B. Zoellick. 2011. Preface. In *World Report on Disability.* Geneva, Switzerland and Washington, DC: World Health Organization and the World Bank. P. xi. https://www.who.int/disabilities/world_report/2011/report.pdf.

Chan, Sewell. 2016. David Cameron Calls Nigeria Corrupt, and Its President Agrees. *New York Times.* May 11. https://www.nytimes.com/2016/05/12/world/europe/david-cameron-calls-nigeria-corrupt-and-its-president-agrees.html.

Chemerinsky, Erwin, and Michael Stokes Paulsen. Common Interpretation: The Preamble. Interactive Constitution. https://constitutioncenter.org/interactive-constitution/interpretation/preamble-ic/interps/37.

Chijioke, Arinze. 2020. Wounded in Battle, Abandoned at Home: Pains of Being a Biafran Soldier. *International Policy Digest.* February 27. https://intpolicydigest.org/wounded-in-battle-abandoned-at-home-pains-of-being-a-biafran-soldier/.

Chinedu, Jude. 2020. Plight of Forgotten Biafran Heroes. *Sun* (Abuja and Lagos). January 17. https://www.sunnewsonline.com/plight-of-forgotten-biafra-heroes/.

Chioma, Unini. 2020. ABU Zaria Denied Me Admission to Study Law Because Of My Disability, Blind Young Man, Deshi Godwin Justin Laments. *Nigeria Lawyer.* October 10. https://thenigerialawyer.com/abu-zaria-denied-me-admission-to-study-law-because-of-my-disability-blind-young-man-deshi-godwin-justin-laments/.

Claasssens, Julie, Leslie Swartz, and Len Hansen, eds. 2013. *Searching for Dignity: Conversations on Human Dignity, Theology[,] and Disability: Conference Proceedings*. Stellenbosch, South Africa: Sun Media Corp.

Clinton, [Bill], and Mrs. [Tipper] Gore. 1999. Combating the Stigma of Mental Illness. Clinton White House. June 5. https://clintonwhitehouse4.archives.gov/textonly/WH/Work/060599.html.

Comstock, Audrey L. 2021. *Committed to Rights: Volume 1: UN Human Rights Treaties and Legal Paths for Commitment and Compliance.* New York: Cambridge University Press.

Constitution of the Federal Republic of Nigeria. 1999. https://www.constituteproject.org/constitution/Nigeria_1999.pdf.

Constitution of the Republic of South Africa, Chapter 2, Bill of Rights. 1996. *South African Government.* https://www.gov.za/documents/constitution/chapter-2-bill-rights#:~:text=This%20Bill%20of%20Rights%20is,in%20the%20Bill%20of%20Rights.

The Convention on the Rights of Persons with Disabilities Training Guide. 2014. Professional Training Series No. 19. New York and Geneva: Office of the UN High Commissioner for Human Rights. https://www.ohchr.org/Documents/Publications/CRPD_TrainingGuide_PTS19_EN%20Accessible.pdf.

Corruption in Nigeria: Patterns and Trends: Second Survey on Corruption as Experienced by the Population. 2019. Vienna, Switzerland: United Nations Office on Drugs and Crime. December. https://www.undoc.org/documents/data-and-analysis/statistics/corruption/nigeria/Corruption-in-Nigeria_2019_standard_res_11MB.pdf.

Council of Ontario Universities. Understanding Barriers to Accessibility. https://www.uottawa.ca/respect/sites/www.uottawa.ca.respect/files/accessibility-cou-understanding-barriers-2013-06.pdf.

Country Background Note: Nigeria. 2019. London: Home Office. Updated December 5. https://assets.publishing.service.gov.uk/government/uploads/system/uploads/attachment_data/file/856368/Nigeria_-_Background_-_CPIN_-_v2.0__January_2020__gov.uk.pdf.

Countries in the World by Population (2020). *Worldometers.* https://www.worldometers.info/world-population/population-by-country/.

Crawford, Sharika. Beyond the Scramble: African Veterans, the Second World War and Decolonization in the World History Classroom. *World History Connected.* https://worldhistoryconnected.press.uillinois.edu/12.1/crawford.html

Crow, Kevin L. 2008. Four Types of Disabilities: Their Impact on Online Learning. Tech Trends: Linking Research and Practice to Improve Learning. 52(1), 51–55. January. https://eric.ed.gov/?id=EJ798639.

Daka, Terhemba. 2019. President Buhari Signs Disability Bill into Law. *Guardian* (Lagos). January 24. https://guardian.ng/news/president-buhari-signs-disability-bill-into-law/24

Devlieger, Patrick, Beatriz Miranda-Galarza, Steven E. Brown, and Megan Strickfaden, eds. 2016. *Rethinking Disability: World Perspectives in Culture and Society*, 2nd Edition. Antwerp, Belgium: Maklu, Garant, and Cyclus.

Devereux, Stephen, and Rachel Sabates-Wheeler. 2004. *Transformative Social Protection.* IDS Working Paper 232. Brighton, Sussex: Institute of Development Studies. October. https://www.ids.ac.uk/download.php?file=files/dmfile/Wp232.pdf.

Difference Between Right and Privilege. 2012. *Difference Between.* July 14. https://www.differencebetween.com/difference-between-right-and-vs-privilege.

Digital Accessibility Benefits Everyone. 2021. *Epic.* May 10. https://epicassist.org/digital-accessibility-benefits-everyone/.

Disability Stigma in Developing Countries. https://assets.publishing.service.gov.uk/media/5b18fe3240f0b634aec30791/Disability_stigma_in_developing_countries.pdf.

Disabled Biafran Veterans Cry Out for Help. 2015. *Vanguard* (Lagos). June 27. https://www.vanguardngr.com/2015/06/disabled-biafran-veterans-cry-out-for-help/.

Discrimination Against Persons with Disabilities (Prohibition) Act. 2018. *Nigeria Health Watch.* https://nigeriahealthwatch.com/wp-content/uploads/bsk-pdf

-manager/2019/02/1244-Discrimination-Against-Persons-with-Disabilities-Prohibition-ACT-2018.pdf.

Doma, Halim. 2020. *Human Rights and Persons with Disabilities in Nigeria: Laws, Policies, and Institutions.* London and Abuja: Adonis & Abbey.

Edward Francis Small Teaching Hospital (The Royal Victory Hospital). https://www.electives.net/hospital/3661/preview.

Egbas, June. 2020. [Four] Things You Should Know about Sharia Law in Nigeria. *Pulse.* August 12. https://www.pulse.ng/news/metro/sharia-in-nigeria-4-things-you-should-know-about-islamic-law/y29g15v.

Eide, Arne, and Benedicte Ingstad, eds. *Disability and Poverty: A Global Challenge*. 2011. Bristol, UK: Policy Press, University of Bristol.

Eleweke, C. Jonah, and Jannine Ebenso. 2016. Barriers to Accessing Services by People with Disabilities in Nigeria: Insights from a Qualitative Study. *Journal of Educational & Social Research.* 6(2), 113–123. doi:10.5901/jesr.2016.v6n2p113.

Enaholo, Patrick. Colonial Footprints: Lagos, Then and Now. Centenary Project. Arts and Culture. https://artsandculture.google.com/story/LAUBxuvCARsA8A.

Enitan, Oluwatobi. 2019. Physically Challenged Protest Buhari's Non-Assent to Disability Bill. *Roots TV* (Nigeria). January 18. https://www.youtube.com/watch?v=8jQhcIEMVG8.

Erunke, Joseph. 2020. Farouq Inaugurates Governing Council of National Commission for Persons with Disabilities. *Vanguard* (Lagos). December 22. https://www.vanguardngr.com/2020/12/farouq-inaugurates-governing-council-of-natl-commission-for-persons-with-disabilities/.

Etieyibo, Edwin. 2021. Social Justice and Persons with Disabilities in Nigeria. In *Africa's Radicalisms and Conservatisms: Politics, Poverty, Marginalization[,] and Education,* eds. Edwin Etieyibo, Obvious Katsaura, and Mucha Musemwa, 143–163. Leiden, The Netherlands: Brill Publishing.

Etieyibo, Edwin, and Odirin Omiegbe. 2017. *Disabilities in Nigeria: Attitudes, Reactions, and Remediation.* Lanham, MD: Hamilton Books.

Ewang, Anietie. 2019. Nigeria Passes Disability Rights Law: Offers Hope of Inclusion, Improved Access. *Human Rights Watch.* January 25. https://www.hrw.org/news/2019/01/25/nigeria-passes-disability-rights-law.

Faal, Courtney. 2009. The Partition of Africa. *Black Past.* February 21. https://www.blackpast.org/global-african-history/partition-africa/.

Falode, Adewunmi James. 2009. The Military and Nation-Building in Nigeria: The General Ibrahim Babangida Regime, 1985–1993. *International Letters of Social and Humanistic Sciences.* 85, 37–48.

Falola, Toyin, and Nic Hamel. 2021. Africanizing Disability: Toward an Articulation of African Disability Studies. In *Disability in Africa: Inclusion, Care, and the Ethics of Humanity,* eds. Toyin Falola and Nic Hamel, 1–46. New York: University of Rochester Press.

Falola, Toyin, and Matthew M. Heaton. 2012. *A History of Nigeria.* New York: Cambridge University Press.

Farley, Alan. 2020. What Does "Guns and Butter" Refer To? *Investopedia.* Updated February 11. https://www.investopedia.com/ask/answers/08/guns-butter.asp.

Faulconbridge, Guy. 2016. Cameron Says Leaders of "Fantastically Corrupt" Countries to Attend UK Anti-Graft Summit. *Reuters.* May 10. https://www.reuters.com/article/us-global-taxavoidance-cameron/cameron-says-leaders-of-fantastically-corrupt-countries-to-attend-uk-anti-graft-summit-idUSKCN0Y11NW.

Federal Ministry of Education. 2019. National Policy on Albinism in Nigeria. Abuja: Federal Ministry of Education. https://albinofoundation.org/wp-content/uploads/2021/09/REVIEWED-NATIONAL-POLICY-ON-ALBINISM-DESIGNED-1.pdf.

Federal Ministry of Education. 2012. *National Policy on Albinism in Nigeria.* Abuja: Federal Ministry of Education. https://albinofoundation.org/wp-content/uploads/2017/04/National-Policy-on-Albinism-Implementatio-Guideline.pdf.

Federal Ministry of Women Affairs and Social Development [MWASD]. https://socialprotection.org/connect/stakeholders/nigeria-federal-ministry-women-affairs-and-social-development

Federal Republic of Nigeria. 2017. *Economic Recovery and Growth Plan.* Abuja, Nigeria: Ministry of Budget and Planning. February. https://estateintel.com/wp-content/uploads/2017/03/Nigeria-Economic-Refom-Plan-2.pdf.

Federal Republic of Nigeria. 2013. *National Policy on Education, 6th ed.* Lagos: Nigerian Educational Research and Development Council (NERDC). https://educatetolead.files.wordpress.com/2016/02/national-education-policy-2013.pdf.

Fertman, Carl I., Myrna M. Delgado, and Susan L. Tarasevich. 2013. *Promoting Child and Adolescent Mental Health.* Burlington, MA: Jones & Bartlett Publishers.

FG Unveils National Draft Policy on Inclusive Education. 2016. *Vanguard* (Lagos). February 22. https://guardian.ng/news/fg-unveils-national-draft-policy-on-inclusive-education/.

The First World War and Its Consequences in Africa. *UNESCO Courier.* https://en.unesco.org/courier/news-views-online/first-world-war-and-its-consequences-africa.

Foley, John Miles. Oral Tradition. *Encyclopedia Britannica.* https://www.britannica.com/topic/oral-tradition.

Foster, Vivien, and Nataliya Pushak. 2011. *Nigeria's Infrastructure: A Continental Perspective* Washington, DC: World Bank Group. June. https://doi.org/10.1596/1813-9450-5686.

Frank, Etim O., and Wilfred I. Ukpere. 2012. The Impact of Military Rule on Democracy in Nigeria. *Journal of Social Sciences.* 33(3), 285–92. https://www.researchgate.net/publication/261672856_The_Impact_of_Military_Rule_on_Democracy_in_Nigeria.

The Gambia: Disability Bill is Key Step toward Greater Inclusion in Society. 2021. *Article 19.* September 10. https://www.article19.org/resources/the-gambia-disability-bill-is-a-key-step-towards-greater-inclusion-in-society/.

Gänsler, Katrin. 2019, Nigeria Looks Back on 20 Years of Sharia Law in the North. *DW.* October 27. https://www.dw.com/en/nigeria-looks-back-on-20-years-of-sharia-law-in-the-north/a-51010292.

Gavin, Michelle. 2019. The Post-Presidential Legacy of Nigeria's Goodluck Jonathan. Council on Foreign Relations. July 16. https://www.cfr.org/blog/post-presidential-legacy-nigerias-goodluck-jonathan.

Global Center for the Responsibility to Protect. 2022. Nigeria. March 1. https://www.globalr2p.org/countries/nigeria/.

Goffman, Erving. 2009. *Stigma: Notes on the Management of Spoiled Identity.* New York: Simon and Schuster.

Gold Coast Government. 1955. *Report on the Enquiry into Begging and Destitution in the Gold Coast 1954.* Accra, Ghana: Government Printer.

Goldstein, Daniel, and Gregory Care. 2012. Disability Rights and Access to the Digital World: An Advocate's Analysis of an Emerging Field. *Federalist Lawyer.* December. 54–59. https://lawreview.law.miami.edu/wp-content/uploads/2013/02/Goldstein-Care-Disability-Rights-and-Access-to-the-Digital-World.pdf.

Government and Disability Activism in Nigeria. 2016. *Poor Magazine.* July 1. https://www.poormagazine.org/node/5549.

Groce, Nora Ellen. 1999. Guest Editorial: Framing Disability Issues in Local Concepts and Beliefs. *Asia Pacific Disability Rehabilitation Journal.* 10(1), 1–6. https://discovery.ucl.ac.uk/id/eprint/15160/1/15160.pdf.

Hanifen, Katharine. Living with Disabilities in Nigeria. Borgen Project. https://borgenproject.org/disabilities-in-nigeria/.

Harding, T.W. 2000. Human Rights Law in the Field of Mental Health: A Critical Review. *Acta Psychiatr. Scand. Suppl.* 399, 24–30. DOI: 10.1111/j.0902-4441.2000.007s020[dash]6.x.

Haruna, Mohammed Awaisu. 2017. The Problem of Living with Disability in Nigeria. *Journal of Law, Policy[,] and Globalization.* 65, 103–113.

Hasenclever, Andreas, Peter Mayer, and Volker Rittberger. 1997. *Theories of International Regimes.* New York: Cambridge University Press.

Hawking, Stephen W. 2011. "Foreword." In *World Report on Disability.* Geneva Switzerland and Washington, DC: World Health Organization and the World Bank. P. ix. https://www.who.int/disabilities/world_report/2011/report.pdf.

Health Care Services in Colonial Nigeria. 2021. *Wefinder.* July 7. wefinder24.com/2021/07/health-care-services-in-colonial-nigeria.html.

Herbst, Jeffrey. 2001. Political Liberalization in Africa after Ten Years. *Comparative Politics.* 33(3), 357–375.

History. 1991. In *Nigeria: A Country Study*, ed. Helen Chapin Metz. Washington, DC: GPO for the Library of Congress.

The Holy Bible. 2011. New International Version. Colorado Springs, CO.

How NDI Supports the Political Inclusion of Persons with Disabilities. 2019. *National Democratic Institute* (USA). November 27. https://www.ndi.org/our-stories/how-ndi-supports-political-inclusion-persons-disabilities.

Human Rights Council Resolution 37/22 Concerning the Rights of Persons with Disabilities—Inputs by National Human Rights Commission, Nigeria. July 22.

Human Rights Instruments for Children with Disabilities. 2016. *Global Disability Rights Now!* October 17. https://www.globaldisabilityrightsnow.org/es/tools/human-rights-instruments-children-disabilities.

Human Rights Watch. 2011. Nigeria: Post-Election Violence Killed 800. May 16. https://www.hrw.org/news/2011/05/16/nigeria-post-election-violence-killed-800#.
Human Rights Watch. 2004. "Political Sharia?": Human Rights and Islamic Law in Northern Nigeria. New York: Human Rights Watch. September 21. https://www.hrw.org/report/2004/09/21/political-sharia/human-rights-and-islamic-law-northern-nigeria#.
Hunt, Elgin F., and David C. Colander. 2005. *Social Science: An Introduction to the Study of Society, 12th ed.* Boston, New York, and San Francisco: Pearson.
Igomu, Tessy. 2021. Disabled by Fate, Denied Rights to Mobility: Nigerians Living with Disabilities Tell Tales of Anguish Accessing Public Transportation. *Punch* (Lagos). September 12. https://punchng.com/disabled-by-fate-denied-rights-to-mobility-nigerians-living-with-disabilities-tell-tales-of-anguish-accessing-public-transportation/.
Inclusive Futures. 2021. *Consequences of Exclusion: A Situation Report on Organizations of People with Disabilities and COVID-19 in Bangladesh, Nigeria, and Zimbabwe.* London, UK: Inclusive Futures. September. https://www.sddirect.org.uk/media/2268/english-situation-report-opds-covid-19-report-final.pdf.
Infrastructure. *Merriam-Webster.* https://www.merriam-webster.com/dictionary/infrastructure.
Institutionalizing Inclusive Education in Nigeria: A Way to End Poverty. 2019. Human Development Initiatives (HDI) Blog. December 3. https://hdinigeria.org/blog/2019/12/03/institutionalizing-inclusive-education-in-nigeria-a-way-to-end-poverty/.
International Disability Alliance. 2020. [Twenty-Five] Million Lives at Stake: Nigerians with Disabilities During the Pandemic. December 4. https://www.internationaldisabilityalliance.org/blog/25-million-lives-stake-nigerians-disabilities-during-pandemic.
International Justice Resource Center. 2016. African Commission Adopts Draft Protocol on Persons with Disabilities Rights. April 20. https://ijrcenter.org/2016/04/20/african-commission-adopts-draft-protocol-on-persons-with-disabilities-rights/.
International Labor Organization. 2006. ILO Welcomes New UN Convention on Rights of People with Disabilities. Press Release. December 14. https://www.ilo.org/global/about-the-ilo/newsroom/news/WCMS_080627/lang--en/index.html.
Ityavyar, Dennis A. 1987. The State, Class[,] and Health Services in Nigeria. *Africa Spectrum.* 22(3), 285–314. https://www.jstor.org/stable/40174297.
Jackson, Ashley. 2006. *The British Empire and the Second World War.* London: Hambledon Continuum.
Jagoe, Kathryn. The Disability Rights Movement: Its Development in South Africa. Independent Living Institute. https://www.independentliving.org/toolsforpower/tools6.html.
Jones, G.I. 2000. *The Trading States of the Oil Rivers: A Study of Political Development in Eastern Nigeria.* Classics in African Anthropology. Münster, Germany: LIT Verlag.
Justiciability. Legal Information Institute, Cornell Law School. https://www.law.cornell.edu/wex/justiciability.

Leithead, Alastair. 2017. The City That Won't Stop Growing: How Can Lagos Cope with Its Spiraling Population. *BBC News.* August 21. https://www.bbc.co.uk/news/resources/idt-sh/lagos.

Leonard, Major Arthur Glyn. 1906. *The Lower Niger and Its Tribes.* London: Macmillan & Co. Ltd.

Lipson, Charles. 1991. Why are Some International Agreements Informal? *International Organization.* 45, 495–538.

List of Countries Which Have Signed, Ratified/Acceded to the Protocol to the African Charter on Human and Peoples' Rights on the Rights of Persons with Disabilities in Africa. https://au.int/sites/default/files/treaties/36440-sl-PROTOCOL%20TO%20THE%20AFRICAN%20CHARTER%20ON%20HUMAN%20AND%20PEOPLES%E2%80%99%20RIGHTS%20ON%20THE%20RIGHTS%20OF%20PERSONS%20WITH%20DISABILITIES%20IN%20AFRICA.pdf.

Longley, Robert. 2021. What Is a Military Dictatorship? Definition and Examples. *ThoughtCo.* January 29. https://www.thoughtco.com/military-dictatorship-definition-and-examples-5091896.

Lord, Janet, and Michael Ashley Stein. 2013. Prospects and Practices for CRPD Implementation in Africa. *African Disability Rights Yearbook.* 1, 97–113.

Lynch, Gabrielle, and Gordon Crawford. 2011. Democratization in Africa 1990–2010: An Assessment. *Democratization.* 18(2), 275–331.

Kabue, Samuel, Esther Mombo, Joseph Galgalo, and C.B. Peters, eds. 2012. *Disability, Society[,] and Theology: Voices from Africa*. Eldoret, Kenya: Zapf Chancery Publishers.

Kazeem, Yomi. 2019. Flying Blind: African Governments Need to Fix Their Problematic Relationship with Data on Their Own Countries. *Quartz Africa.* October 16; last updated October 18, 2019. https://qz.com/africa/1725537/africa-has-a-data-problem-says-mo-ibrahim-governance-report/.

Kearney, Audrey, Liz Hamel, and Mollyann Brodie. 2021. Mental Health Impact of the COVID-19 Pandemic: An Update. *KFF.* April 14. https://www.kff.org/coronavirus-covid-19/poll-finding/mental-health-impact-of-the-covid-19-pandemic/.

Krasner, Stephen D., ed. 1983. *International Regimes*. Ithaca, NY: Cornell University Press.

Madison, James. 1788. Federalist Paper No. 51. *Reprinted* in Bill of Rights Institute. https://billofrightsinstitute.org/primary-sources/federalist-no-51.

Madobi, Mukhtar Ya'U. Nigerian Roads: Death Traps for Commuters. 2021. *Cable.* November 24. https://www.thecable.ng/nigerian-roads-death-traps-commuters#:~:text=It%20was%20estimated%20that%20about,really%20indicated%20a%20terrifying%20situation

Mahoney, Dennis J., and Kenneth L Karst 1986. Right-Privilege Distinction. *Encyclopedia of the American Constitution.* https://www.encyclopedia.com/politics/encyclopedias-almabacs-transcripts-and-maps/right-privilege-distinction.

Maikudi, Abdullahi. 2021. Nigeria Needs [US]$ 2.3trn To Bridge Infrastructural Deficit–Osinbajo. *The Will.* March 18. https://thewillnigeria.com/news/nigeria-needs-2-3trn-to-bridge-infrastructural-deficit-osinbajo/.

Major, Brenda, and Laurie T. O'Brien. 2005. The Social Psychology of Stigma. *Annual Review of Psychology.* 56 (1), 393–421. doi:10.1146/annurev.psych.56.091103.070137.

Manning, Sherman D. 2016. *American Dream, A Search for Justice*. [place of publication not indicated] American Dream Online Books.

Marchildon, Jackie. 2018. [Five] Facts About Living with a Disability in the Developing World. *Global Citizen.* November 23. https://www.globalcitizen.org/en/content/disability-in-the-developingworld/#:~:text=1)%2080%25%20of%20people%20living,people%20live%20in%20developing%20countries.

Marini, Irmo, Noreen M. Graf, and Michael Millington. 2011. *Psychosocial Aspects of Disability: Insider Perspectives and Strategies for Counselors.* 2nd Ed. New York: Springer Publishing.

Marx, Karl. Theses on Feuerback, Thesis 11 (1845). 1950. In *Selected Works, Vol. 1, Marx Engels.* Moscow: Foreign Languages Publishing House. 13–15

Marx, Karl, and Friedrich Engels. 1998. *The German Ideology, Including Theses on Feuerbach.* Amherst, NY: Prometheus.

Maxfield, Michael G., and Earl R. Babbie. 2015. *Research Methods for Criminal Justice and Criminology,* 7th ed. Stamford, CT: Cengage Learning.

Mayo Clinic. Mental Illness. https://www.mayoclinic.org/diseases-conditions/mental-illness/symptoms-causes/syc-20374968

Mbengue, Makane Moïse. 2006. Preamble. *Max Planck Encyclopedias of International Law.* New York and Oxford: Oxford University Press. https://opil.ouplaw.com/view/10.1093/law:epil/9780199231690/law-9780199231690-e1456.

McCaslin, Jack. 2018. Lord Lugard Created Nigeria 104 Years Ago. Council on Foreign Relations. January 2. https://www.cfr.org/blog/lord-lugard-created-nigeria-104-years-ago.

McNeill, William H. 1976. *Plagues and Peoples.* Garden City, NY: Anchor Press/Doubleday.

Melvin, Don. 2016. David Cameron calls Afghanistan, Nigeria "Fantastically Corrupt." *CNN.* May 11. https://www.cnn.com/2016/05/10/europe/cameron-corrupt-countries-nigeria-afghanistan-queen/index.html.

Mental Disorders. *MedlinePlus.* https://medlineplus.gov/mentaldisorders.html.

Merelli, Annalisa. 2019. No Benevolent Dictators: 150 Years of Data Proves It: Strongmen are Bad for the Economy. *Quartz.* August 19. https://qz.com/1688397/data-proves-it-authoritarian-leaders-are-bad-for-the-economy/.

Merrick, Joav, Ariel Tenenbaum, Mohammed Morad, and Eli Carmeli. 2018. A Short History of Disability Aspects from Israel. In *The Routledge History of Disability,* eds. Roy Hanes, Ivan Brown, and Nancy E. Hansen, 94–114. London and New York: Routledge.

Message from Donna E. Shalala, Secretary of Health and Human Services. 1999. In *Mental Health: A Report of the Surgeon General.* Rockville, MD: U.S. Department of Health and Human Services. https://collections.nlm.nih.gov/ext/document/101584932X120/PDF/101584932X120.pdf.

Minor, Kyle. 2012. *There Was a Country*, Chinua Achebe's Long-Awaited Memoir of Biafra. *Salon.* November 8. https://www.salon.com/2012/11/08/there_was_a_country_chinua_achebes_long_awaited_memoir_of_biafra/.

Models of Disability: An Overview. MIUSA: Mobility International USA. https://www.miusa.org/resource/tipsheet/disabilitymodels.

Mojekwu, Christopher C. 1979. Nigerian Constitutionalism. In *Constitutionalism,* eds. J. Roland Pennock and John W. Chapman, 163–186. New York: New York University Press.

Montinola, Gabriella R. Political Corruption. *Encyclopedia.com*. https://www.encyclopedia.com/international/legal-and-political-magazines/political-corruption.

Mordi, Emmanuel Nwafor. 2019. Nigerian Forces Comforts Fund, 1940–1947: "The Responsibility of the Nigerian Government to Provide Funds for the Welfare of Its Soldiers." *Itinerario: Journal of Imperial and Global Interactions.* 43(3) 516–542. December. https://doi.org/10.1017/S0165115319000585.

Moses, Lauren. Nigerian Disability Advocates Conduct First-Ever Election Accessibility Audits. *Democracy Works.* https://www.demworks.org/nigerian-disability-advocates-conduct-first-ever-election-accessibility-audits.

Musoke, Grace, and Priscille Geiser, eds. 2013. Linking CRB, Disability, and Rehabilitation. CRB Africa Network. http://www.fatoafrique.org/site/IMG/pdf/cbr_africa_final.pdf

National Bureau of Statistics (Nigeria). https://www.devex.com/organizations/national-bureau-of-statistics-nigeria-143915.

National Center for Health Statistics, US CDC. 2008. International Classification of Functioning, Disability[,] and Health (ICF). January 24. http://www.cdc.gov/NCHS/about/otheract/icd9/icfhome.htm.

National Democratic Institute (USA). 2019. How NDI Supports the Political Inclusion of Persons with Disabilities. November 27. https://www.ndi.org/our-stories/how-ndi-supports-political-inclusion-persons-disabilities.

National Democratic Institute (USA). 2019. Nigerians with Visual Impairments Vote Independently for the First Time. April 23. https://www.ndi.org/our-stories/nigerians-visual-impairments-vote-independently-first-time.

National Government of South Africa. Department of Women, Youth[,] and Persons with Disabilities (DWYPD). https://nationalgovernment.co.za/units/management/31/department-of-women-youth-and-persons-with-disabilities-dwypd.

National Health Act of 2014. 2014. Federal Republic of Nigeria Official Gazette. 101(145) October 27. https://nigeriahealthwatch.com/wp-content/uploads/bsk-pdf-manager/2018/07/01_-Official-Gazette-of-the-National-Health-Act-FGN.pdf.

National Human Rights Commission of Nigeria. 2013. October 17. https://www.upr-info.org/sites/default/files/document/nigeria/session_17_-_october_2013/nhrc-nigeria_upr17_nga_e_main.pdf.

National Institute of Health (USA). 2021. HIV and AIDS: The Basics. Last reviewed August 16. https://hivinfo.nih.gov/understanding-hiv/fact-sheets/hiv-and-aids-basics.

The National Integrated Infrastructure Master Plan. 2020. Abuja: Federal Ministry of Finance, Budget, and National Planning.

New State Ice Co. v. Liebmann. 1932. 285 U.S. 262.

Ngai, Karen K.H., Simon W.K. Wu, and Joanna L.P. Chung. 2018. A Journey of Change—History of Disability in Hong Kong[,] 1841–2014. In *The Routledge History of Disability,* eds. Roy Hanes, Ivan Brown, and Nancy E. Hansen, 163–203. London and New York: Routledge.

Niger River. *New World Encyclopedia.* https://www.newworldencyclopedia.org/entry/Niger_River.

Nigeria. 2020. *Freedom in the World 2020: Country Report.* Washington, DC: Freedom House. https://freedomhouse.org/country/nigeria/freedom-world/2020

Nigeria. IDMC: Internal Displacement Monitoring Center. https://www.internal-displacement.org/countries/nigeria.

Nigeria: Children and Young People with Disabilities. 2021. London: Asylos and ARC Foundation. October.

Nigeria Fact Sheet. 2012. United States Embassy in Nigeria. January. https://photos.state.gov/libraries/nigeria/487468/pdfs/Nigeria%20overview%20Fact%20Sheet.pdf.

Nigeria IDP Figures Analysis. 2016. IDMC. September 13. http://www.internal-displacement.org/sub-saharan-africa/nigeria/figures.analysis.

Nigeria Independence Act, 1960. 1960. 1960 Ch. 55 8 and 9 Eliz. July 29. https://www.legislation.gov.uk/ukpga/1960/55/pdfs/ukpga_19600055_en.pdf.

Nigeria Issues New Data Protection Regulation. 2019. Hunton Andrews Kurth. April 5. https://www.huntonprivacyblog.com/2019/04/05/nigeria-issues-new-data-protection-regulation/.

Nigeria—Location, Size, and Extent. *Nations Encyclopedia.* https://www.nationsencyclopedia.com/Africa/Nigeria-LOCATION-SIZE-AND-EXTENT.html.

Nigeria's Loss of ₦557 bn to Contract Inflation. 2021. *Blueprint.* October 7. https://www.blueprint.ng/nigerias-loss-of-n557bn-to-contract-inflation/.

Nigeria Needs $100 Billion Annually to Address Infrastructural Deficit–Emefiele. 2021. *The Will.* September 25. https://thewillnigeria.com/news/nigeria-needs-100bn-annually-to-address-infrastructural-deficit-emefiele/.

Nigeria Population (Live). *Worldometers.* https://www.worldometers.info/world-population/nigeria-population/.

Nigeria Republic Act, 1963. 1963. 1963 Ch. 57. December 18. https://www.legislation.gov.uk/ukpga/1963/57/enacted.

Nigeria Situational Analysis Version II–June 2020. 2020. *Inclusive Futures: Promoting Disability Inclusion.* Brighton, UK: Institute of Development Studies. July. https://opendocs.ids.ac.uk/opendocs/bitstream/handle/20.500.12413/15561/DID%20SITAN%20Nigeria%20V2%20July%202020.pdf?sequence=1&isAllowed=y.

Nigeria Social Insurance Trust Fund Decree 1993 (No. 73 of 1993). 1993. August 23. Published in *Federal Republic of Nigeria Official Gazette*, 80(24), A811-A27. September 1 Reprinted in Laws Africa: Legislation Commons. https://commons.laws.africa/akn/ng/act/1993/73/eng@2002-12-31.pdf.

Nigerian Muslims Welcome Sharia Law. 2000. *BBC News.* January 27. news.bbc.co.uk/2/hi/Africa/620058.stm.

Nigerians with Disability Decree. 1993. GLADNET Collection. Paper 133. http://digitalcommons.ilr.cornell.edu/gladnetcollect/133.

Nigerians with Visual Impairments Vote Independently for the First Time. 2019. *National Democratic Institute* (USA). April 23. https://www.ndi.org/our-stories/nigerians-visual-impairments-vote-independently-first-time.

Njung, George N. 2020. Amputated Men, Colonial Bureaucracy, and Masculinity in Post-World War I Colonial Nigeria. *Journal of Social History.* 53(3), 620–643. Spring.

Njung, George. 2019. *Amputated Men: The British Nigerian Disabled Men of the First World War and Their Crisis of Masculinity.* Lecture at the University of Nottingham, UK. December 10. https://www.nottingham.ac.uk/home/featureevents/2019/amputated-men-the-british-nigerian-disabled-men-of-the-first-world-war.aspx.

Nwokorie, Okechukwu V., and Patrick J. Devlieger, "We Only Got Coca-Cola": Disability and the Paradox of (Dis)empowerment in Southeast Nigeria. *African Journal of Disability.* 8(444) (2019). doi: 10:4102/ajod.v8i0.444.

Number of Deaths Due to AIDS in Nigeria as of 2020. 2022. *Statista.* February 1. https://www.statista.com/statistics/1262130/deaths-due-to-aids-in-nigeria/#:~:text=As%20of%202020%2C%201.7%20million,adults%2C%20with%2020%20thousand%20deaths.

Number of Internally Displaced Persons (IDP) in Nigeria from 2013 to 2020. *Statista.* https://www.statista.com/statistics/1237374/number-of-internally-displaced-persons-in-nigeria/.

Obadare, Ebenezer. 2022. Nigeria's All Too Familiar Corruption Ranking Begs Broader Questions Around Normative Collapse. Council on Foreign Relations (Blog). February 24. https://www.cfr.org/blog/nigerias-all-too-familiar-corruption-ranking-begs-broader-questions-around-normative-collapse.

Office of the Auditor-General for the Federation. https://www.oaugf.ng/about-us/about-oaugf.

Office of the UN High Commissioner for Human Rights. 2012. *The United Nations Human Rights Treaty System: An introduction to the Core Human Rights Treaties and the Treaty Bodies.* Fact Sheet No. 30/Rev. 1. August. https://www.refworld.org/docid/5289d3e84.html.

Office of the UN High Commissioner for Human Rights. 2010. *Monitoring the Convention on the Rights of Persons with Disabilities: Guidance for Human Rights Monitors.* Professional Training Series No. 17. Geneva and New York: Office of the UN High Commissioner for Human Rights.

Office of the UN High Commissioner for Human Rights. 2010. *National Human Rights Institutions: History, Principles, Roles[,] and Responsibilities.* Professional Training Series No. 4. Geneva and New York: Office of the UN High Commissioner for Human Rights. https://www.ohchr.org/sites/default/files/Documents/Publications/PTS-4Rev1-NHRI_en.pdf.

Office of the UN High Commissioner for Human Rights. 2008. Frequently Asked Questions on Economic, Social[,] and Cultural Rights. December. https://www.ohchr.org/documents/publications/factsheet33en.pdf.

Office of the UN High Commissioner for Human Rights. 2007. *From Exclusion to Equality: Realizing the Rights of Persons with Disabilities.* Handbook for Parliamentarians No. 14. New York: Office of the UN High Commissioner for Human Rights.

Ogundola, Olusola. 2020. Disability Narratives in the News Media: A Spotlight on Africa. In *The Routledge Companion to Disability and Media,* eds. Katie Ellis, Gerard Goggin, Beth Haller, and Rosemary Curtis, 169–176. New York and London: Routledge.

Ogundipe, Samuel. 2019. Buhari Signs Law Banning Discrimination Against Persons with Disability. *Premium Times* (Abuja). January 23. https://www.premiumtimesng.com/news/headlines/307474-buhari-signs-law-banning-discrimination-against-persons-with-disability.html.

Ogunlesi, Adegboyega O., and Adegboyega Ogunwale. 2012. Mental Health Legislation in Nigeria: Current Leanings and Future Years. *International Psychiatry.* 9(3), 62–64. August.

Ojewale, Oluwole. 2021. Rising Insecurity in Northwest Nigeria: Terrorism Thinly Disguised as Banditry. Brookings (Blog). February 18. https://www.brookings.edu/blog/africa-in-focus/2021/02/18/rising-insecurity-in-northwest-nigeria-terrorism-thinly-disguised-as-banditry/.

Oji River Leprosy Settlement: Chapel of the Transfiguration, Built Largely by Patients, 1956. ArchiveSearch. https://archivesearch.lib.cam.ac.uk/repositories/2/archival_objects/171271.

Olasupo, Abisola. 2020. Why Nigeria Needs to Sign Digital Right and Freedom Bill into Law as the World Goes Digital. *Guardian* (Lagos). July 2. https://guardian.ng/features/why-nigeria-needs-to-sign-digital-right-and-freedom-bill-into-law-as-the-world-goes-digital/.

Omeni, Akali. 2015. The Almajiri in Northern Nigeria: Militancy, Perceptions, Challenges, and State Policies. *African Conflict and Peacebuilding Review.* 5(2), 128–142. doi:10.2979/africonfpeacrevi.5.2.128.

Omiegbe, Odirin. 2021. Poverty and Persons Living with Disabilities in Nigeria. In *Africa's Radicalisms and Conservatisms: Politics, Poverty, Marginalization[,] and Education,* eds. Edwin Etieyibo, Obvious Katsaura, and Mucha Musemwa, 164–185. Leiden, The Netherlands: Brill Publishing.

Onyeji, Ebuka. 2021. PWDs Not Benefitting Enough from Social Protection Programs in Four Nigerian States—Survey. *Premium Times* (Abuja). May 14. https://www.premiumtimesng.com/news/more-news/461527-pwds-not-benefitting-enough-from-social-protection-programmes-in-four-nigerian-states-survey.html.

Open Society Justice Initiative. African Commission on Human and Peoples' Rights. https://www.justiceinitiative.org/publications/african-commission-human-and-peoples-rights.

Organization of African Unity (OAU). 1990. African Charter on the Rights and Welfare of the Child. CAB/LEG/24.9/49. July 11. https://www.refworld.org/docid/3ae6b38c18.html.

Organization of African Unity (OAU). 1981. African Charter on Human and Peoples' Rights ("Banjul Charter"). June 27. CAB/LEG/67/3 rev. 5, 21 I.L.M. 58 (1982). https://www.refworld.org/docid/3ae6b3630.html.

Ostien, Philip, and Albert Dekker. 2010. Sharia and National Law in Nigeria. In *Sharia Incorporated: A Comparative Overview of the Legal Systems of Twelve Muslim Countries in Past and Present*, ed. Jan Michiel Otto, 553–612. Zuid-Holland, Netherlands: Leiden University Press.

Ostein, Philip, compiler and editor. 2007. *Sharia Implementation in Northern Nigeria 1999–2006: A Sourcebook.* Sharia in Africa.net. http://www.sharia-in-africa.net/media/publications/sharia-implementation-in-northern-nigeria-volume-six/Chapter%208%20Part%20II.pdf.

Other Benefits. Social Protection and Human Rights. https://socialprotection-human-rights.org/key-issues/social-protection-systems/other-benefits/.

Ottaway, Marina. 1999. *Africa's New Leaders: Democracy or State Reconstruction?* Washington, DC: Carnegie Endowment for International Peace.

Ottaway, Marina, ed. 1997. *Democracy in Africa: The Hard Road Ahead.* SAIS African Studies Library. Boulder and London: Lynne Rienner Publishers.

Ovadiya, Mirey, and Giuseppe Zampaglione. 2009. *Escaping Stigma and Neglect: People with Disabilities in Sierra Leone.* Working Paper No. 164. Washington, DC: World Bank.

Partnership for Advocacy in Child and Family Health at Scale. 2021. *[Fifteen Percent] Benchmark to Health Sector in Nigeria—The Journey So Far.* Abuja: PACFaH@Scale. April. https://drpcngr.org/15-benchmark-to-health-sector-in-nigeria-the-journey-so-far/.

Patton, Steven. 2019. The Peace of Westphalia and it[s] [E]ffects on International Relations. Diplomacy and Foreign Policy. *Histories.* 10(1), 91–99. https://digitalcommons.lasalle.edu/cgi/viewcontent.cgi?article=1146&context=the_histories.

Physical Disability. Education to Employment. https://web.archive.org/web/20130724013228/http://pubsites.uws.edu.au/ndco/employment/what/physical.htm.

People with Disabilities and Politics in Nigeria. 2013. *World Pulse.* September 23. https://www.worldpulse.com/community/users/vweta/posts/28511.

Petrila, John, and Thomas Brink. 2001. Mental Illness and Changing Definitions of Disability Under the Americans with Disabilities Act. *Psychiatric Services.* 52(2), 626–630. May.

Pillay, Navanethem. 2014. Foreword. In *The Convention on the Rights of Persons with Disabilities.* Training Guide. Professional Training Series No. 19. New York and Geneva: United Nations. https://www.ohchr.org/Documents/Publications/CRPD_TrainingGuide_PTS19_EN%20Accessible.pdf.

Pillay, Navanethem Pillay. 2010. Foreword. In *Monitoring the Convention on the Rights of Persons with Disabilities Guidance for Human Rights Monitors.*

Professional Training Series No. 17. New York and Geneva: Office of the UN High Commissioner for Human Rights.

Pilling, David. 2022. What is Nigeria's Government for? *Financial Times* (UK). January 31. https://www.ft.com/content/c4025da8-7951-4ed1-bccd-5d546f86786c.

Political Violence. *Your Dictionary*, https//www.yourdictionary.com/political-violence.

Powell, Anita. 2021. Pandemic Takes Unique Toll on South Africa's Disabled. *VOA News*. March 10. https://www.voanews.com/a/covid-19-pandemic_pandemic-takes-unique-toll-south-africas-disabled/6203126.html.

Protocol to the African Charter on Human and Peoples' Rights on the Rights of Persons with Disabilities in Africa. 2018. January 29. https://au.int/sites/default/files/treaties/36440-treaty-protocol_to_the_achpr_on_the_rights_of_persons_with_disabilities_in_africa_e.pdf.

Purohit and Moore v. The Gambia. 2003. Communication No. 241/2001. https://africanlii.org/afu/judgment/african-commission-human-and-peoples-rights/2003/49.

Quinn, Gerard, and Theresia Degener. 2002. *Human Rights and Disability: The Current Use and Future Potential of United Nations Human Rights Instruments in the Context of Disability*. New York and Geneva: United Nations.

Raja, Deepti Samant. 2016. *Digital Dividends: Bridging the Disability Divide through Digital Technologies*. Background Paper, World Development Report 2016. Washington, DC: World Bank. https://thedocs.worldbank.org/en/doc/123481461249337484-0050022016/original/WDR16BPBridgingtheDisabilityDividethroughDigitalTechnologyRAJA.pdf.

Ratification Status for CESCR—International Covenant on Economic, Social and Cultural Rights. UN Treaty Body Database. https://tbinternet.ohchr.org/_layouts/15/TreatyBodyExternal/Treaty.aspx?Treaty=CESCR&Lang=en.

Ratification Status for Nigeria. UN Treaty Body Database. Office of the High Commissioner for Human Rights. https://tbinternet.ohchr.org/_layouts/15/TreatyBodyExternal/Treaty.aspx?CountryID=127&Lang=EN.

Read into (Something). *Free Dictionary*. https://idioms.thefreedictionary.com/read+into

The Rectification of Names. *Cultural China*. http://www.cultural-china.com/chinaWH/History/en/165History878.html.

Reinforcing and Cross-Cutting Cleavages. *Desart*. http://desart.us/courses/3180/cleavages.html.

Renne, Elisha P. 2012. Polio in Nigeria. *History Compass*. 10(7), 496–511. https://citeseerx.ist.psu.edu/viewdoc/download?doi=10.1.1.818.5571&rep=rep1&type=pdf.

Renne, Elisha P. 2010. *The Politics of Polio in Northern Nigeria*. Bloomington and Indianapolis: Indiana University Press.

Rivara, Frederick. 2019. The Effects of Violence on Health. *Health Affairs* (Millwood). 38(10) (October), 1622–1629. https://doi.org/10.1377/hlthaff.2019.00480.

Robertson, Gabrielle Udoka. 2021. *Explanatory Models of Autism in Nigeria: Exploring Sociocultural Beliefs to Inform Systems of Care*. Honor Thesis,

University of Mississippi. April. https://egrove.olemiss.edu/cgi/viewcontent.cgi?article=2862&context=hon_thesis.

Rohwerder, Brigitte. 2018. Disability Stigma in Developing Countries. *K4D Helpdesk Report.* May 9. 4, 12–13. https://opendocs.ids.ac.uk/opendocs/bitstream/handle/20.500.12413/13795/Disability_stigma_in_developing_countries.pdf?sequence=1.

Rose, M. Lynn. 2018. The Courage of Subordination: Women and Intellectual Disability in the Ancient Greek World. In *The Routledge History of Disability,* eds. Roy Hanes, Ivan Brown, and Nancy E. Hansen, 35–47. London and New York: Routledge.

Rose, Martha L. 2013. *The Staff of Oedipus: Transforming Disability in Ancient Greece.* Ann Arbor: University of Michigan Press.

Ross, Will. 2021. Boko Haram War Has Led to 350,000 Deaths—UN. BBC World Service. June 24. https://www.bbc.com/news/topics/c50znx8v435t/boko-haram.

Royal Victoria Teaching Hospital, Banjul. http://www.accessgambia.com/information/rvh.html.

Sadowsky, Jonathan. 1999. *Imperial Bedlam: Institutions of Madness in Colonial Southwest Nigeria.* Berkeley, Los Angeles, and London: University of California Press.

Sango, Precious. 2013. Visible but Invisible: People Living with Disability in Nigeria. *Books2Africa.* November 13. https://books2africa.org/visible-but-invisible-people-living-with-disability-in-nigeria/.

Sani Abacha: Nigerian Military Leader. 2022. *Encyclopedia Britannica.* Last updated March 3. https://www.britannica.com/biography/Sani-Abacha

Sani Abacha. Religion and Public Life, Harvard Divinity School. https://rpl.hds.harvard.edu/faq/sani-abacha.

Scott-Emuakpor, Ajovi. 2010. The Evolution of Health Care Systems in Nigeria: Which Way Forward in the Twenty-First Century. *Nigerian Medical Journal.* 51(2), 53–65. https://www.nigeriamedj.com/article.asp?issn=0300-1652;year=2010;volume=51;issue=2;spage=53;epage=65;aulast=Scott-Em.

Senu-Oke, Helen. 2011. *A Genealogy of Disability and Special Education in Nigeria: From the Pre-Colonial Era to the Present.* Ed.D. Dissertation in Educational Leadership, Miami University.

Shakespeare, Tom. 1996. Disability, Identity, and Difference. In *Exploring the Divide: Illness and Disability*, eds. Colin Barnes and Geof Mercer, 94–113. Leeds, UK: The Disability Press.

Sheetz, Kathleen. Slave Coast. *Encyclopedia Britannica*. https://www.britannica.com/place/Slave-Coast.

Silwimba, Felix. Possibilities of Independent Living of Persons with Disabilities in Africa. Independent Living Institute. https://www.independentliving.org/toolsforpower/tools5.html.

The Six Regions of the African Union. West Africa Brief. http://www.west-africa-brief.org/content/en/six-regions-african-union.

Smith, Daniel Jordan. 2007. *A Culture of Corruption: Everyday Deception and Popular Discontent in Nigeria.* Princeton, NJ: Princeton University Press.

Smith, David. 2015. Muhammadu Buhari: Reformed Dictator Returns to Power in Democratic Nigeria. *Guardian* (London). March 31. https://www.theguardian.com/world/2015/mar/31/muhammadu-buhari-military-dictator-nigeria-new-democratic-president.

Sodiq, Olayinka. 2022. [Ten] Best African Countries to Invest in 2022. *Business Insider Africa.* February 5. https://africa.businessinsider.com/local/markets/10-best-african-countries-to-invest-in-2022/whvt6nq.

Soyinka, Wole. 2019. Lessons from Nigeria's Militarized Democratic Experiment. *New York Times*, Op-Ed. October 19. https://www.nytimes.com/2019/10/09/opinion/nigeria-militarized-democratic-experiment.html.

Staples, James, and Nikita Mehrota. 2016. Disability Studies: Developments in Anthropology. In *Disability in the Global South: The Critical Handbook*, eds. Shaun Grech, and Karen Soldatic, 35–49. Cham, Switzerlnd: Springer.

Stocker, John. 1951. *Nigerian Railway Jubilee, 1901–1951: An Illustrated and Descriptive History of the Nigerian Railway.* Lagos: Railway Printer. Digitized August 8, 2006, by the University of Michigan.

Sutter, Daniel. 1999. Legitimacy and Military Intervention in a Democracy: Civilian Government as a Public Good. *American Journal of Economics and Sociology.* 58(1), 129–143.

Tignor, Robert L. 1998. *Capitalism and Nationalism at the End of Empire: State and Business in Decolonizing Egypt, Nigeria, and Kenya, 1945–1963.* Princeton, NJ: Princeton University Press.

Toumi, Marika, Ikponwosa Ero, and Herbert Tawata. 2021. *Report: Regional Action Plan on Ending Attacks and Human Rights Violations Against Persons with Albanism in Africa, 2017–2021: Action on Albinism*. July 1. https://www.ohchr.org/Documents/Issues/Albinism/RAP_Report_01-07_21_EN.pdf.

Transparency International. What is Corruption? https://www.transparency.org/en/what-is-corruption.

Trivundža, Ilija Tomanić, Hannu Nieminen, Nico Carpentier, and Josef Trappel. 2018. Concluding Remarks. In *The Routledge History of Disability,* eds. Roy Hanes, Ivan Brown, and Nancy E. Hansen, 500–501. London and New York: Routledge.

[Twenty Seventeen] Disability Status Report. 2019. Cornell University. https://www.disabilitystatistics.org/StatusReports/2017-PDF/2017-StatusReport_US.pdf.

Types of Physical Disabilities. Carehome.Co.UK. https://www.carehome.co.uk/advice/types-of-physical-disabilities.

Types of Sensory Disabilities. *Aruma.* https://www.aruma.com.au/about-us/about-disability/types-of-disabilities/types-of-sensory-disabilities/.

Types of Social Protection. GSDRC. https://gsdrc.org/ topic-guides/social-protection/types-of-social-protection/.

Ubah, C.N. 1992. Hope for the Despondent: A Colonial Health Care Scheme at Uzuakoli, Eastern Nigeria. *Transafrican Journal of History.* 21, 51–68.

Udodiong, Inemesit. 2018. Here Are the Countries with the Best and Worst Roads in Africa. *Pulse.* December 10. https://www.pulse.ng/bi/lifestyle/lifestyle-here-are-the-countries-with-the-best-and-worst-roads-in-africa/3d6jeng.

Ugochukwu, Obianuju, Nkechi Mbaezue, Saheed Akinmayowa Lawal, Chris Azubogu, Taiwo Lateef Sheikh, and Frédérique Vallières. 2020. The Time is Now: Reforming Nigeria's Outdated Mental Health Laws. *Lancet*, 8(8)E989-990. August. https://doi.org/10.1016/S2214-109X(20)30302-8.

Umeh, Ngozi C. and Ramola Adeola. 2013. Nigeria. *African Disability Rights Yearbook*. 1, 277–290.

UN Department of Economic and Social Affairs. Convention on the Rights of Persons with Disabilities (CRPD). https://www.un.org/development/desa/disabilities/convention-on-the-rights-of-persons-with-disabilities.html.

UN Department of Economic and Social Affairs. *Toolkit on Disability for Africa: Disability-Inclusive Development*, Module 3. https://www.un.org/esa/socdev/documents/disability/Toolkit/Disability-inclusive-development.pdf.

UN Department of Economic and Social Affairs. *Toolkit on Disability for Africa: Culture, Beliefs, and Disability*, Module 13. https://www.un.org/esa/socdev/documents/disability/Toolkit/Cultures-Beliefs-Disability.pdf.

UN Department of Economic and Social Affairs. Factsheet on Persons with Disabilities. https://www.un.org/development/desa/disabilities/resources/factsheet-on-persons-with-disabilities.html.

UN Department of Economic and Social Affairs. Frequently Asked Questions regarding the Convention on the Rights of Persons with Disabilities. https://www.un.org/development/desa/disabilities/convention-on-the-rights-of-persons-with-disabilities/frequently-asked-questions-regarding-the-convention-on-the-rights-of-persons-with-disabilities.html#neg1.

UN Department of Economic and Social Affairs. [Tenth] Anniversary of the Adoption of Convention on the Rights of Persons with Disabilities (CRPD). https://www.un.org/development/desa/disabilities/convention-on-the-rights-of-persons-with-disabilities/the-10th-anniversary-of-the-adoption-of-convention-on-the-rights-of-persons-with-disabilities-crpd-crpd-10.html.

UN Department of Economic and Social Affairs. African Decade of Disabled Persons (2000–2009). https://www.un.org/esa/socdev/enable/disafricadecade.htm.

UN General Assembly. About the General Assembly. https://www.un.org/en/ga/about/background.shtml#:~:text=The%20Assembly%20is%20empowered%20to,of%20people%20throughout%20the%20world.

UN General Assembly. 2015. Transforming Our World: The 2030 Agenda for Sustainable Development. September 25. https://www.un.org/ga/search/view_doc.asp?symbol=A/RES/70/1&Lang=E

UN General Assembly. 2006. Convention on the Rights of Persons with Disabilities. A/RES/61/106, Annex I. December 13. https://www.refworld.org/docid/4680cd212.html.

UN General Assembly. 2006. Optional Protocol to the Convention on the Rights of Persons with Disabilities. A/RES/61/106, Annex II. December 13. https://www.refworld.org/docid/4680d0982.html.

UN General Assembly. 1993. Standard Rules on the Equalization of Opportunities for Persons with Disabilities. Resolution No. A/RES/48/96. December 20. https://www.refworld.org/docid/3b00f2e80.html.

UN General Assembly. 1991. Principles for the Protection of Persons with Mental Illness and the Improvement of Mental Health Care. Resolution No. 46/119. December 17. https://www.who.int/mental_health/policy/en/UN_Resolution_on_protection_of_persons_with_mental_illness.pdf.

UN General Assembly. 1982. World Program of Action concerning Disabled Persons. A/RES/37/52. December 3. https://www.equalrightstrust.org/sites/default/files/ertdocs//world%20program%20of%20action%20on%20disabled%20persons.pdf.

UN General Assembly. 1975. Declaration on the Rights of Disabled Persons. A/RES/3447 (XXX). December 9. https://www.refworld.org/docid/3b00f1c18.html.

UN General Assembly. 1966. International Covenant on Economic, Social and Cultural Rights. United Nations, Treaty Series, Vol. 993, 3. December 16. https://www.refworld.org/docid/3ae6b36c0.html.

UN General Assembly. 1965. International Convention on the Elimination of All Forms of Racial Discrimination. United Nations, Treaty Series, Vol. 660, 195. December 21. https://www.refworld.org/docid/3ae6b3940.html.

UN General Assembly. 1948. Universal Declaration of Human Rights. 217 A (III). December 10. https://www.refworld.org/docid/3ae6b3712c.html.

Unah, Linus. 2020. Leprosy Lives on in Nigeria, 20 Years after Its "Elimination" as a Public Health Problem. *Devex*. January 15. https://www.devex.com/news/leprosy-lives-on-in-nigeria-20-years-after-its-elimination-as-a-public-health-problem-96345.

UNAIDS. 2019. New Survey Results Indicate that Nigeria Has an HIV Prevalence of 1.4%. Press Release. March 14. https://www.unaids.org/en/resources/presscentre/pressreleaseandstatementarchive/2019/march/20190314_nigeria#:~:text=New%20survey%20results%20indicate%20that%20Nigeria%20has%20an%20HIV%20prevalence%20of%201.4%25,-14%20March%202019&text=ABUJA%2FGENEVA%2C%2014%20March%202019,national%20HIV%20prevalence%20of%202.8%25.

UNICEF. Social Protection. https://www.unicef.org/social-policy/social -protection.

United Nations. 2018. *The Report on the World Social Situation 2018*. September. New York: United Nations. doi: https://doi.org/10.18356/c107798c-en.

United Nations Development Program. 2016. *Leaving No One Behind: A Social Protection*. New York, NY: United Nations Development Program. October 6.

United Nations Enable. International Norms and Standards Relating to Disability. https://www.un.org/esa/socdev/enable/comp303.htm#:~:text=Groups%20with%20Disabilities-,3.1%20African%20Human%20Rights%20Instruments,its%20recognition%20of%20collective%20rights.&text=The%20other%20distinctive%20feature%20is%20the%20recognition%20of%20the%20right%20to%20development.

United Nations Enable. Fact Sheet on Persons with Disabilities. https://www.un.org/disabilities/documents/toolaction/pwdfs.pdf.

U.S. Department of State. 2021. Nigeria. In *2020 Country Reports on Human Rights Practices*. March 30.

Uzuakoli (Nigeria). International Leprosy Association—History of Leprosy. https://leprosyhistory.org/geographical_region/site/uzuakoli.

Van Tol, Deanne. 2007. Mothers, Babies, and the Colonial State: The Introduction of Maternal and Infant Welfare Services in Nigeria, 1925–1945. *Spontaneous Generations.* 1(1), 110–131.

Wada, Yusuf Hassan, Linus Rajwani, Emmanuel Anyam, Evelyn Karikari, Mitchell Njikizana, Lilian Srour, and Garba M. Khalid. 2021. Mental Health in Nigeria: A Neglected Issue in Public Health. *Public Health in Practice*, 2 (2021), 1–3.

Wangare, Jackline. 2021. Colonialism in Nigeria: Positive and Negative Impacts of Nigerian Colonization. *Legit.* October 25. https://www.legit.ng/1131998-colonialism-nigeria-positive-negative-impacts.html.

What Does Democracy Mean for You? 2015. *Everyday Democracy.* June 12. https://www.everyday-democracy.org/news/what-does-democracy-mean-you.

What Does ECOSOC Do? https://www.un.org/en/ecosoc/meetings/2005/hl2005/ECOSOCinfo%20rev%20et.pdf.

What is Accessibility? Case Western Reserve University. https://case.edu/accessibility/what-accessibility

What is a Physical Disability? *Achieve Australia.* https://achieveaustralia.org.au/ndis-overview-and-faqs/physical-disability/#:~:text=A%20physical%20disability%20is%20a,and%20visual%20impairments%20and%20more.

What is a Sensory Disability? *Achieve Australia.* https://achieveaustralia.org.au/ndis-overview-and-faqs/what-is-sensory-disability/.

What is the Difference Between Common Law and Civil Law. 2014. Washington University in St. Louis School of Law. January 28. https://onlinelaw.wustl.edu/blog/common-law-vs-civil-law/#:~:text=The%20main%20difference%20between%20the,law%20systems%2C%20codified%20statutes%20predominate

What is the Difference between Signing, Ratification[,] and Accession of UN Treaties? Dag Hammarskjöld Library. https://ask.un.org/faq/14594.

What to Know about Intellectual Disability. *Medical News Today*, https://www.medicalnewstoday.com/articles/intellectual-disability.

Why It's Important to Raise Awareness Around Disabilities. Weaver Industries (Blog). https://www.weaverindustries.org/blog-details/why-its-important-to-raise-awareness-around-disabilities#:~:text=Creating%20acceptance%20is%20a%20vital,posts%20with%20friends%20and%20family.

Wilson, Frank L. 1996. *Concepts and Issues in Comparative Politics: An Introduction to Comparative Analysis.* Upper Saddle River, NJ: Prentice Hall.

Wilson, Mary E. 1995. Travel and the Emergence of Infectious Diseases. *Emerging Infectious Diseases.* 1(2), 39–46. doi:10.3201/eid0102.950201.

Wiseman, John A. 1996. *The New Struggle for Democracy in Africa.* Aldershot, Brookfield, Singapore, and Sydney: Ashgate.

World Bank. 2020. *Social Protection and Labor Overview*. Washington, DC: World Bank. Last updated April 20. https://www.worldbank .org/en/topic/socialprotection/overview#1

World Bank. 2020. *Disability Inclusion in Nigeria: A Rapid Assessment.* Washington, DC: World Bank. https://doi.org/10.1596/34073.

World Bank. 2020. A More Accessible and Sustainable World: A Disability-Inclusive Response to COVID-19. December 1. https://www.worldbank.org/en/news/feature/2020/12/01/a-more-accessible-and-sustainable-world-a-disability-inclusive-response-to-covid-19.

World Bank. 2019. World Bank Group Commitments on Disability-Inclusive Development. July 24. https://www.worldbank.org/en/topic/socialsustainability/brief/world-bank-group-commitments-on-disability-inclusion-development.

World Bank. 2018. World Bank Group Announces New Commitments on Disability Inclusion. Press Release No. 2018/012/SUR. July 24. https://www.worldbank.org/en/news/press-release/2018/07/24/world-bank-group-announces-new-commitments-on-disability-inclusion.

World Bank. 2018. World Bank Group Commitments on Disability-Inclusive Development. Brief. July 24. https://www.worldbank.org/en/topic/socialsustainability/brief/world-bank-group-commitments-on-disability-inclusion-development.

World Health Organization. 2002. *Toward a Common Language for Functioning, Disability[,] and Health ICF*. Geneva, Switzerland: World Health Organization. https://www.who.int/classifications/icf/icfbeginnersguide.pdf.

World Health Organization. 2001. *International Classification of Functioning, Disability and Health.* Geneva, Switzerland: World Health Organization.

World Report on Disability. 2011. Geneva Switzerland and Washington, DC: World Health Organization and the World Bank. https://www.who.int/disabilities/world_report/2011/report.pdf.

Yohanna, Timothy Ali. *They Call Us Senseless Beggars.* Abuja: Grassroots Researchers Association. https://www.grassrootresearchers.org/wp-content/uploads/2019/01/disability_challenges.pdf.pdf.

Index

About the Authors

Philip C. Aka is former Professor and Dean of the Faculty of Law, International University of Sarajevo; and a member of the Illinois State Bar. Professor Aka received a Doctor of Juridical Science (SJD) degree from Indiana University Robert H. McKinney School of Law at Indianapolis; a Ph.D. degree in political science from Howard University; a Juris Doctorate (JD) degree from Temple University Beasley School of Law; an LL.M. (summa cum laude) degree from IU Robert H. McKinney School of Law at Indianapolis; an M.A. degree in political science from the University of North Texas; a B.A. (magna cum laude) degree in political science from Edinboro University of Pennsylvania; and a Certificate in Conflict Resolution from Cornell University.

In Spring 2020, Dr. Aka was a Visiting Professor at Southern Illinois University School of Law at Carbondale. He has authored or coauthored more than 100 publications. His recent books include: *Humor in Pedagogy in Tertiary Education in the Age of COVID-19: Bosnia in Comparative Perspective* (Lexington Books, 2022); *The Political Economy of Universal Healthcare in Africa: Evidence from Ghana* (2022); *Healthcare and Economic Restructuring: Nigeria in Comparative Perspective* (2022); *Bosnia as Civic State and Global Citizen: Alternative Futures Outside the EU* (Rowman & Littlefield, 2021); *Genetic Counseling and Preventive Medicine in Post-War Bosnia* (Palgrave Macmillan, 2020); and *Human Rights in Nigeria's External Relations: Building the Record of a Moral Superpower* (Lexington Books, 2017).

Joseph Abiodun Balogun is a retired Distinguished Professor and former Dean of the College of Health Sciences at Chicago State University; Emeritus Professor of Physiotherapy at the University of Medical Sciences, Ondo City, Nigeria; a Visiting Professor and Program Consultant at the Center of Excellence in Reproductive Health Innovation, University of Benin, Nigeria; and founder and CEO of Joseph Rehabilitation Center, a social service organization that provides community-integrated living arrangement services for adults with disabilities at Tinley Park, Illinois, in the United States.

Professor Balogun received a Ph.D. in Exercise Physiology and an M.S. in Orthopedic and Sports Physical Therapy from the University of Pittsburgh, as well as a B.Sc. in Physiotherapy from the University of Ibadan, Nigeria. He is a recipient of over a dozen academic fellowships, including: the Academy of Medicine Specialist (FAcadMedS), the Royal Society for Public Health (FRSPH), the Institute of Management Consultants (FIMC), the Academy of Science (FAS), the Nigeria Society of Physiotherapy (FNSP), and the American College of Sports Medicine (FACSM).

His recent publications include *Healthcare and Economic Restructuring: Nigeria in Comparative Perspective* (2022) (with Philip C. Aka); *The Nigerian Healthcare System: Pathway to Universal and High-Quality Health Care* (2022); *Contemporary Obstetrics, and Gynecology for Developing Countries* (with Friday Okonofua et al., 2021); *Health Professions in Nigeria: An Interdisciplinary Analysis* (2021); and *Healthcare Education in Nigeria: Evolutions and Emerging Paradigms* (2020).

www.ingramcontent.com/pod-product-compliance
Ingram Content Group UK Ltd.
Pitfield, Milton Keynes, MK11 3LW, UK
UKHW041836031026
15587UKWH00002B/820

9 781666 914177